IMAGES
of America

DAPHNE

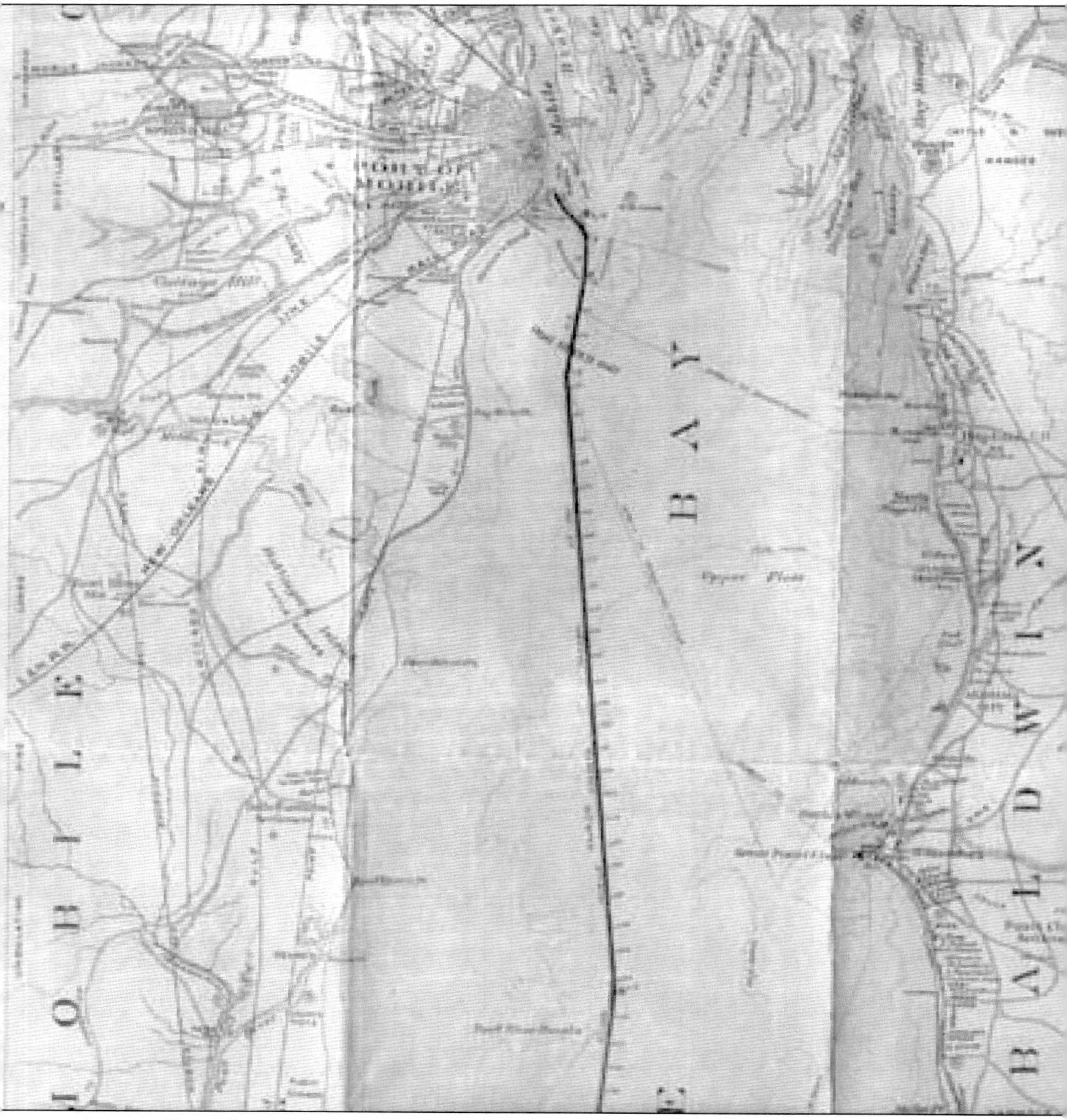

MOBILE BAY. This 1889 map of Mobile Bay shows the bayfront of Daphne during the years when bay boats were the primary means of travel across the water to Mobile. (Old Methodist Church Museum of Daphne.)

ON THE COVER: The celebration of May Day has long been associated with the bayfront town of Daphne. This is one of the earliest celebrations held at the Daphne Normal School. The building previously served as the county courthouse. (Old Methodist Church Museum of Daphne.)

IMAGES
of America

DAPHNE

Harriet Brill Outlaw
and Penny H. Taylor

ARCADIA
PUBLISHING

ISBN 978-0-7385-9116-2

Published by Arcadia Publishing
Charleston, South Carolina

Printed in the United States of America

Library of Congress Control Number: 2011935492

For all general information, please contact Arcadia Publishing:
Telephone 843-853-2070
Fax 843-853-0044
E-mail sales@arcadiapublishing.com
For customer service and orders:
Toll-Free 1-888-313-2665

Visit us on the Internet at www.arcadiapublishing.com

This work is dedicated to Al Guarisco, whose efforts to preserve the heritage of Daphne are unlimited.

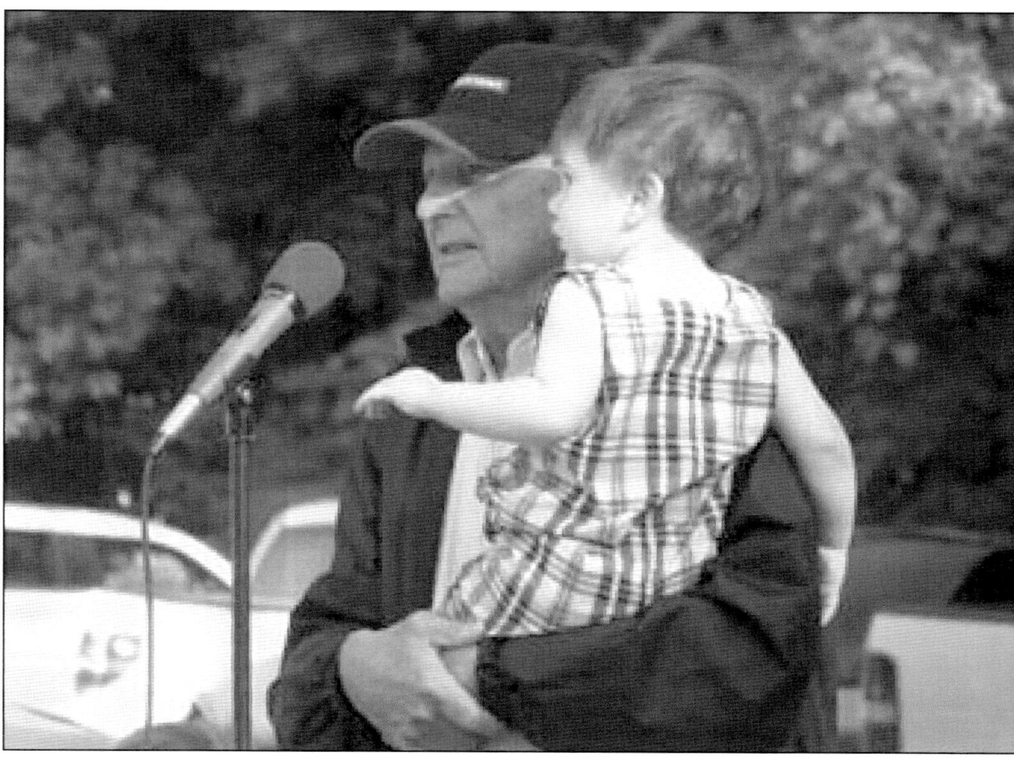

Contents

Foreword

The perseverance of one Alfred (Al to all) Guarisco is the force majeure behind this book. For about 15 years, Al has labored with a love of history, specifically, his and his ancestors' history of Daphne, Alabama. The story of Daphne and its surroundings sparkles with the telling from a nearly photographic memory of place, people, preservation, and purpose. Early Italian settlers from the boot, Sicily, northern Italy, and Rome settled in Daphne after sensing the purpose of America from living off its bounteous riches in distant locations. For a few dollars, an acre of dirt was pure resource to be farmed and built upon and trusted to the growing of the grape. Business, or commerce, came to town as well with the opening of post offices, sawmills, retail shops, cotton gins, and kilns for firing clay pottery. Before 1900, the Eastern Shore's wharves handled the boat (bay boats, as they were known) traffic between prosperous Mobile (across Mobile Bay) and Ecor Rouge—the highest bluff between the East and West—and hotels for the summer guests on the lookout for gentle breezes, freedom from yellow fever, and a getaway. Al saw many of these wharves in his youth and witnessed the bay boats in action until they died out shortly after the opening of the Spanish Fort Causeway to Mobile in 1927. Progress and modernity slid quietly into Daphne as the years went by. The pictures and descriptions you will see as you turn the pages tell the Daphne tale from its modest beginning in the 1830s. Present-day Daphne is known as the "Jubilee City" after the unique occurrence known as the "jubilee"—when an unusual combination of bay tides, temperatures, winds, and a shortage of oxygen in the water forces many sea creatures, like crabs, to climb ashore to be scooped up by lucky fishermen. The Daphne party is just beginning. We thank you, Al.

—Kennard Balme, president
Old Methodist Church Museum of Daphne

ACKNOWLEDGMENTS

A work of this nature depends on the historical insight of many culturally-aware people who treasure their heritage. The authors appreciate the willingness of citizens to share their family photographs. Many of the photographs, including the Davis and Stokes collections, were donated to the Daphne Museum. Dick Scott, whose parents were also avid collectors of historical memorabilia, has graciously shared the Mary Owen Carney collection. The works used from this collection are designated as the Carney Collection. The Baldwin County Training School alumni have created an outstanding museum dedicated to the history of black education in Baldwin County. The authors are in debt to Gartrelle Agee, Glenita Andrews, Robert Andrews, and a host of others who worked to preserve and share this unique history. John Lewis of The Gallery in Bay Minette deserves credit for his preservation of the Willison Duck collection of photographs and for permission to use some of them in this book. Thanks go to the descendants of the early Italian families—the Guariscos, Mancis, Cortes, Allegris, and others—who cleaned out attics and garages for new revelations. The work grew with contributions of residents along the bayfront whose families date back to the 1830s. Charles "Chuck" Philipp has been a collector of Spanish Fort photographs for most of his life. His willingness to share them has preserved them for the future.

Information for the captions was also gleaned from personal anecdotes of residents and from the previously published works of historians, which are listed in the bibliography. *A Tour of Historic Olde Towne Daphne* was updated by David Manci Gardner as an Eagle Scout project. Baldwin County Public Schools, Fairhope Museum, Baldwin County Heritage Museum, and the University of South Alabama were all supportive and most helpful. Many of the photographs are from the Old Methodist Church Museum of Daphne (OMCMD), also referred to as the Daphne Museum.

Several collections have been donated to the museum. John Davis donated photographs he used in the yearbook for the normal school, the *Nymph*. These are listed as courtesy of the Davis Collection. Kennard Balme, president of the Daphne Museum, and his volunteers, many of whom are lifelong residents, helped secure images and information. The authors also wish to thank Simone Monet-Williams of Arcadia Publishing for her support and guidance. Most importantly, credit goes to Al Guarisco, to whom this work is dedicated. His perseverance is the reason the history of Daphne has been preserved.

Introduction

The city of Daphne watches the sun rise over the rich farmlands to the east and set on the glimmering waters of Mobile Bay to the west. She is home to people whose stories are as rich as the soil and as bountiful as the waters. Her bayfront is where the rare phenomenon known as "jubilee" occurs, when sea life makes its way to the shoreline in the wee hours of the morning. The cry of "jubilee!" awakens residents, who grab gigs and buckets and harvest the fresh shrimp, crab, and flounder that come ashore. Perhaps the rich gifts of the water brought the town its first peoples; shell middens along the shoreline tell the story of the Native Americans who came to garner shellfish during the fishing season.

As Europeans began to explore the Gulf Coast, the Spaniard Alonso Alvarez de Pineda sailed through the mouth of the bay he named Espiritu Santo, or Bay of the Holy Ghost. He wrote of a red bluff high on the Eastern Shore, Ecor Rouge, which became a landmark for sailors in the bay. During his 40-day stay, Pineda recorded information on a large Indian village and told of more than 40 additional Native American settlements along the rivers to the north.

After an unsuccessful attempt at Spanish colonization by Tristan de Luna, French explorers Bienville and D'Iberville Le Moyne established a colony named Mobile, which included the eastern shore of Espiritu Santo. The community, known as "the Village," served as the major crossing point between the east and west sides of the bay. The site at the Village had a bounteous freshwater spring and had long been a spot for ships taking on fresh water; here, a pottery, a brickyard, and a sawmill were established. The land route to Pensacola, now known as the Old Spanish Trail, connected with Mobile at the Village as well. Under British control, Comdr. Thomas Durnford established a plantation south of the Village. During the Revolutionary War, Spanish forces joined with the colonists against the British, and a bloody battle took place on the soil of Baldwin County. Gen. Bernardo de Galvez once again wrested control of the area for Spain.

The D'Olives and the Rochans, who managed large plantations by the early 1800s under Spanish land grants, owned some of the earliest homes along the shore. The D'Olives even opened a hotel named La Belle Rose. During the Creek Indian Wars, Andrew Jackson was summoned to the Gulf Coast, where he met with men under the command of Maj. Uriah Blue. Under the spreading limbs of a stately oak tree at the Village, he addressed the men before they headed out to fight in the Battle of New Orleans.

In the 19th century, riverboat and bay boat travel directed the course of growth in Daphne. The high ground, with such plentiful resources, grew into the major point of entry into Baldwin County. Many residents of Mobile built lovely summer homes on the bayfront, and several hotels were opened to welcome guests. One such resident, Maj. Lewis Starke, and his wife, Louisa D'Olive, ran a brickwork factory and plantation at the point, labeled as Starke's Bluff on early maps. Another prominent resident was a Connecticut sea captain named William Howard, better known as Uncle Billy. He first discovered the area when taking on fresh water from a spring. He returned, purchased 123 acres, and built a lovely home and hotel. The Howard Hotel became famous for the hospitality of its hosts and for the wonderful springwater, which reportedly had healing properties. In addition to managing the hotel, Howard also sold fresh water to vessels, ran a delivery service to ships, and became the first postmaster. He is said to have named the town Daphne because the many laurel trees found there brought to mind the Greek myth: a nymph named Daphne spurned the love of the god Apollo. As he pursued her through the forest, she became weak and tired and could run no more. Just as Apollo reached her, she cried to the heavens for help and was turned into a laurel tree.

Another story states that Daphne was so named to honor a local slave. Daphne was an African American woman who nursed many residents through the terrible yellow fever epidemic that claimed many lives.

Next to the Howard Hotel, Gavin Yuille purchased 72 acres and built a house and farm that he named Magnolia Hill. The Yuilles were some of several bayfront residents who constructed long piers and operated docks for bay boats.

Other bayfront homes were built further south of Daphne in the historic community of Montrose, high on the red bluffs of Ecor Rouge.

By the time of the Civil War, the Daphne Methodist Episcopal Church had been erected and was used as a resting place for Union soldiers on the way to the Battle of Spanish Fort and Blakeley. The original Spanish Fort had been reinforced as Fort McDermott, one of the forts used to help protect Mobile. Here, Union soldiers lay siege in a battle that lasted several days before moving north to Blakeley.

After the war, Major Starke deeded land to several of his former slaves to establish a house of worship. The Little Bethel Baptist Church was built and its cemetery was the resting place for many early African American residents. In 1868, the Baldwin County seat was moved from the defunct town of Blakeley to Daphne. A building was constructed facing the bay, as well as a separate jailhouse. Daphne was the center of all county activity until the railroad was completed across the Mobile Bay delta, when train travel rivaled bay boat access to Mobile. The city of Bay Minette successfully won the legislative designation of county seat in 1900 but had to remove the official court records by somewhat questionable means in 1901. Daphne still refers to the removal of the records as the "night the courthouse was stolen."

In 1899, the Eastern Shore Missionary Baptist Association founded a school in Daphne, which, by 1916, had been transferred to the Baldwin County School System and eventually became Baldwin County Training School. This was the only secondary school for black students in the county until another black high school was built in Douglasville, near Bay Minette in 1950. Baldwin County Training School had dormitories, athletic teams, and an outstanding curriculum, including liberal arts as well as industrial sciences.

By the end of the 1800s, the bayfront had grown by tremendous strides. Not only were African American communities thriving, there was an influx of new residents who were enticed by the ideal living conditions. A colony of Italian residents was encouraged by the efforts of Alesandro Mastro-Valerio, who purchased land in 1888 to assist fellow Italians with finding homes outside of the large cities where most immigrants congregated. Many of the Italians who purchased land here settled east of town in what is today known as Belforest.

Another significant colonization effort was initiated by Jason Malbis, who developed an agricultural plantation just east of Daphne for the purpose of employing and training young Greek men in America. The colony was self-sufficient, with communal housing for workers, a religious establishment, electric power plant, cannery, dairy, icehouse, and large farm holdings. A Greek Orthodox Church was built in 1965 to honor Jason Malbis and his vision. Constructed by old country artisans using materials from the homeland, it is a landmark in architecture for the county.

The earliest schools in Daphne were private schools in homes and hotels. Before grades one through twelve were educated as part of the normal school program in the former courthouse, there were one-room public schools on Randall Avenue and downtown. The Alabama State Teacher College on Mobile Bay, also called the State Normal School, operated from 1907 until

1940. Students were then housed at various locations while the most modern school in Alabama was under construction on North Main Street. Daphne Junior High opened in 1938 for students in grades one through nine. A springtime May Day festival began in 1917 at the Daphne Normal School. Pageants, games, entertainment, and a processional of the May court were the highlight of the year. May Day activities were also held at the Baldwin County Training School. Parents and community members worked diligently each year to make the events successful fundraisers and celebrations.

As automobiles became more readily available, Daphne's downtown area gradually shifted from the bayfront to Main Street. The bay boat landing at Daphne was the jump-off for all points north, as well as the Old Spanish Trail, the road that connected Mobile to Pensacola. The downtown area was filled with a bustling trade, with stores such as Trione's Grocery, Bertagnolli's Store, Russell Garage, Dryer's Drug Store, a barbershop, a doctor's office, banks, and restaurants. Russell Dick, the son of a former slave, was a prominent citizen of Daphne. Dick was industrious and a wise entrepreneur who worked hard and eventually owned a major portion of the downtown area. A main source of employment in Daphne was the pottery industry, housed in several successful operations, the last of which was operated by Clarence Dryer until the mid-20th century.

When the causeway was opened in 1927, connecting the Eastern Shore to Mobile by way of Spanish Fort (Bridgehead), the bay boat era began to fade, but the road running through the hill at Spanish Fort aided in the growth of the community there, which was primarily developed by George and David Fuller.

Daphne was incorporated on July 8, 1927, with a population of 500. The old-town atmosphere was maintained until the new Highway 98 bypassed Main Street. For a while, growth occurred more on the outskirts of downtown. New schools, new developments such as Lake Forest, major highway improvements, the opening of Interstate 10, new businesses, and an influx of new residents increased the population, making Daphne the largest city in Baldwin County today. And Main Street is once again the hub of the town. Parks flank restaurants, offices, and city hall. Bay access is enhanced by the improvement of two public launches and piers, where residents gather to talk about the old days.

The story of Daphne is one of people coming together—under an oak tree, at the courthouse, at the grocery store, on the bayfront, at schools, at churches, or in the wee hours before dawn to gather the beached seafood during a jubilee.

One

The Early Years
The First Settlers

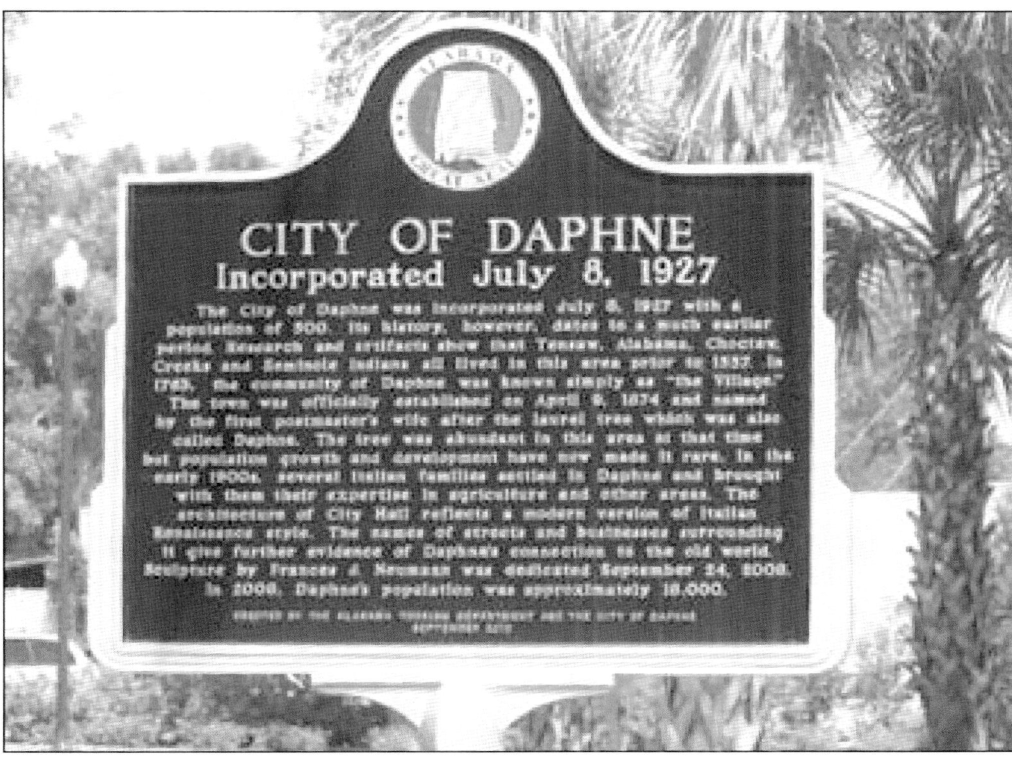

City of Daphne. From the time of the discovery of Mobile Bay by Spanish explorers, the east side of the bay has beckoned to settlers. Before Europeans came, it was a gathering place for Native Americans, who left shell mounds along the shore. Since then, settlers have gathered on the shores to build lives for their families. (Photograph by Penny Taylor.)

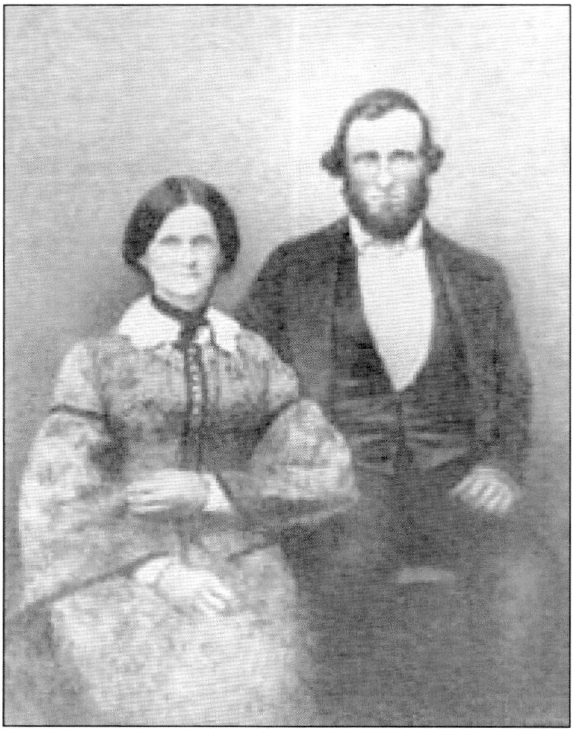

Early Plantations. Among the earliest settlers in Daphne were the D'Olives, a French family from Mobile. Pictured are Aurelia Hall and Louis D'Olive, who operated a large plantation during the years when the community was dubbed "the Village." D'Olive's original plantation stemmed from a 1787 Spanish land grant of approximately 800 acres. The D'Olives also built a hotel, La Belle Rose, which flourished until the War of 1812. (Dick Scott.)

D'Olive Family Cemetery. The family plot has tombstones dating back to the early 1800s. Several members of the family are buried here, including Louisa D'Olive and her husband, Maj. Lewis Starke. The historic cemetery, surrounded by a historic ironwork fence, is preserved and located at Village Point Park Preserve in Daphne. (Dick Scott, Carney Collection.)

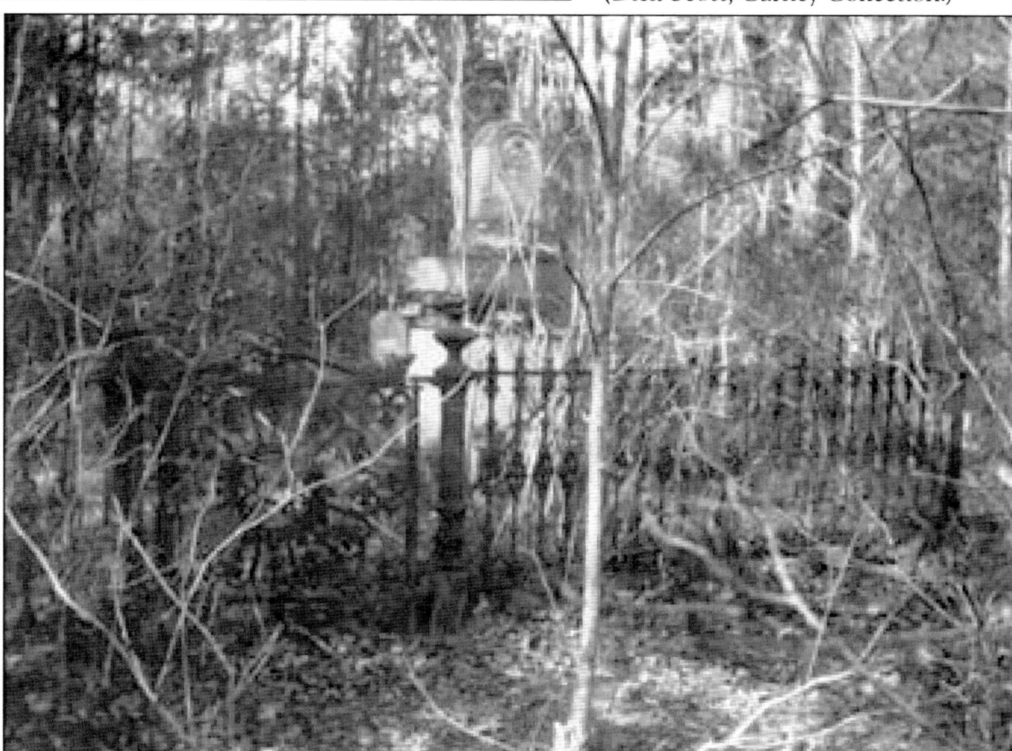

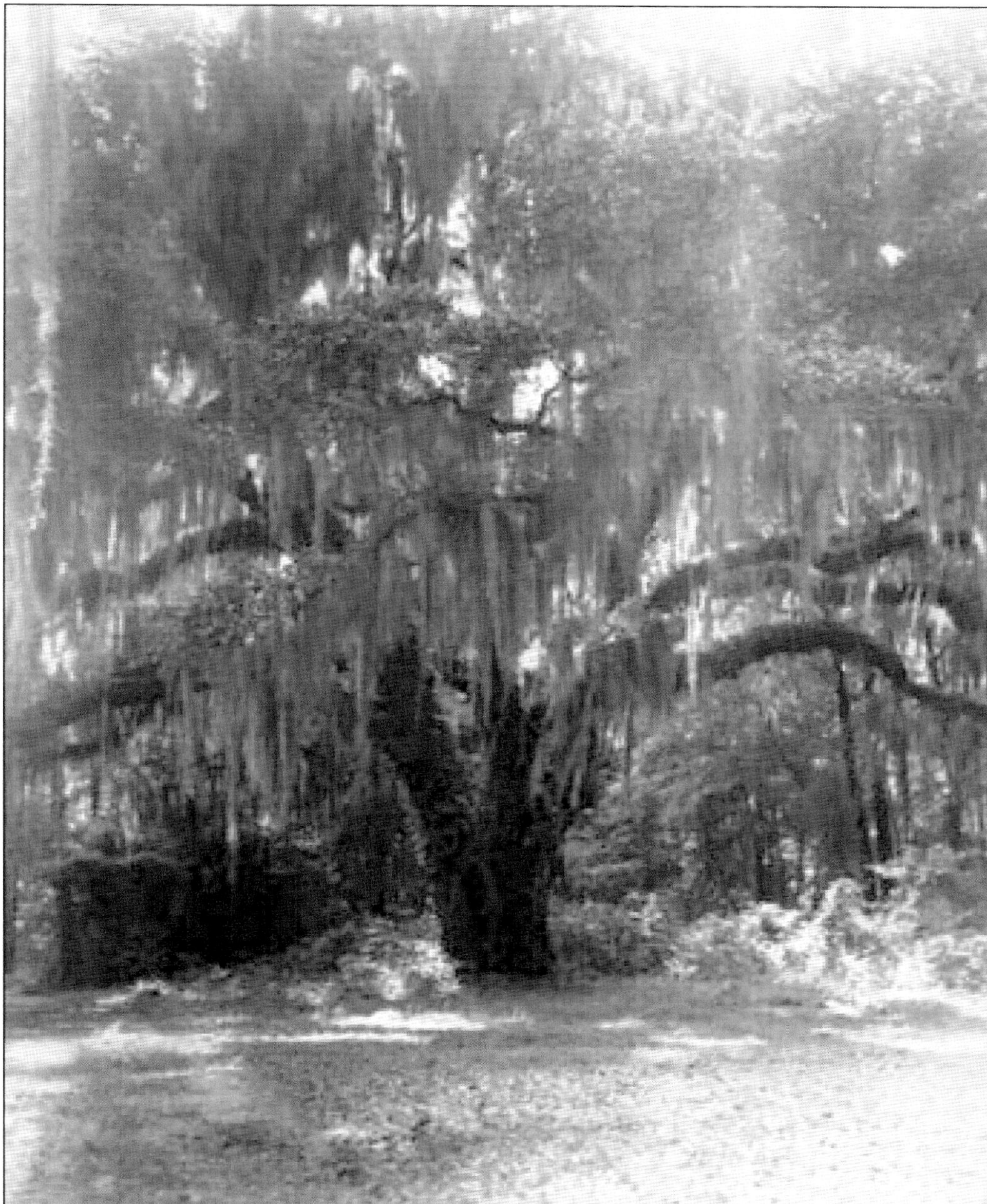

JACKSON'S OAK. The area known as the Village was the site of a famous event during the War of 1812. Andrew Jackson was reputed to have addressed the troops beneath the branches of a towering oak tree before heading to the Battle of New Orleans, in which he soundly defeated the British at Chalmette. Since that time, it has been called "Jackson's Oak." (Dick Scott, Carney Collection.)

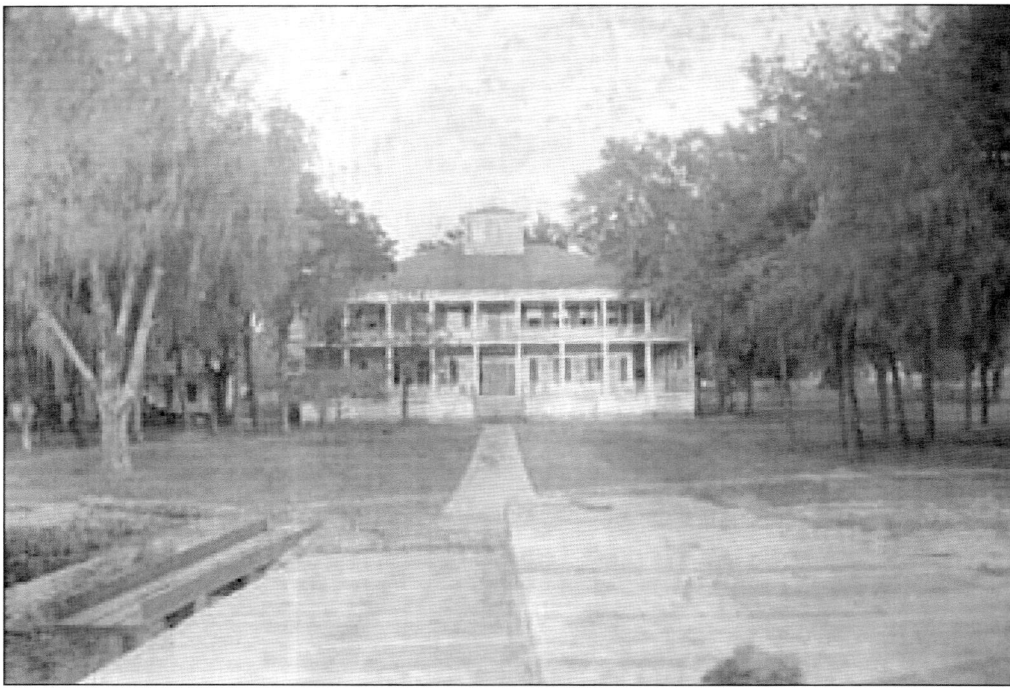

HOWARD HOTEL. Capt. William Howard brought his bride, Elizabeth, to Daphne after learning about the town while taking on supplies for his ship. They built a two-story hotel, which became a popular spot for "taking the waters" and escaping big-city life for a spell. During the Civil War, a cannonball went completely through the hotel and lodged in a cedar tree in the yard. After the death of "Uncle Billy," his wife, "Aunt Betty," sold the hotel to William Dryer, who changed the name to Daphne Springs Hotel (and later to the Dryer Hotel). The second-story porch was removed, and dormers were added later. (Above, OMCMD; below, Dick Scott, Carney Collection.)

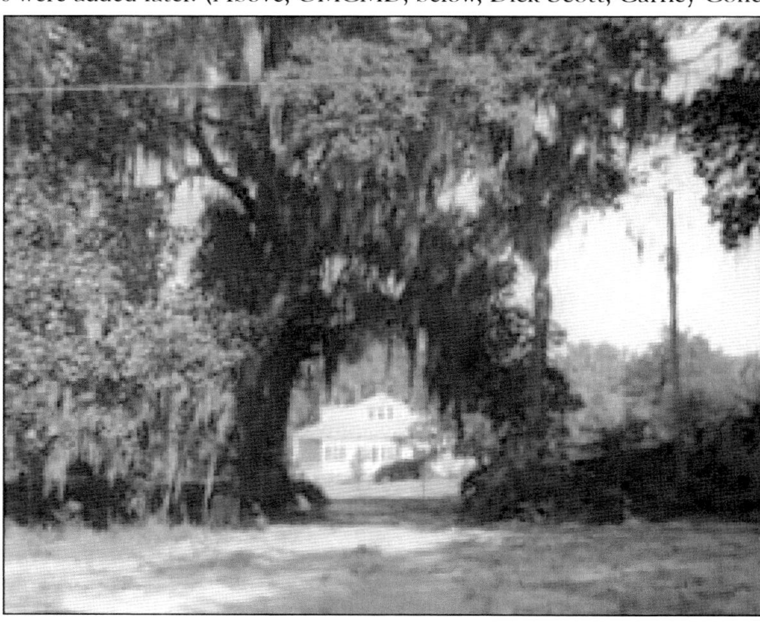

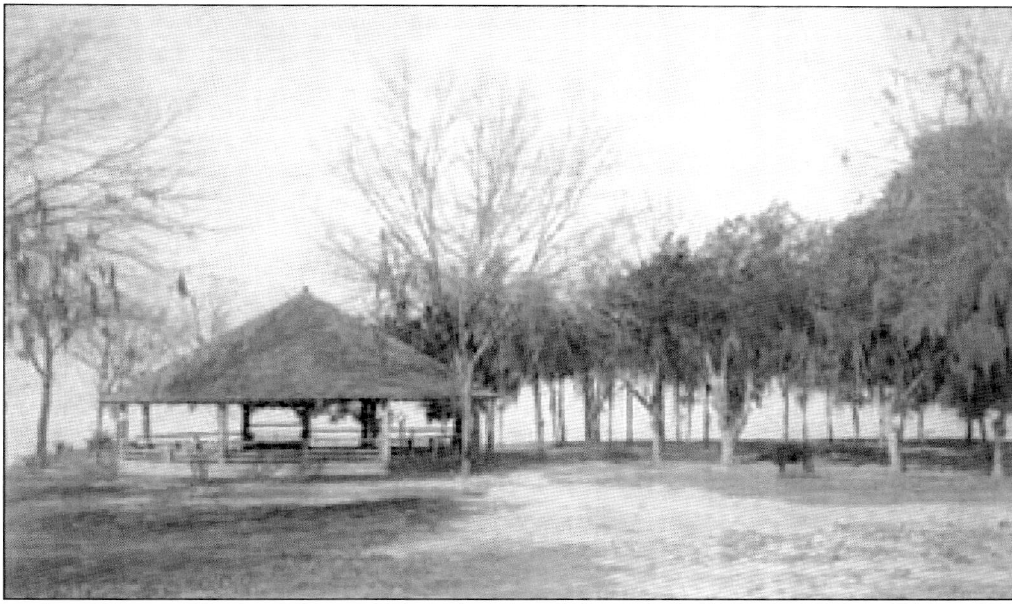

Howard Hotel Pavilion. The Howard Hotel was enhanced by the beautiful view from the pavilion. Bay breezes cooled visitors as they sat in the shade drinking their afternoon tea. The steps down the bluff to the shoreline offered excursion opportunities for the more adventurous. Eventually, bathing in the bay waters became as fashionable as partaking of the benefits of the freshwater spring located on the property. In fact, Billy and Betty Howard built a flume to transport springwater to the boats docking at the pier. Billy also ran a service that delivered fresh water to ships too large to dock at the Howard Pier. (Above, OMCMD; below, OMCMD.)

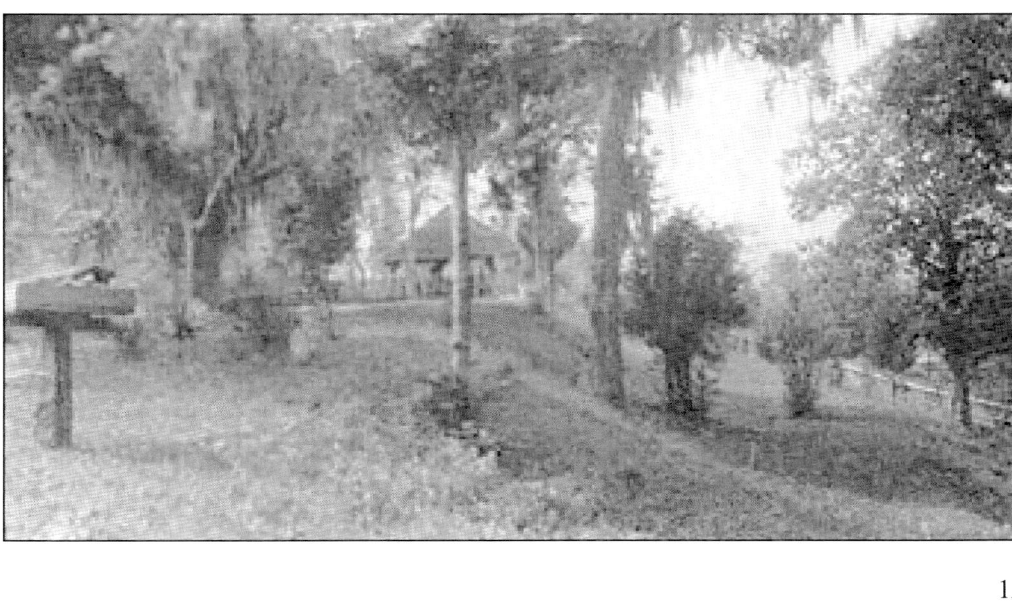

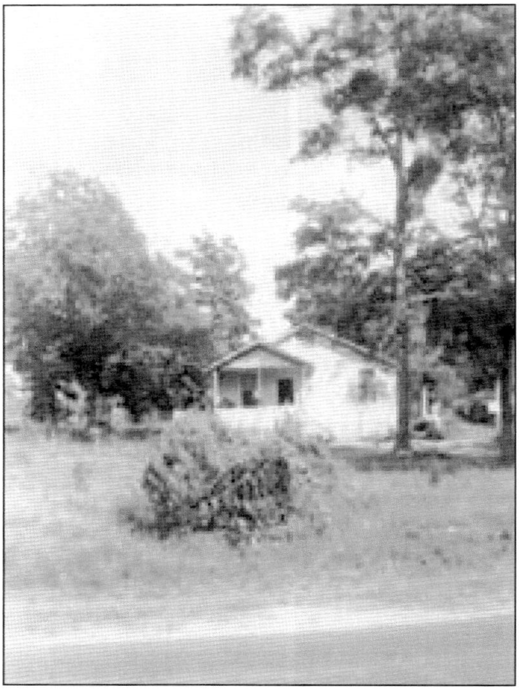

PATTERSON GRAVE. The 1847 grave of the mysterious William A. Patterson sits beside the highway. After losing his cotton gin and mercantile in a fire, the bachelor died at age 30. The tombstone, of unknown origin, reads: "Her sorrow weeps on virtue's sacred dust/Our tears become us and our grief is just. Such were the tears she shed who gratefully pays/This last sad tribute of her love and praise." (Dick Scott, Carney Collection.)

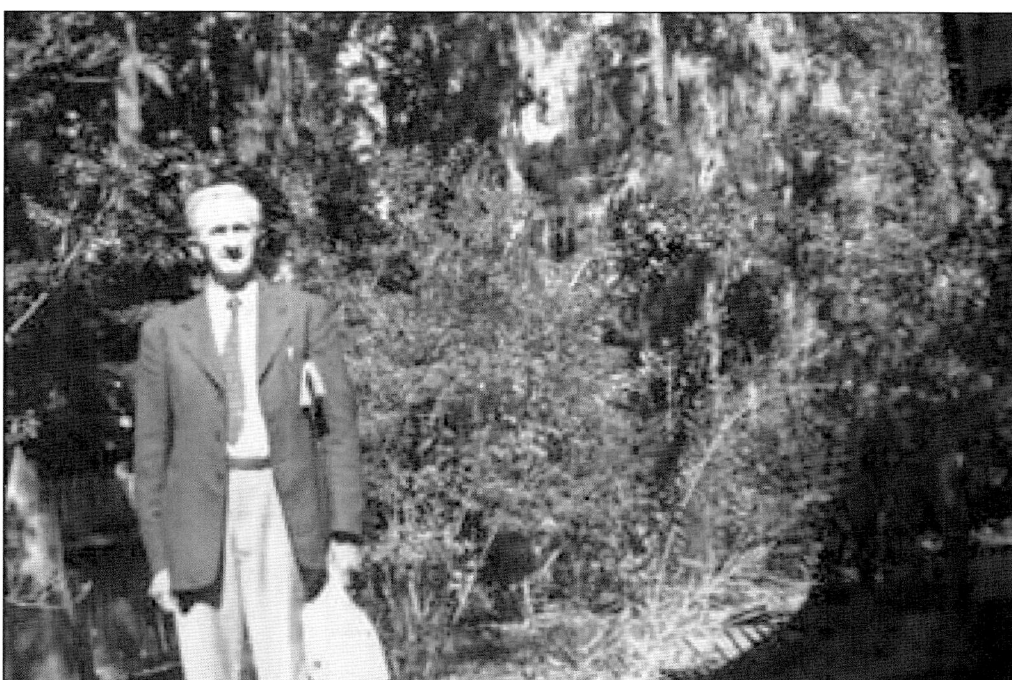

JAMES A. CARNEY. Carney was the grandson of Louis and Aurelia Hall D'Olive. His father, James A. Carney Sr., made a considerable fortune in lumber and turpentine investments. James Jr. married Mary Owen in 1927 and they had one son, Marshall. James Jr. continued his family enterprises and was the owner of at least four bay boats. (Dick Scott, Carney Collection.)

Down in Daphne. Mary Owen came from Butler County in 1924 to teach at the normal school, and in 1926, she was asked to return as the music program director. Owen was the vice president of the Women's Study Club, which she helped organize in 1924. She photographed and documented historic sites along the Eastern Shore of the bay and composed the sheet music pictured at right. (Dick Scott, Carney Collection.)

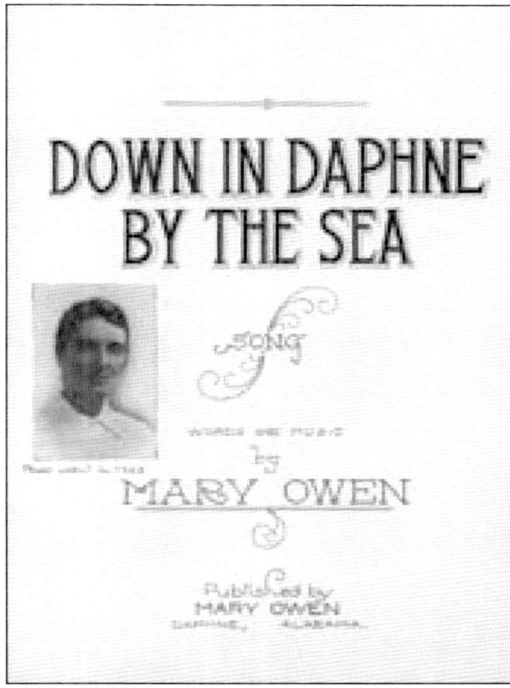

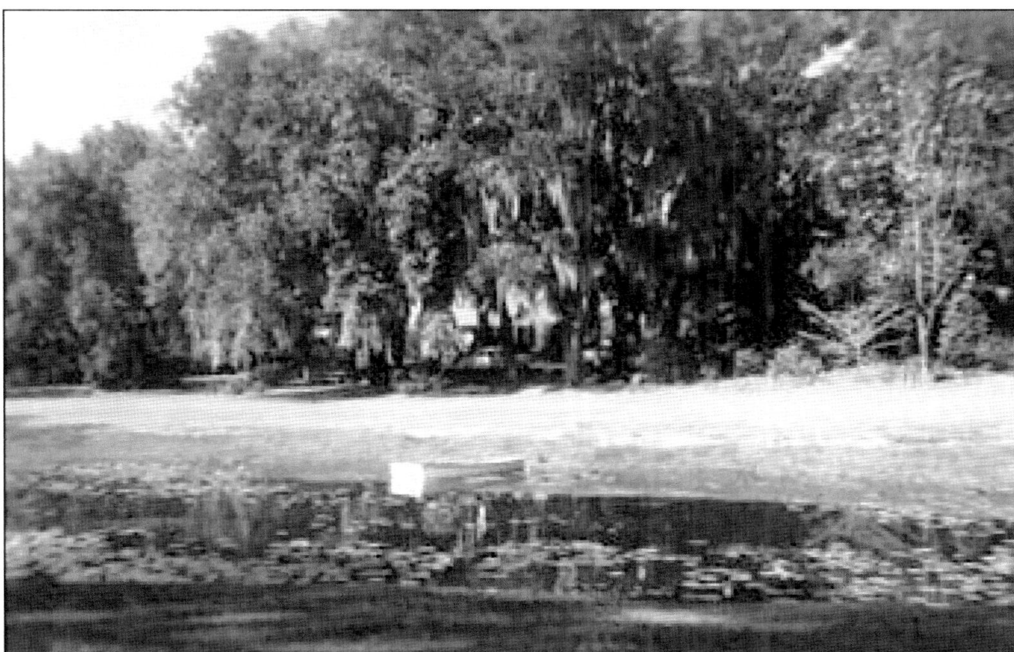

Short's Hotel. Thomas Short ran an 1867 advertisement that read: "EASTERN SHORE, being prepared to accommodate those who wish to spend the summer 'Over the Bay,' I would inform the public that my house is now open for the reception of visitors." Short's Hotel, on Maj. Lewis Starke's plantation property, also had several cottages. The hotel burned in the 1870s. After 1890, the Kesslers, Newmans, and Morrills each lived on this site. (Dick Scott, Carney Collection.)

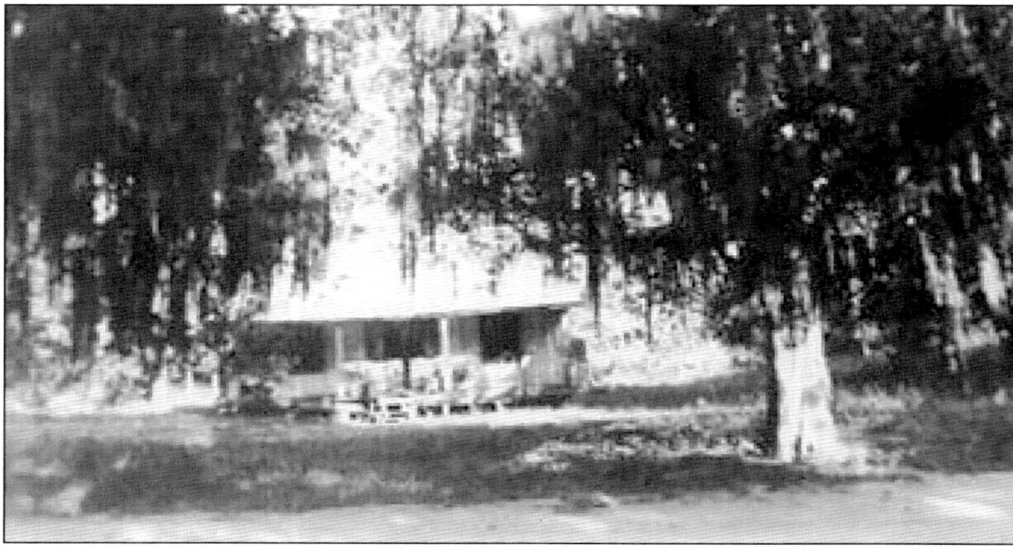

O'Neal Cottage. In 1872, Capt. James O'Neal, an Irish immigrant, purchased 120 acres of bayfront property. The O'Neal Cottage shown here was built in 1835 and is one of the oldest standing structures in Daphne. The home features a "sleeping porch," which means that the eaves extend well beyond the norm, providing protection from rain and wind. (Dick Scott, Carney Collection.)

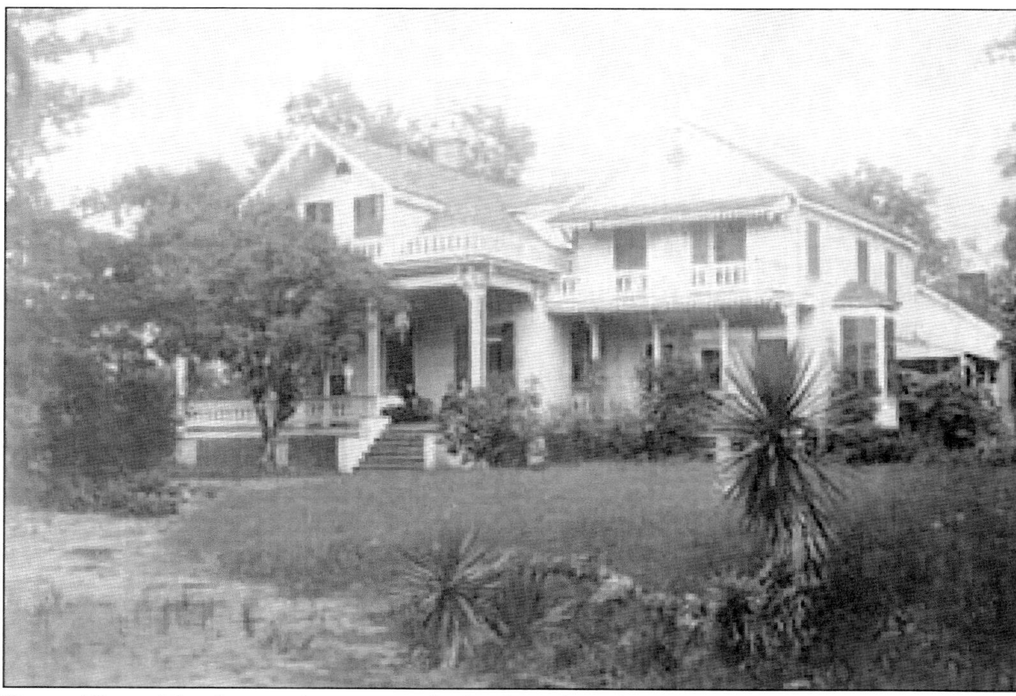

Yuille Home. This historic home is on the land purchased by Gavin Yuille from William Weeks, of Fish River, in 1845. The 72 acres were between the lands of Lewis Starke and William Howard. Yuille sold 35 acres to Davidella G. Cullum, for what would later be the site of the Lea Home. Yuille and his wife, Ann, named the place Magnolia Hill and reared their children there. (OMCMD.)

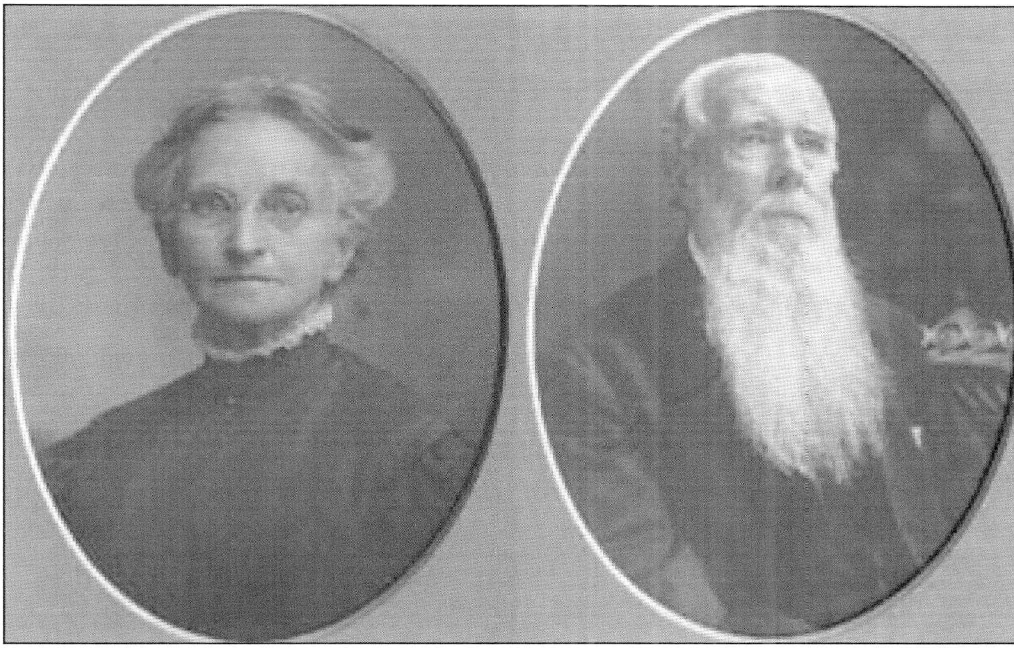

The Yuilles. The Yuille family became permanent residents of Daphne. Gavin Yuille continued to run the family bakery in Mobile, staying in that city during some of the winter months. His wife, Ann, wrote to family in Scotland of the "pretty place on a high bank on the side of the water." (OMCMD.)

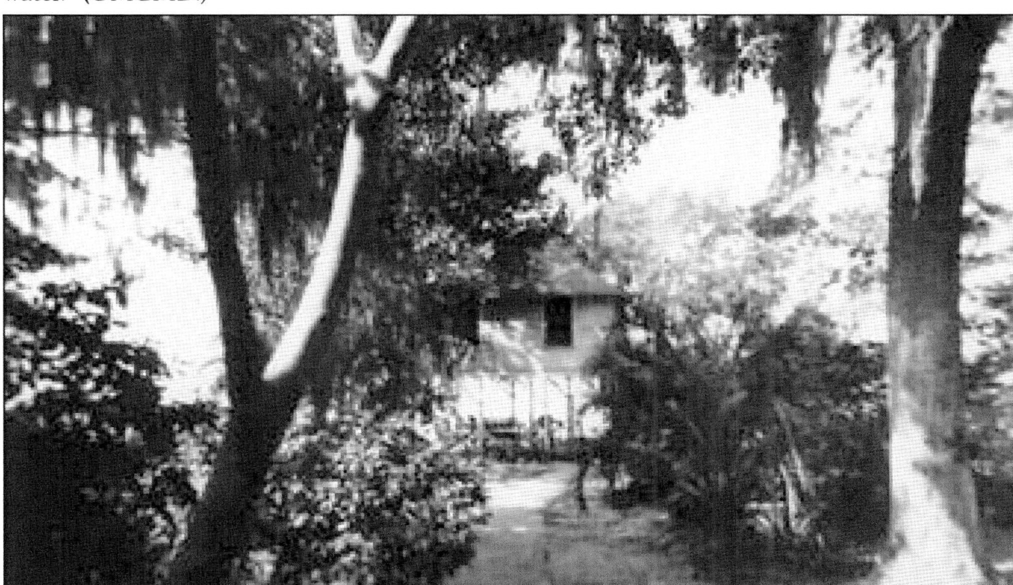

Hollywood Hotel. Willard F. Freeman ran the Hollywood Hotel, which was situated on 46 acres on the bay. Operating during the antebellum years, the one-and-a-half-story building had spacious halls through the center (to take advantage of the bay breezes) and one of the longest wharves in Daphne, which extended far enough into the water for passengers to disembark conveniently. (Dick Scott, Carney Collection.)

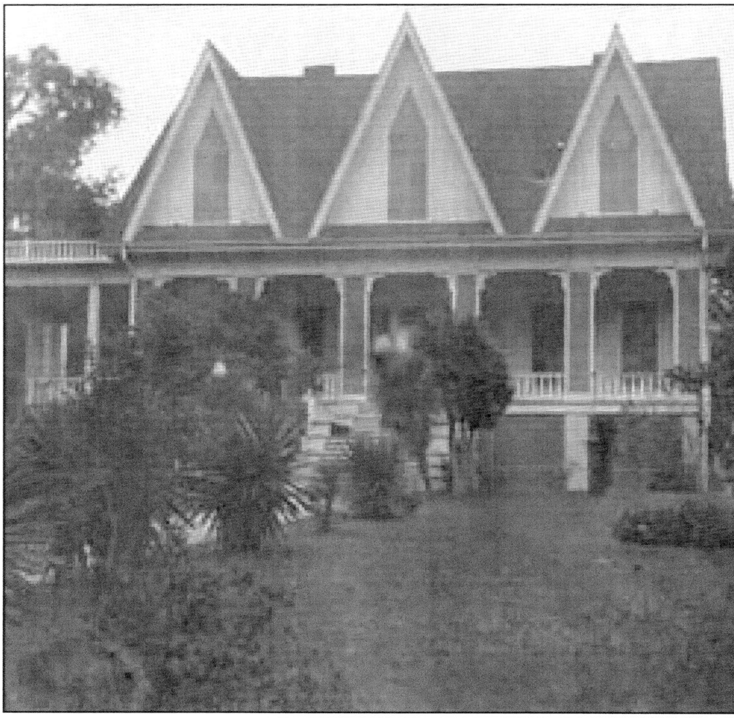

Shonts Home. A bayside home on the north side of town was purchased by Edward Quincy Norton, who was involved in locating the Fairhope Single Tax Colony and edited the *Standard* from 1901 until 1907. Next to Norton's house, T.P. Shonts built this distinctive summer home. Shonts, a New York railroad magnate, was chairman of the Panama Canal Commission from 1905 to 1907. The home burned down around 1920. (OMCMD.)

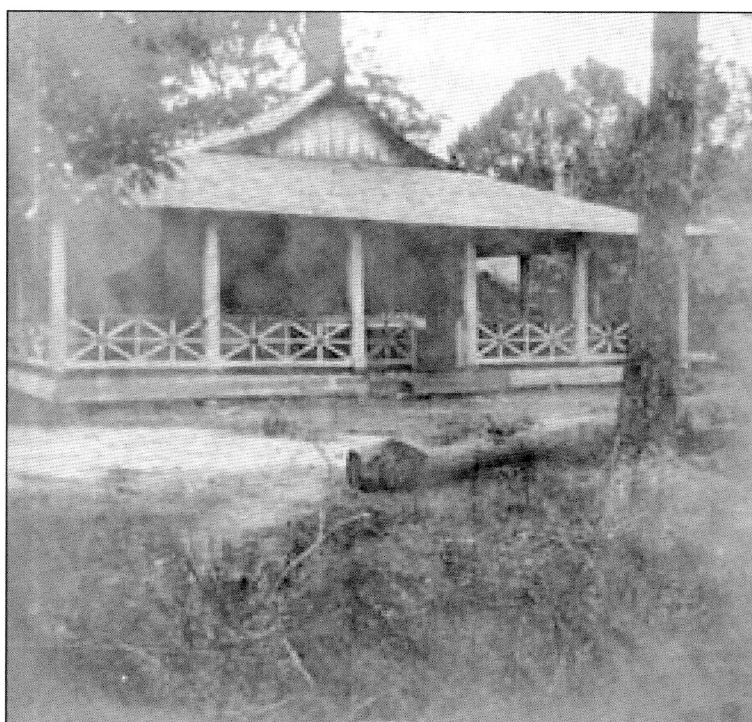

Stokes Home. Before the Civil War, Samuel Stokes operated a successful plantation. He answered the call to serve in the war and returned to find his home burned and his wife and three children dead. He built this home on the original homesite in 1868 and remarried. The cemetery on the homesite is the resting place of many of the Stokes family members. (OMCMD.)

STOKES FAMILY. Samuel Stokes rebuilt his life in Daphne with the help of Rose Jenkins, who came to work for him. He remarried and had six daughters. One of the daughters, Elizabeth, married William Yuille at the family home. After a period of residence in Mobile, Miss Bessie (Elizabeth) and her husband returned to live in the Daphne home and, later, in a cottage located on the property. (OMCMD.)

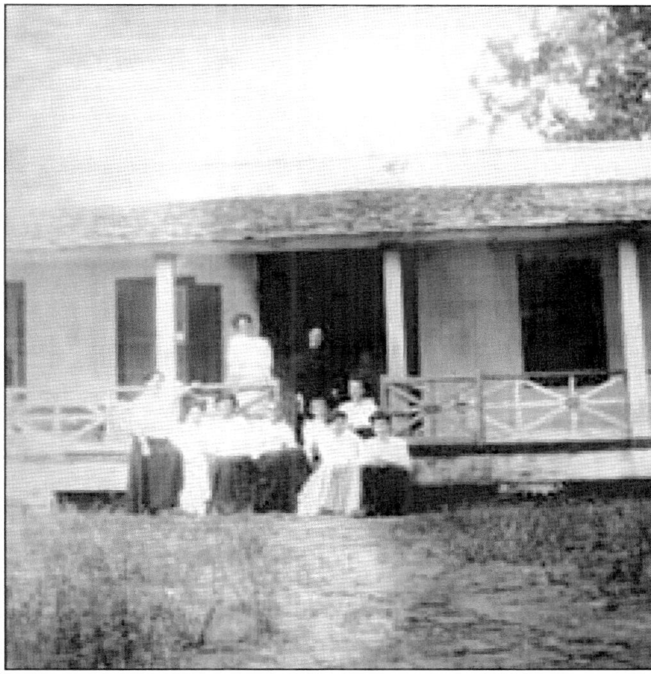

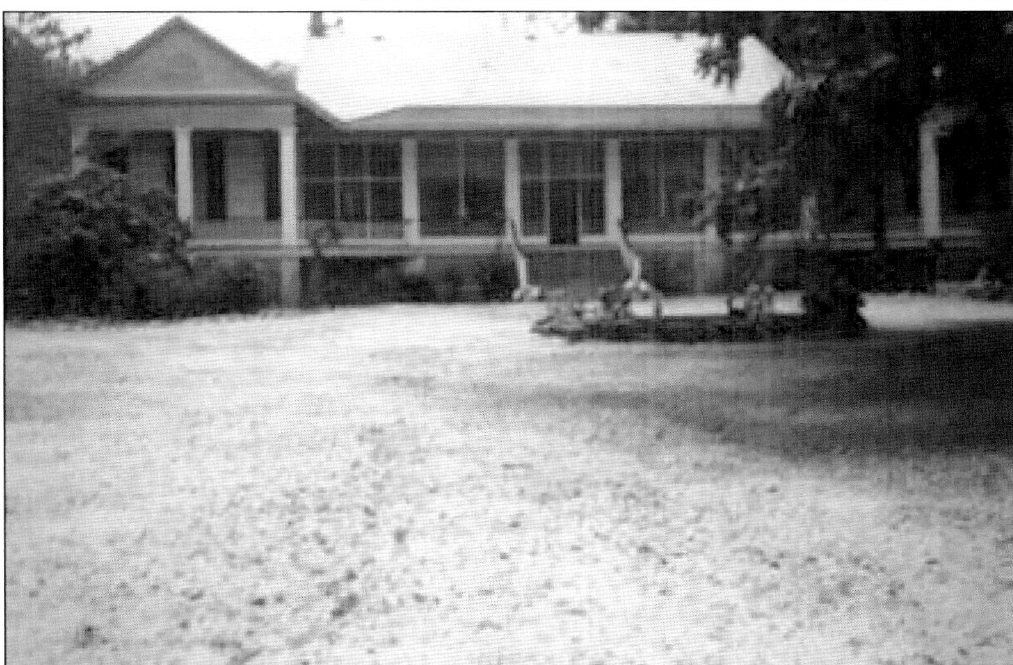

LEA-CAFFEY HOME. The Lea Home is also one of the oldest residences still standing. Davidella G. Cullum, who purchased the property from the Yuilles, built the Creole-style home in 1846. William Jones moved into the house about 1850 and left his mark with improvements that included four marble mantels. His nephew William Jones Lea, the next resident of the home, moved into the house after the Civil War. (Kit Caffey.)

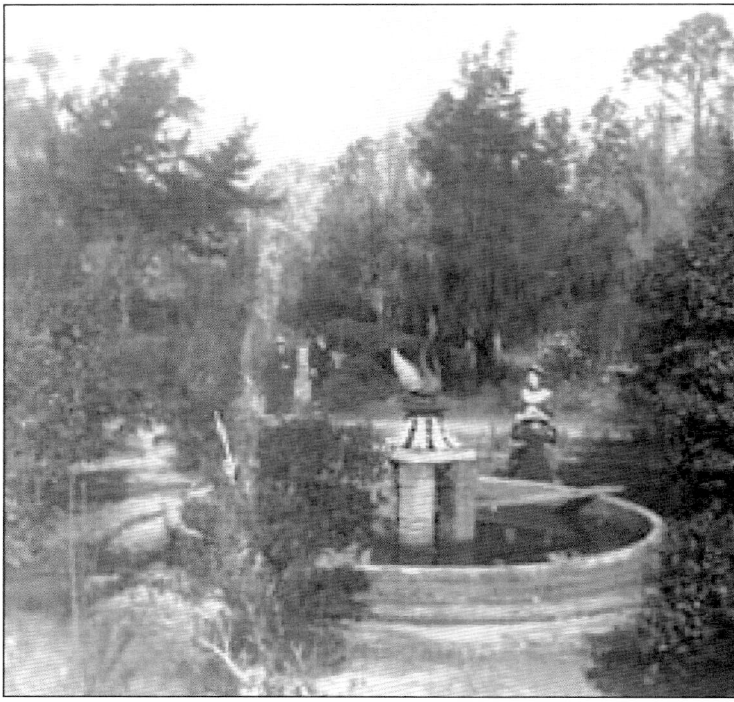

THE SCREAMING SWAN. The Lea home had extensive formal gardens, which featured the famous "Screaming Swan," as Florence Scott described the graceful bronze fountain surrounded by clipped hedges and a profusion of azaleas and camellias. A ram was used to pump water from the clear stream up to the house for the fountain and for general use. (OMCMD, Davis Collection.)

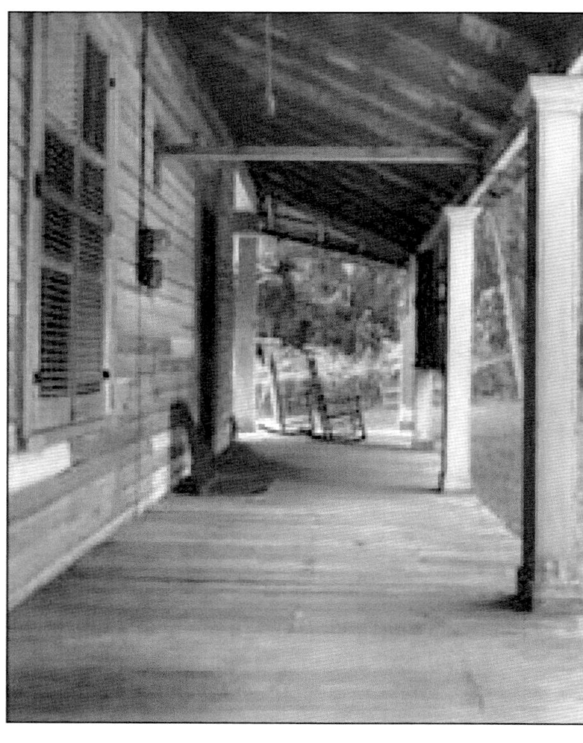

LEA HOME PORCH. When the Trimbles purchased the Lea home in the 1960s, the porches were reminiscent of the grandeur that had once been. The wings were probably added a few years after the original Creole cottage was built in 1846, as evidenced by the change in saw blade marks and a difference in lathing style. The home, now restored to its original beauty, is truly one in which the walls do talk. Mrs. Lea told author Florence Scott that the house was used as a hospital during the Civil War and that shutters were removed and used as stretchers. The rest of the story includes the years that the house was inhabited by the family of Judge William G. Caffey, who moved there in 1976. Kit Caffey, a local historian, spent hours lovingly caring for the grounds and preserving the home. Later residents included the Hendricks and the McMurphy families. (Kit Caffey.)

Two

ON THE BAYFRONT
LIFE ON THE WATER

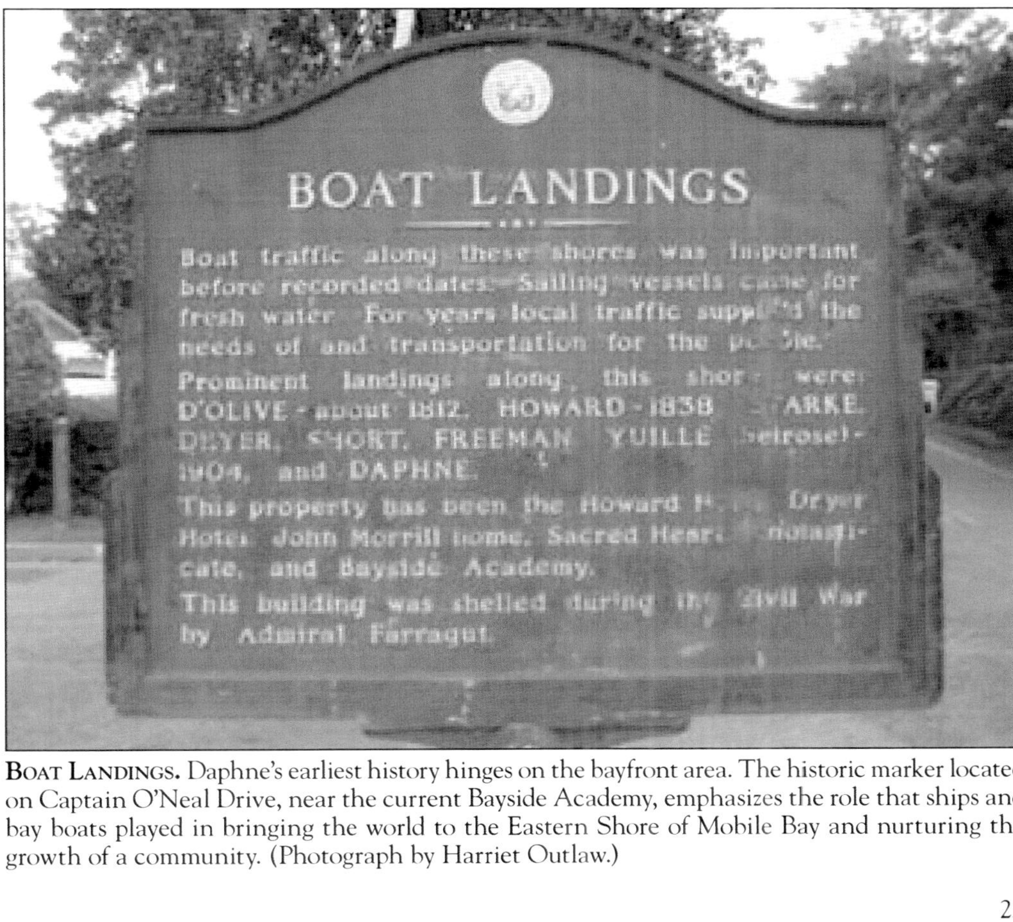

BOAT LANDINGS. Daphne's earliest history hinges on the bayfront area. The historic marker located on Captain O'Neal Drive, near the current Bayside Academy, emphasizes the role that ships and bay boats played in bringing the world to the Eastern Shore of Mobile Bay and nurturing the growth of a community. (Photograph by Harriet Outlaw.)

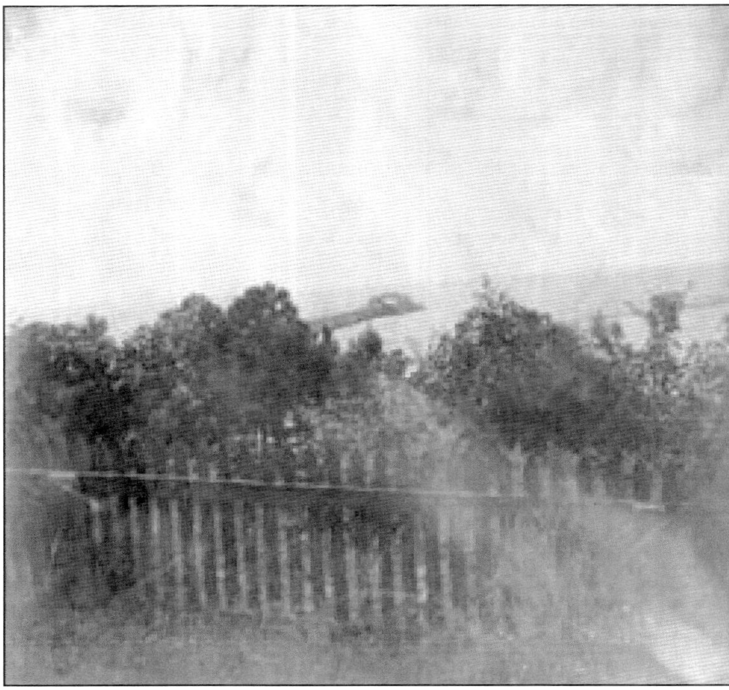

Longest Pier. Most residents in Daphne depended on the piers for access to all communication. The length of this pier is evident from this photograph, taken from one of the bluffs in Daphne. The bay depth averages only five feet, and long piers had to be constructed to accommodate larger vessels. Most homes and all hotels along the bayfront had such piers. (OMCMD.)

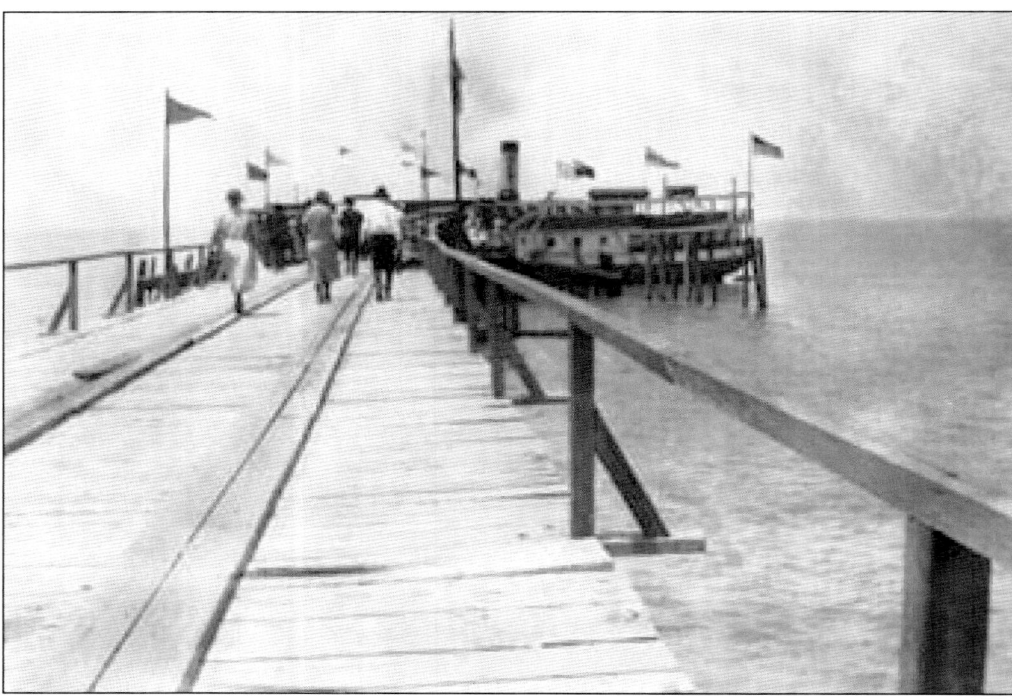

Transport on the Pier. A close-up view of the Wharf Street Pier shows the construction, which used lumber from Daphne sawmills. The rail is designed for a narrow-gauge cart that was pulled by mules to deliver passengers and goods to and from the bluff. However, the Shorts Hotel pier had a cart operated by sails to run the pier traffic. (OMCMD, Davis Collection.)

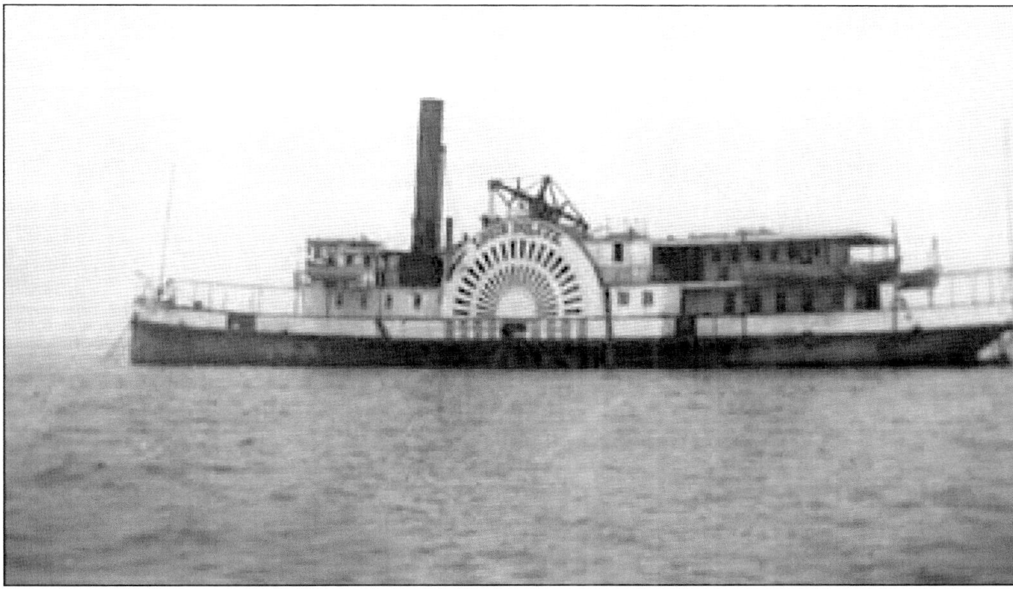

THE *LOUIS D'OLIVE*. Owner James Carney named this ship for his grandfather, who was among the earliest plantation owners in Daphne. Carney also owned the *Heroine*, which had been a blockade-runner, and the *Caloosa*. On most weekdays, bay boats left Daphne in the mornings and returned in the late afternoon. Some traveled south to Point Clear, Magnolia Springs, and Bon Secour. (Dick Scott.)

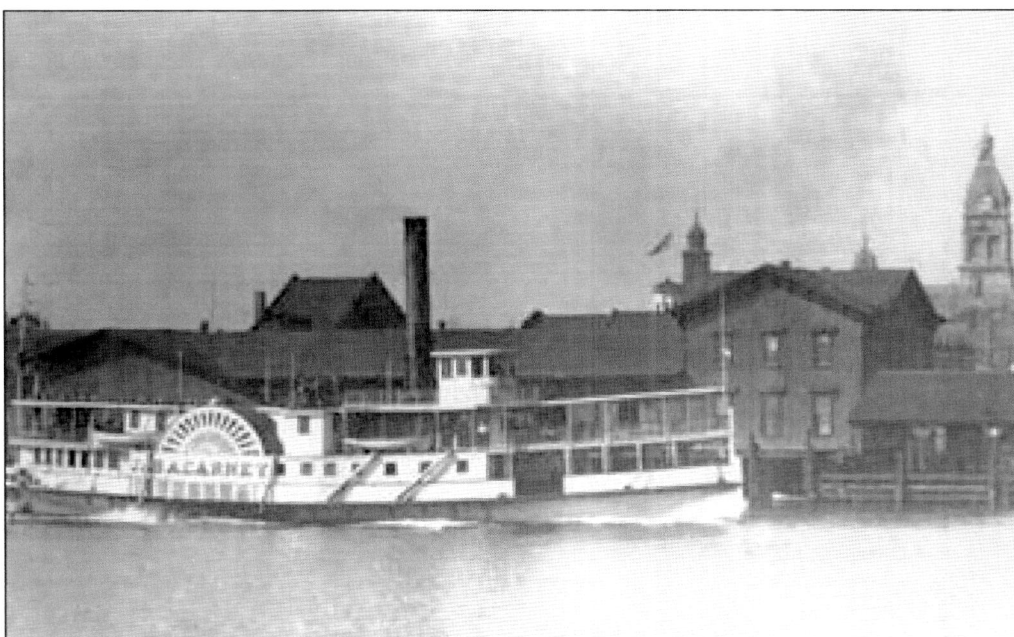

THE *JAMES CARNEY*. The 1890s were the years that saw the most bay traffic. The *James A. Carney* was one of four bay boats owned by James Carney and was named for his father. The 150-foot side-wheeler transported the first Single Tax Colonists from Mobile to Fairhope. She was destroyed beyond repair in the 1916 hurricane. (Dick Scott.)

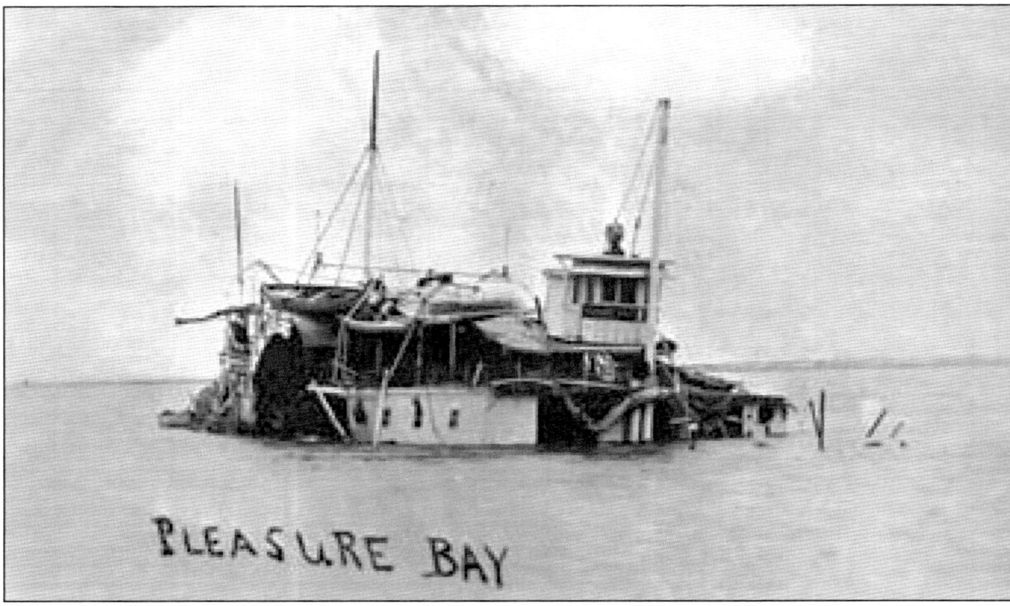

HURRICANE OF 1916. Gulf Coast history is peppered with stories of destruction caused by hurricanes. Three significant, legendary hurricanes arrived almost exactly a decade apart—in 1906, 1916, and 1926. The hurricane of 1906 destroyed the town of Navy Cove on the Fort Morgan peninsula, after which the Nelson family salvaged their home and moved it by barge to Daphne. The photographs on this page show some results of the 1916 hurricane in Daphne. Boats near the shoreline were broken from anchors and thrown onto each other. Some were grounded in the mud and thrashed to bits. The *Pleasure Bay*, pictured above, offered regular runs and excursions to Fort Morgan, Palmetto Beach, and Blakeley. She was salvaged after the hurricane only to burn in Lake Pontchartrain. Homes along the bluff were damaged during all of the storms—mostly from falling trees—but Hurricane Camille, in 1969, was the worst to hit the area until the infamous Frederic virtually redesigned most of Baldwin County in 1979. (Above, Dick Scott; below, OMCMD.)

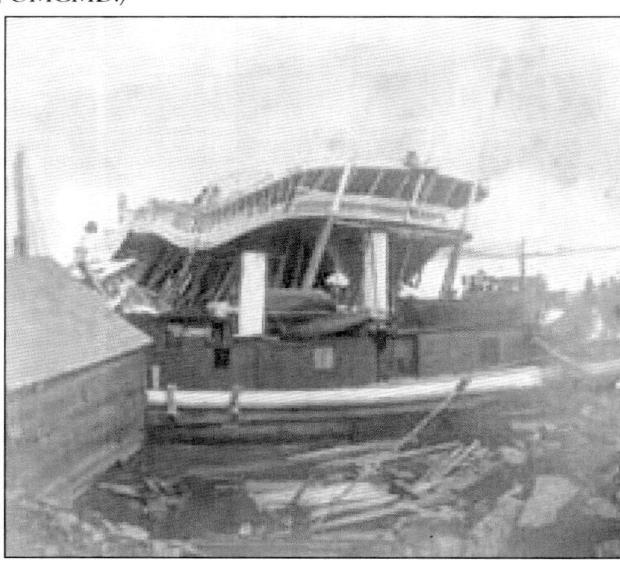

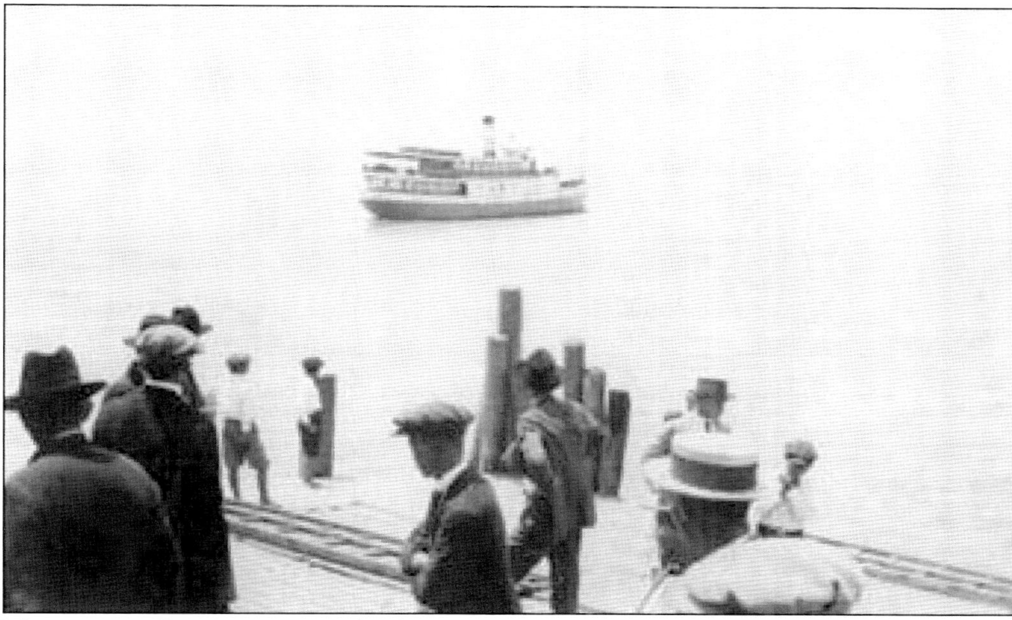

MEETING THE BAY BOAT. Many bayfront residents came to the Eastern Shore for the summer months, bringing everything they might need for comfortable living—including the family cow. Passengers rode in the front of the boat and livestock was transported at the rear. The town of Daphne sprang to life each afternoon with the arrival of the boats. Carts collected ordered goods, guests for hotels, and visiting friends and relatives. Boat traffic continued, for a while, even after the road to Mobile opened in 1927. The last steamboat to make the run was the *Eastern Shore* in October 1933. (Both, OMCMD, Davis Collection.)

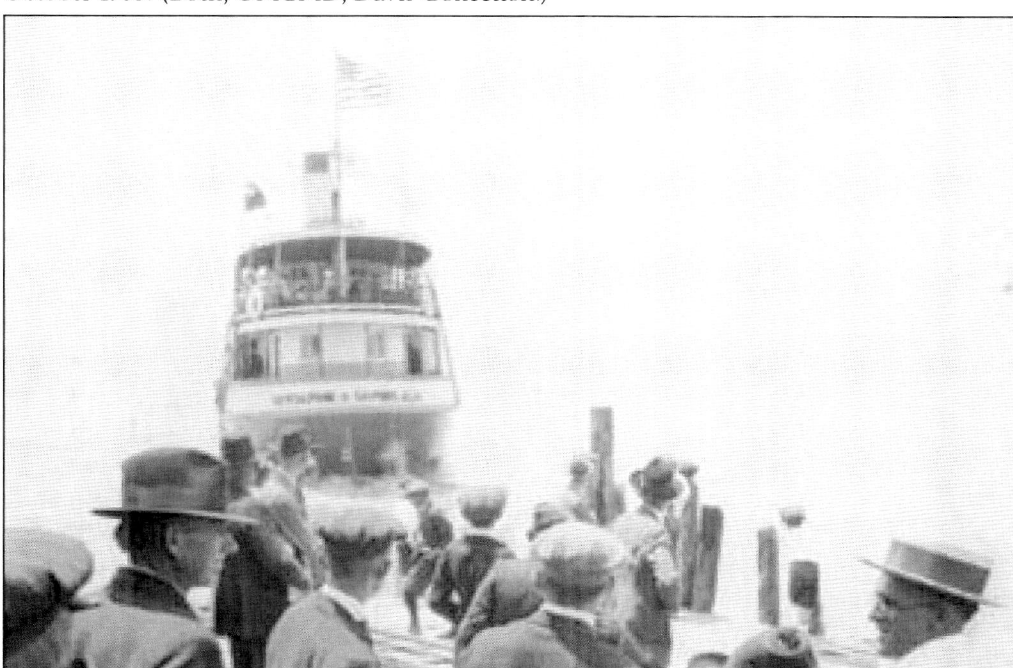

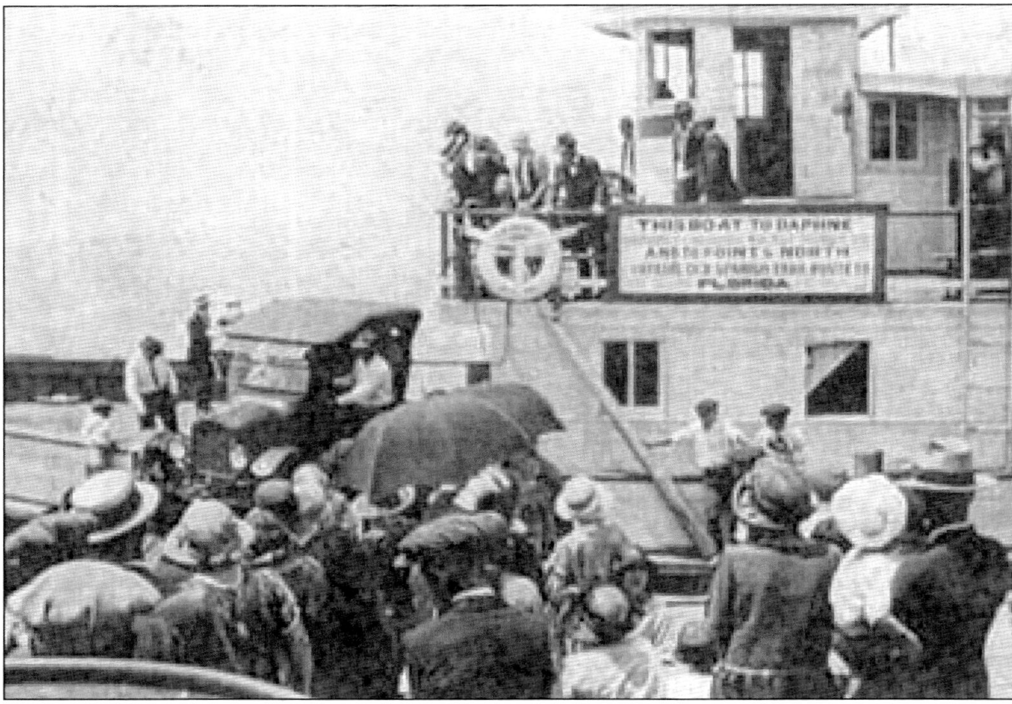

THE *NEW DAPHNE*. The bay boat *New Daphne* was chosen as the transport for the first automobiles brought across for the opening of the official Spanish Trail highway connecting Mobile and Pensacola. The trail had long been used but was newly upgraded and completed as US Highway 90. When the highway cut through Daphne, it became Main Street, and the town center moved from the bayfront to downtown. (John Lewis.)

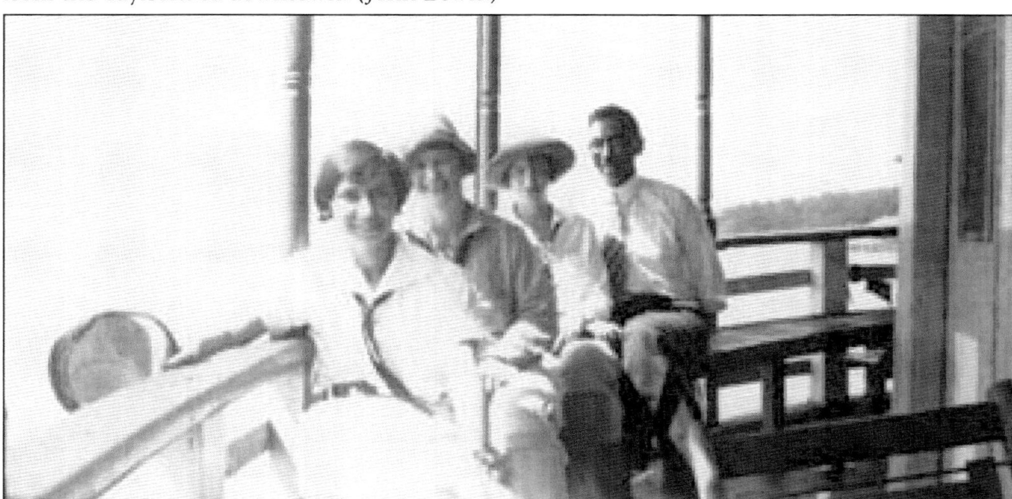

DAY TRIP. Edna Rae Davis is pictured here (left front) with three friends on a day excursion to Mobile. Many people took the boat to Mobile for work, for federal court dates or to visit friends. Many were heading for a day of shopping or perhaps a visit to Monroe Park in Mobile. The fare was 25¢, and the trip took 90 minutes. On Saturdays, the route ran from Mobile to Daphne in the mornings. (OMCMD, Davis Collection.)

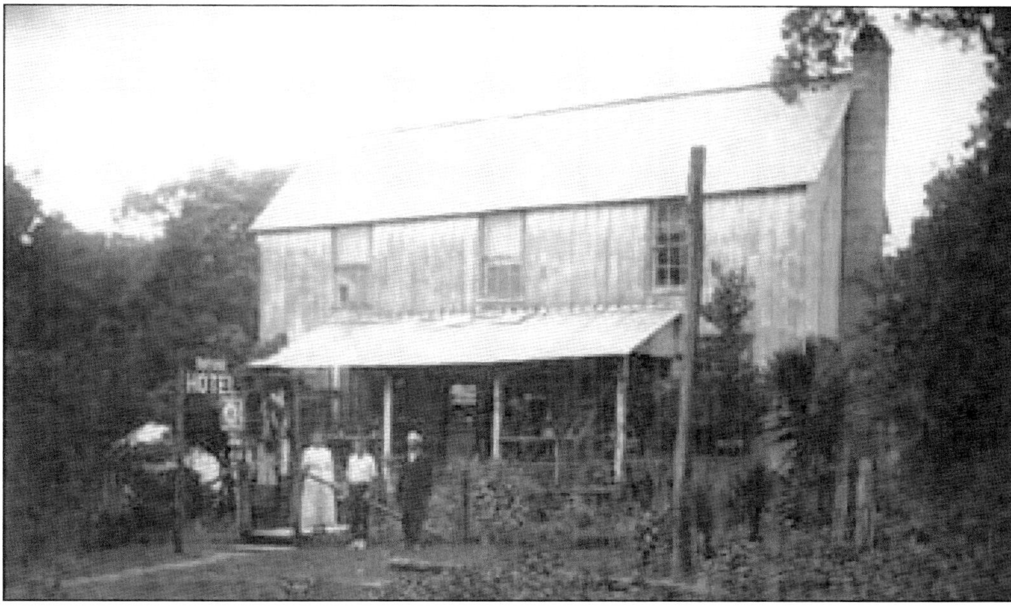

Davis Hotel. Dora K. Davis (left), son Johnnie V., and Warren C. Davis, pictured here in the early 1900s, ran one of the longest-existing hotels in Daphne. The first telephone in town was located here. Many visitors liveried wagons and teams here before journeying to Mobile. (OMCMD.)

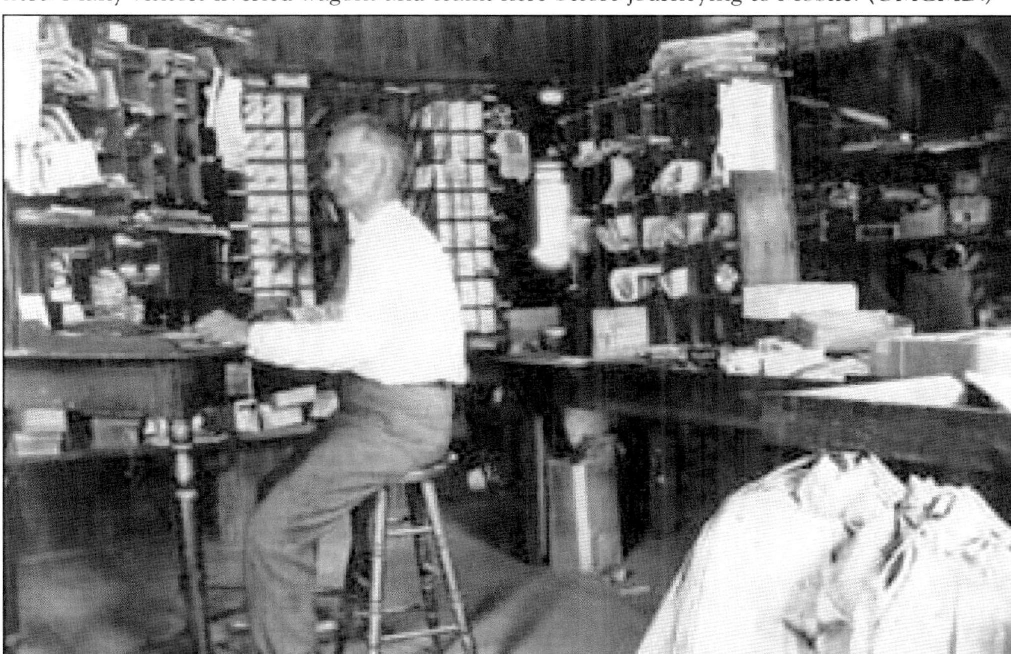

Reception Desk. The Davis family ran the hotel for more than 50 years. It housed jurors when the county seat was located at Daphne, and served as a boarding house for female students at the Daphne Normal School until the death of Dora Davis made it improper for young ladies to board there. It continued to offer accommodations to overnight guests until the middle of the century; today, it is a private home. (OMCMD, Davis Collection.)

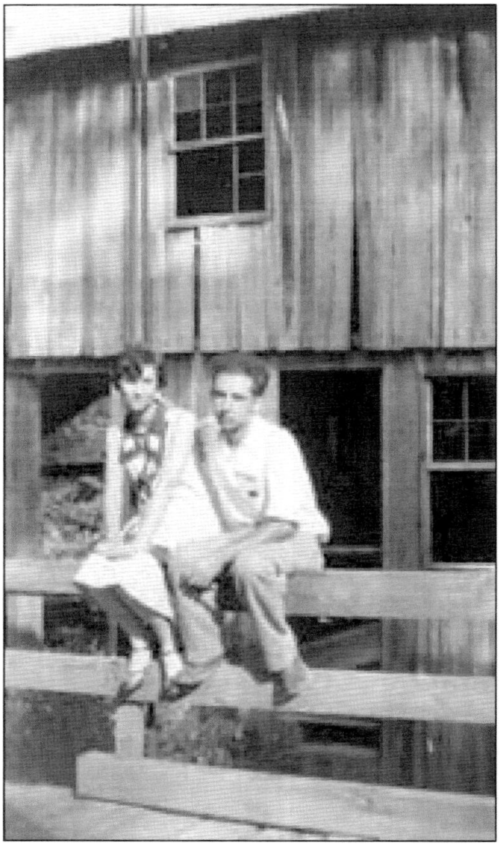

Johnnie and Edna. Johnnie Davis, the little boy in the photograph of the Davis Hotel on page 29, grew up in Daphne, attended the normal school, and then went to University of Alabama, where he earned a degree in engineering. His research earned him a patent in the chroming process, and he was a successful businessman. He and his wife, Edna, spent many hours at Johnnie's home near the bayfront. Their photograph albums have become virtual history books about the bayfront era. (OMCMD, Davis Collection.)

Walking Trail. The trail connecting the three major hotels and other homes along the bayfront provided wonderful walking paths. Each home or hotel site had a swinging gate at either side of the property, and all were welcome to pass through. The trail also extended over the gullies thanks to homemade trestles. The Davis family album includes this image of a group on the bridge, dangling their feet and whiling away the day. (OMCMD, Davis Collection.)

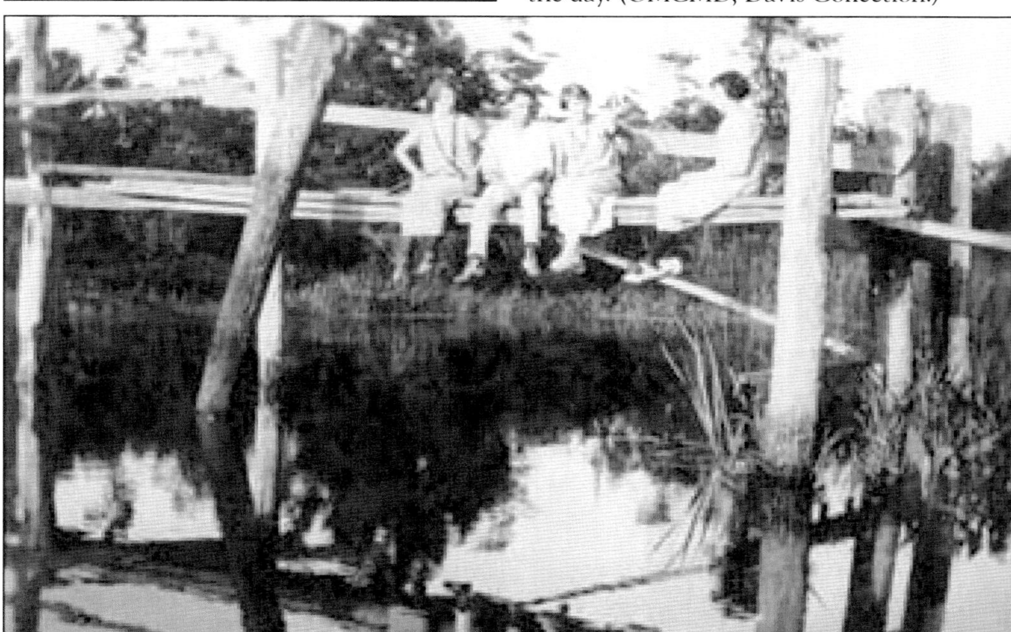

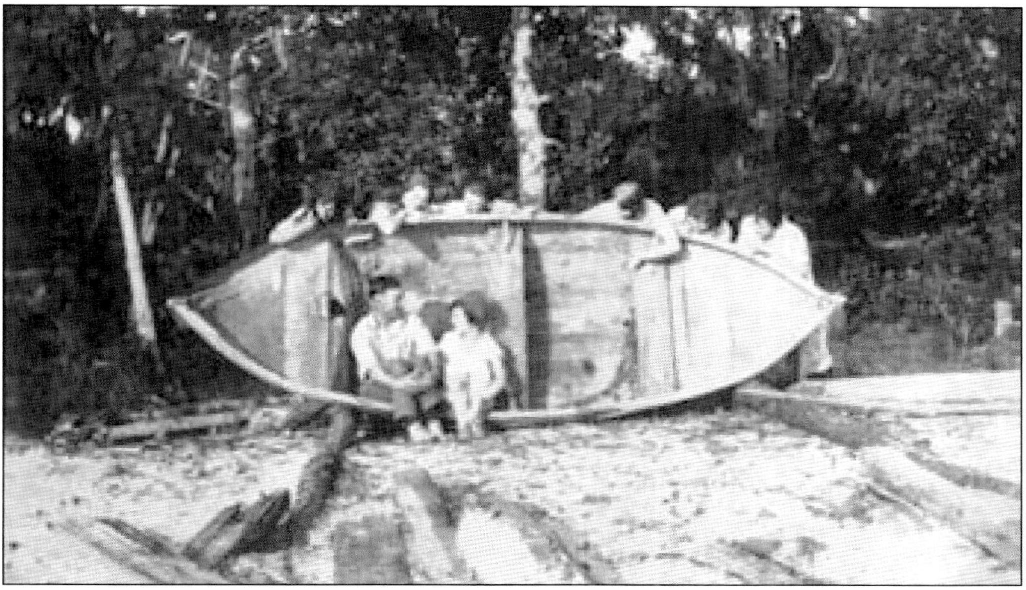

Under the Old Wooden Boat. Many young people courted and spent afternoons walking on the trails. Several homes had steps leading down to the beach, and many young people simply scaled the bluffs. Almost everyone had a boat, even if it was just a rowboat like this one, which provided a neat resting place for a group of the Davises' friends on the beach. (OMCMD, Davis Collection.)

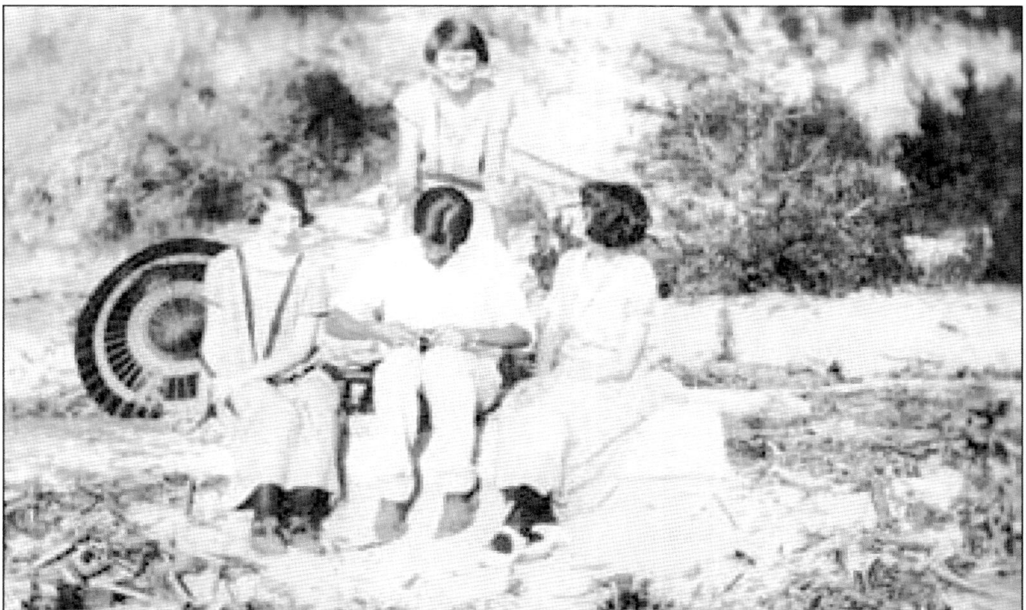

Friends at the Beach. People spent afternoons on the beach enjoying the bay breezes. They met to watch the sunset, talk, play games, and maybe steal a kiss or two. The love story of Johnnie and Edna is the stuff dreams are made of. They met while she was a student at Daphne Normal School, and the rest is a fairy tale. (OMCMD, Davis Collection.)

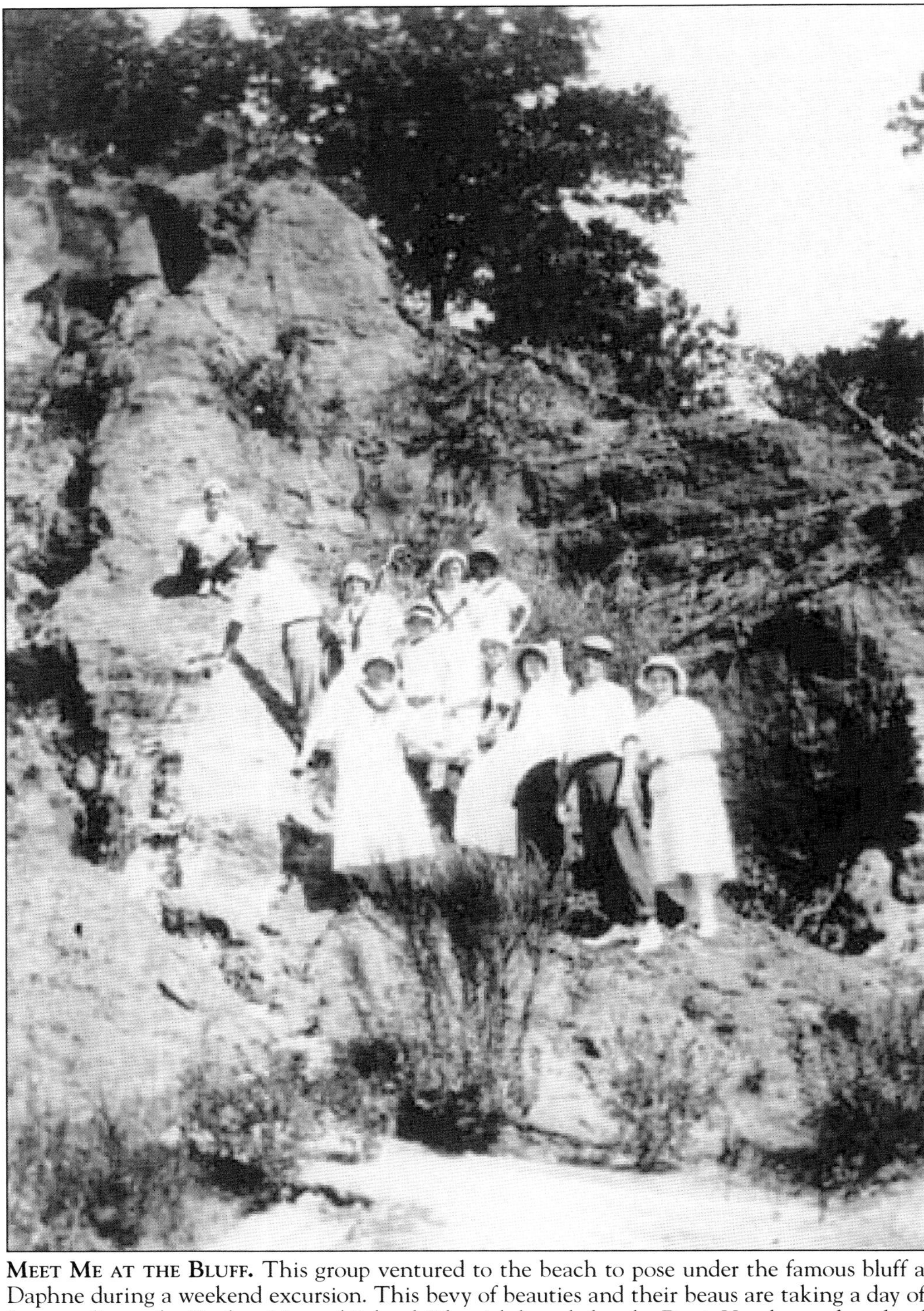

Meet Me at the Bluff. This group ventured to the beach to pose under the famous bluff at Daphne during a weekend excursion. This bevy of beauties and their beaus are taking a day off from studies at the Daphne Normal School. The girls boarded at the Davis Hotel near the school. (Doy Leale McCall Rare Book and Manuscript Library, University of South Alabama.)

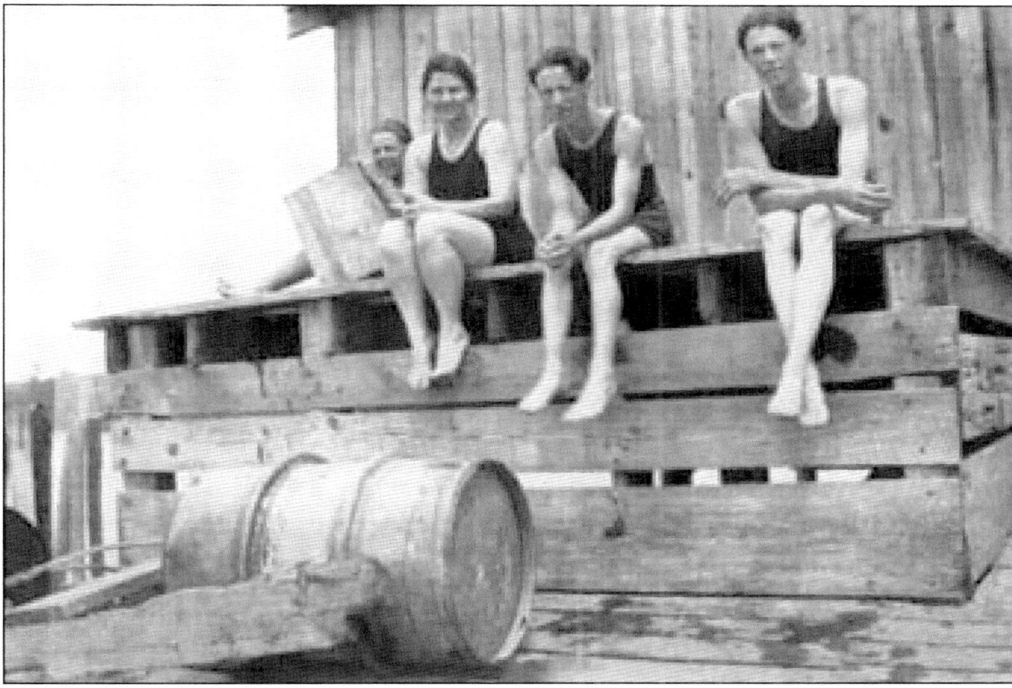

Fashionable Swimwear. Friends of Johnnie Davis sport the modern fashion in swimwear in the 1920s. Not only did men begin to appear in public in swimsuits, but women also began showing more than ever before! This group posed on the pier near "the Casino," as the gym was called. (OMCMD, Davis Collection.)

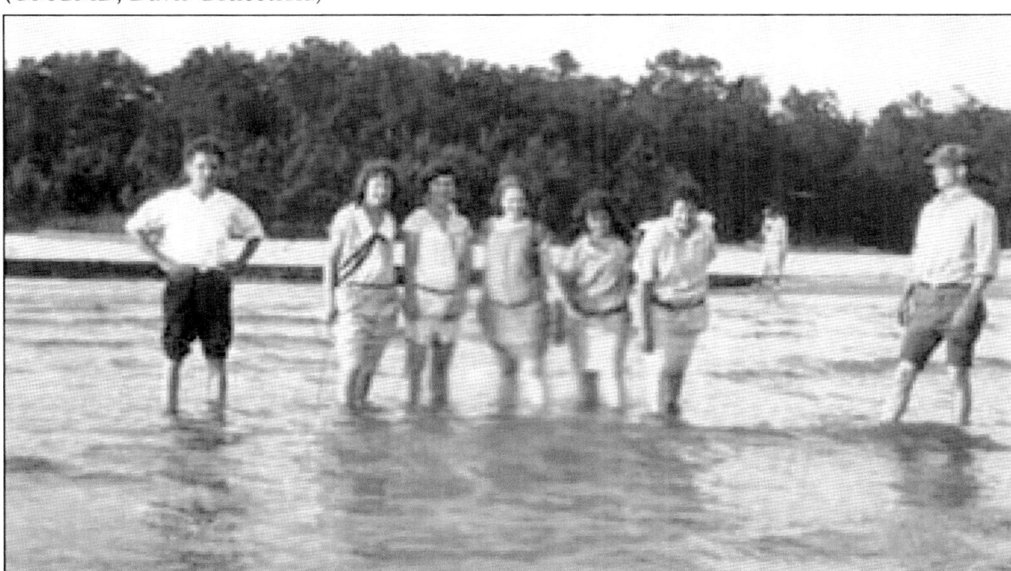

Knee-Deep in the Bay. These folks were evidently not prepared for swimming but could not resist rolling up their pants and taking a dip in the bay. At the time, the bay was only a few feet deep for almost a mile out from the shore of Daphne. Mobile Bay is a nursery bay, providing estuarine resources that engender excellent breeding conditions for sea life. (OMCMD, Davis Collection.)

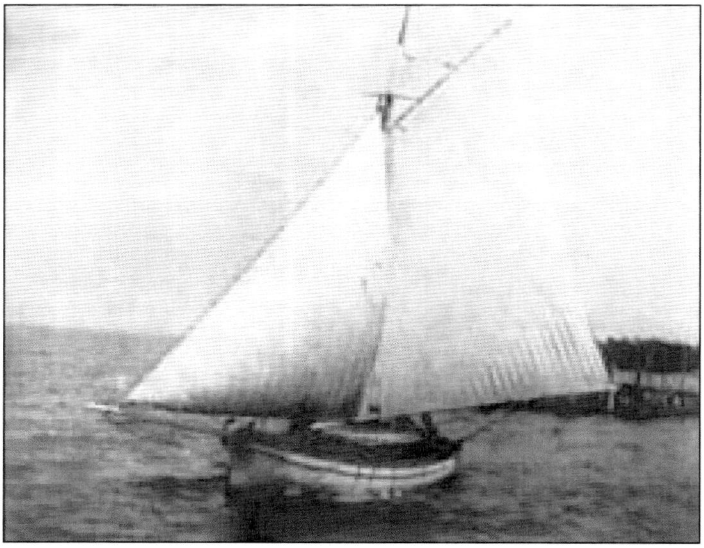

Pleasure Sailing and Racing. Sailing has always been a means of transportation in the bay. However, sailing as a sport was probably more prevalent. Races were held often, but little is known of a formal yacht or sailing club, as most sailors had their own homes on the bayfront. By the 1950s, the Lake Forest Yacht Club and the Fairhope Yacht Club had been established and the Dauphin Island Regatta had become an annual event. (OMCMD.)

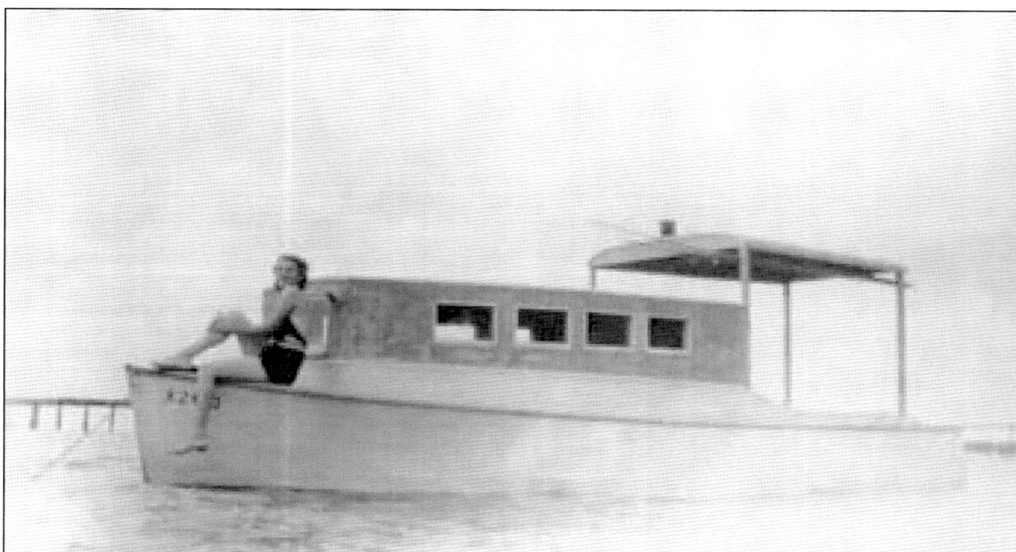

Edna, Ready to Launch. This small, gasoline-powered boat is called a launch, and Edna Davis poses on the hull, basking in the sun. Wooden-boat building was a skill that not many mastered, but Stauter-built boats became a legendary name in the Mobile Bay area. Launches were built for speed and could make the trip to Mobile much faster than steamboats could, so many people used them to commute. (OMCMD, Davis Collection.)

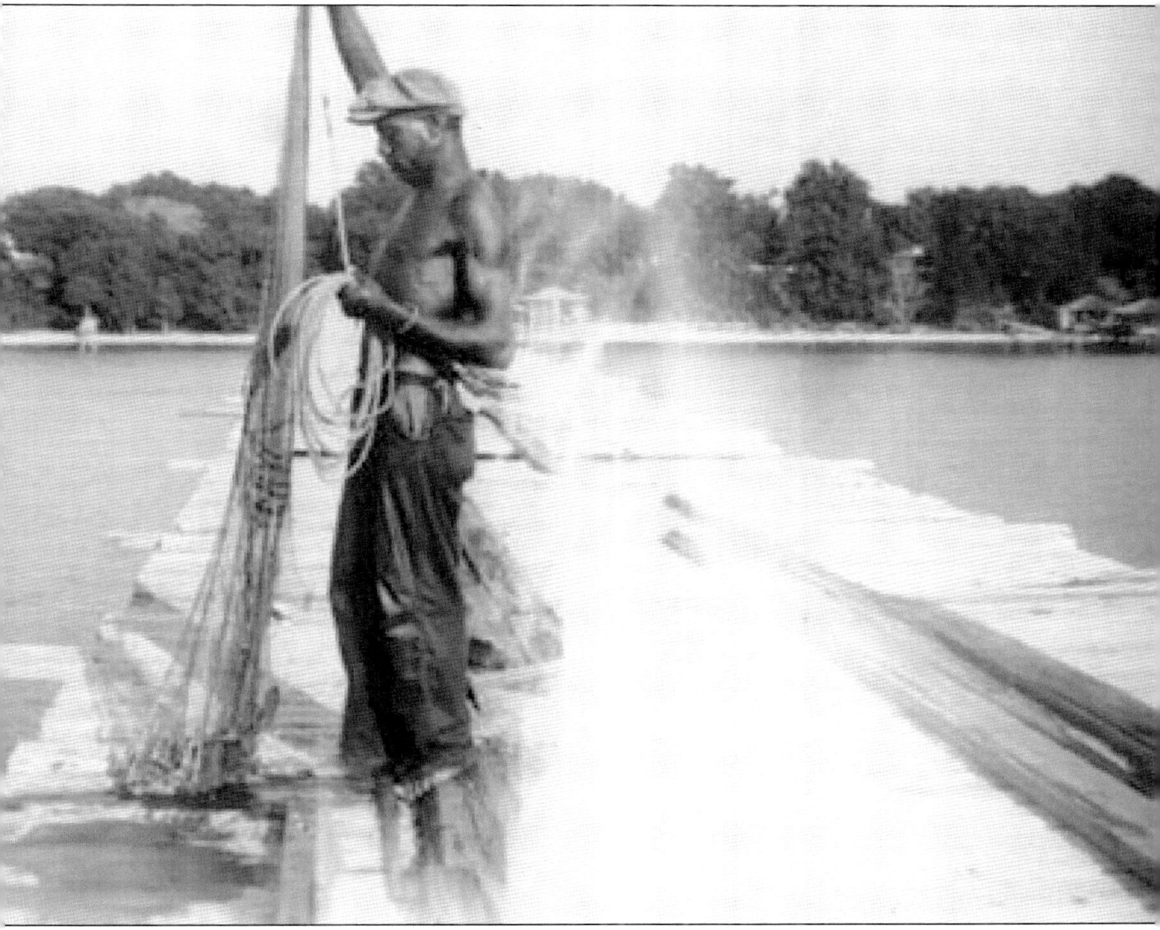

WINDING THE NET. Fishing has always been popular along the bay. Here, a fisherman readies his cast net by looping over his left arm. The right hand holds an edge to lead the toss. Many people hold one of the weights in their mouth to spread out the net, which works, if the fisherman remembers to open his mouth at the right time; if not, he loses a couple cf teeth. (OMCMD, Davis Collection.)

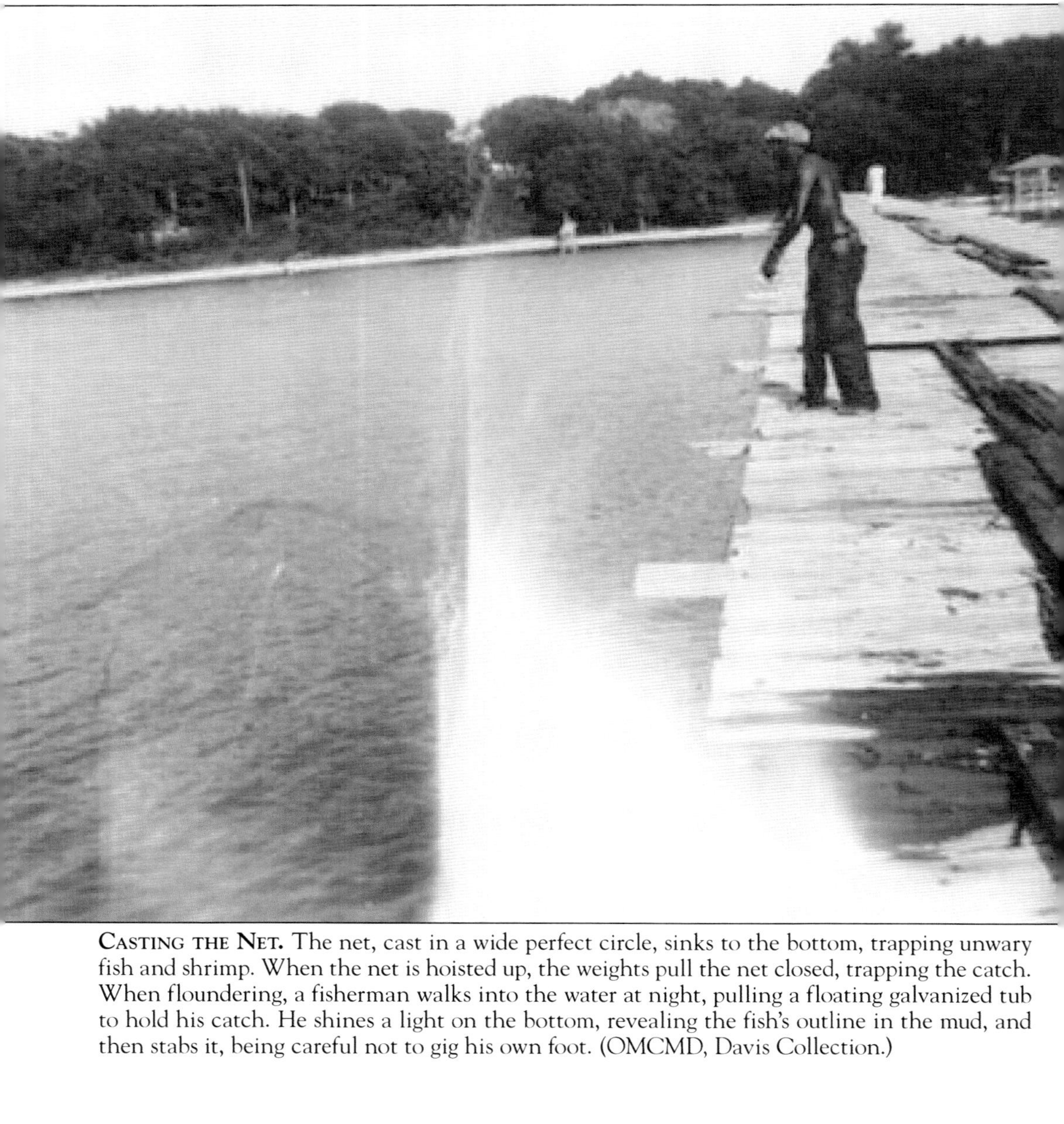

Casting the Net. The net, cast in a wide perfect circle, sinks to the bottom, trapping unwary fish and shrimp. When the net is hoisted up, the weights pull the net closed, trapping the catch. When floundering, a fisherman walks into the water at night, pulling a floating galvanized tub to hold his catch. He shines a light on the bottom, revealing the fish's outline in the mud, and then stabs it, being careful not to gig his own foot. (OMCMD, Davis Collection.)

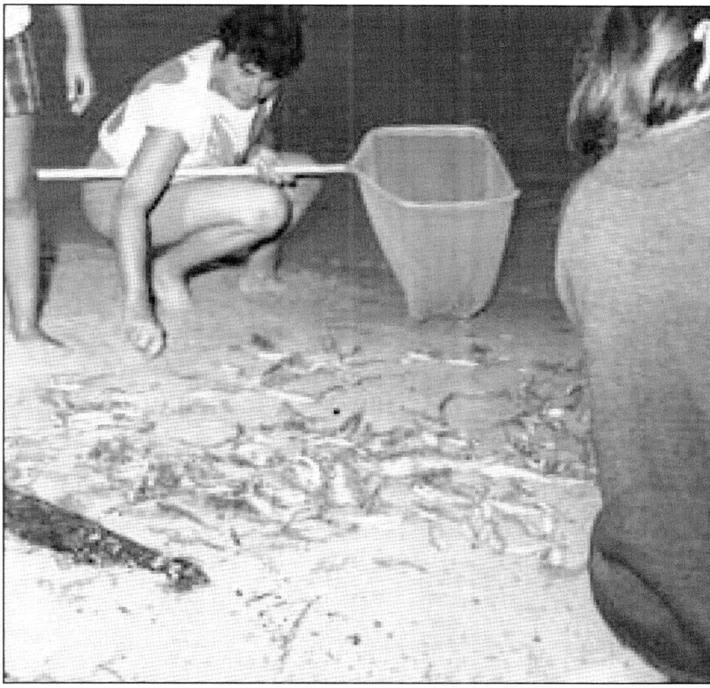

Jubilee! Jubilee! When the "jubilee!" cry is heard in the predawn hours of a summer morning, people jump from their slumbers and head to the shore. There, they see crabs, fish, eel, and shrimp that come incredibly close to shore—sometimes onto the beach. Experts say a jubilee is the result of a lack of oxygen in the water, which can occur when the tides, wind, and temperature are all just right. (Right, Elberta Heritage History Museum; below, OMCMD.)

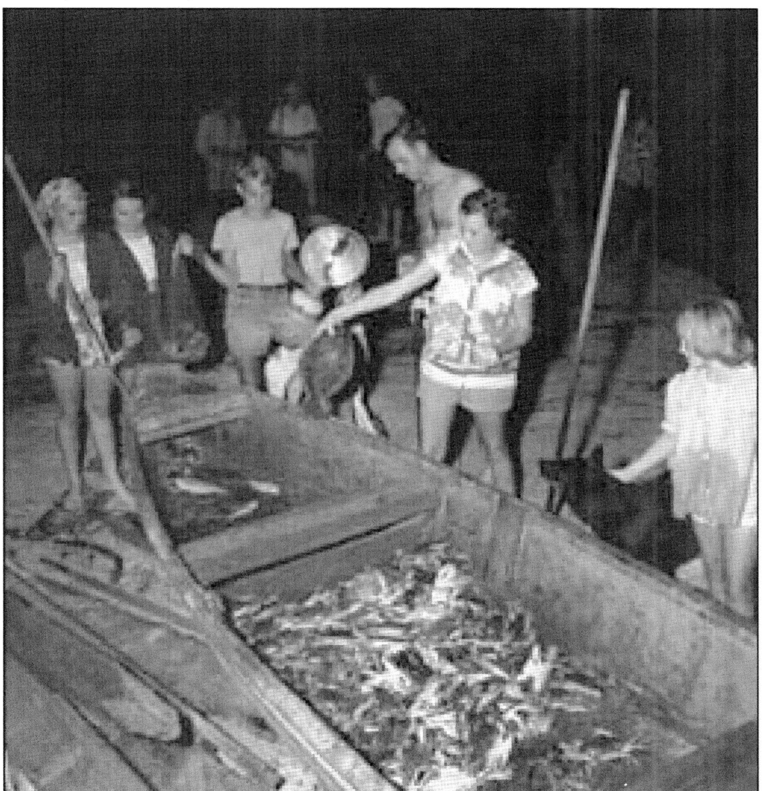

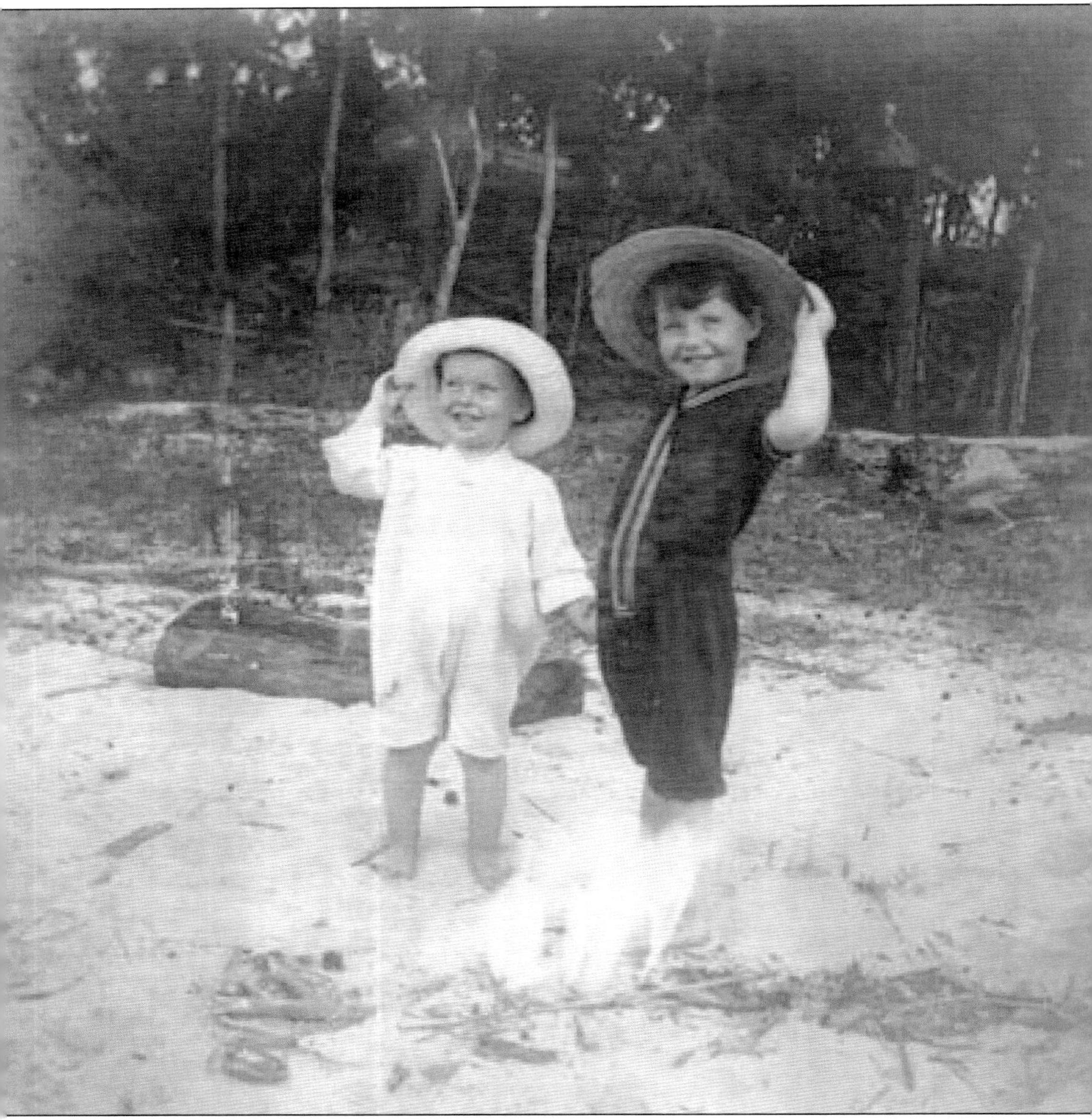

Portraits by the Bay. The picturesque bayfront creates a perfect setting for family portraits. This photograph of two unknown boys from a local family album is typical of portraits taken at the beach. (OMCMD.)

Three

A Community is Built
The Jubilee Town

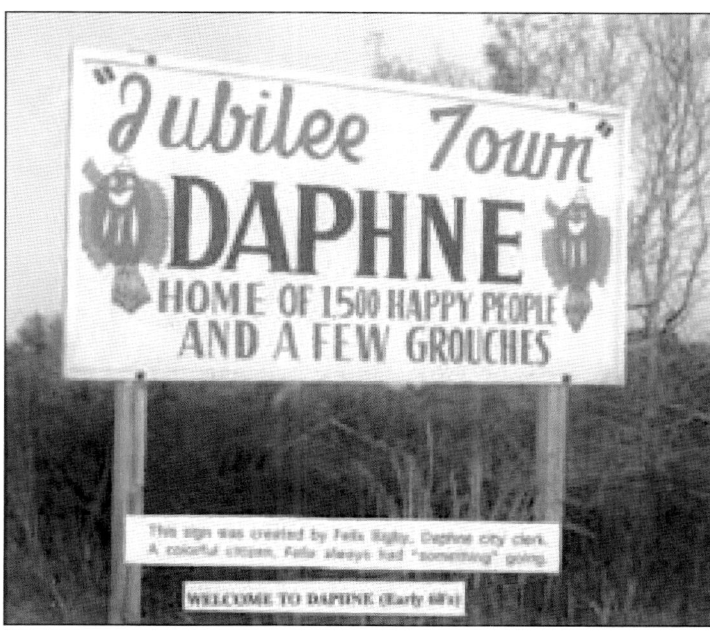

Welcome to Daphne. Daphne city clerk Felix Bigby created this welcome sign, which stood at the town limits on Highway 98, in the early 1960s. By 2000, Daphne was the largest city in Baldwin County. When Highway 98 was improved in the 1980s, it bypassed the old Main Street, which then seemed abandoned. Today, Main Street is once again the lively center of a vibrant community. (OMCMD.)

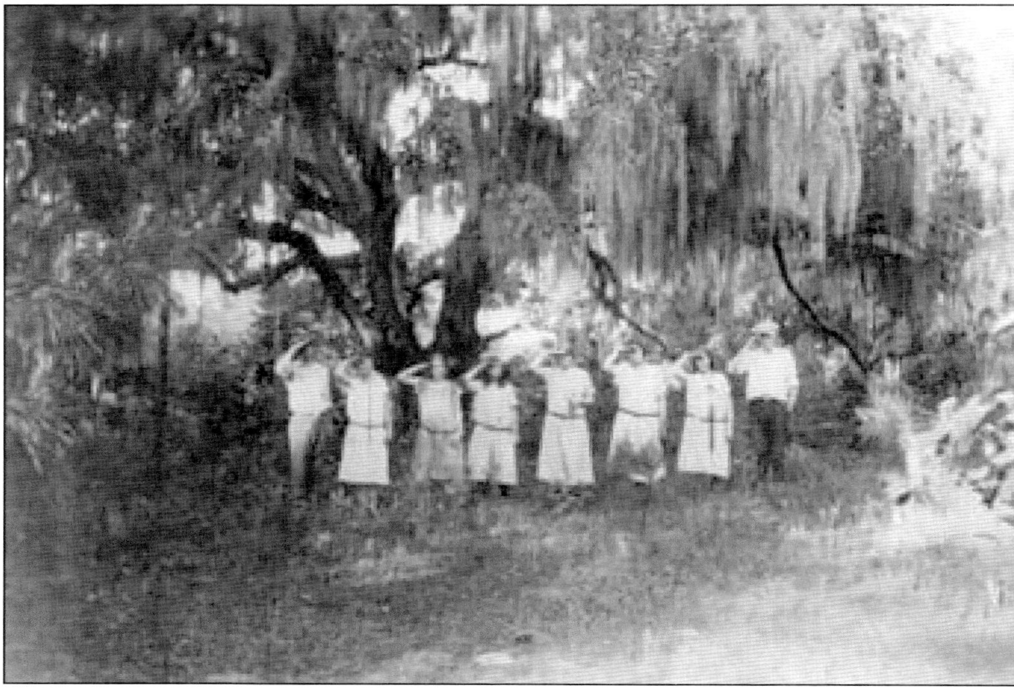

Meet Me at the Tree. Jackson's Oak has borne witness to the history of Daphne from the days of Indian powwows. Here, the hiking club of the Daphne Normal School gathered at the tree for a formal picture; the group was learning the history of the area through a literal field trip. Today, this tree is preserved at the Village Point Park Preserve. (OMCMD, Davis Collection.)

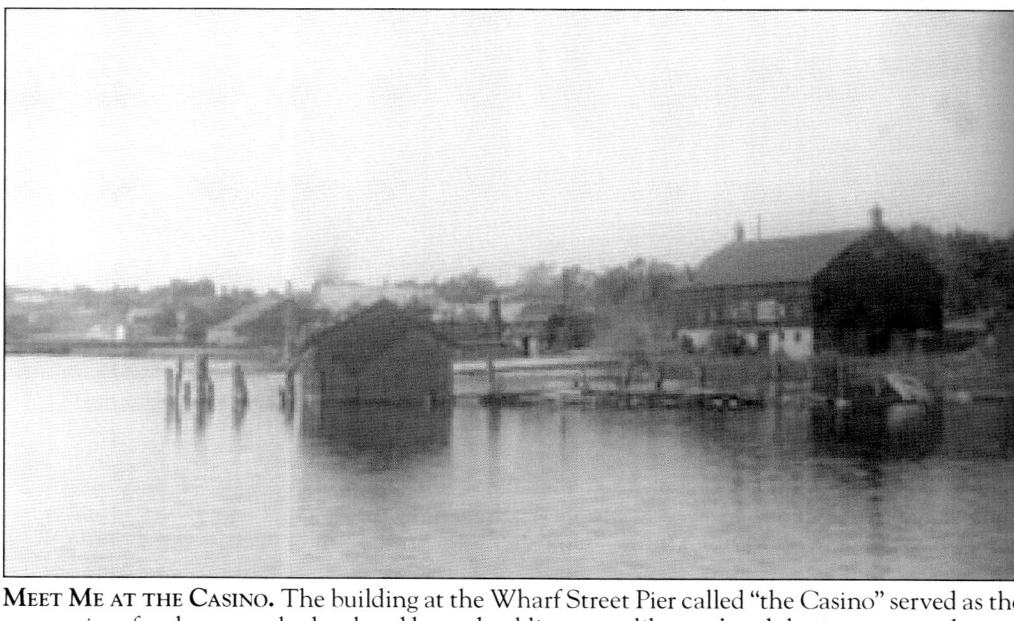

Meet Me at the Casino. The building at the Wharf Street Pier called "the Casino" served as the gymnasium for the normal school and hosted public events like weekend skating parties, dances, basketball games, and even boxing matches. A snack bar was open here during the summers for visitors who had come for an outing at the beach. (OMCMD, Davis Collection.)

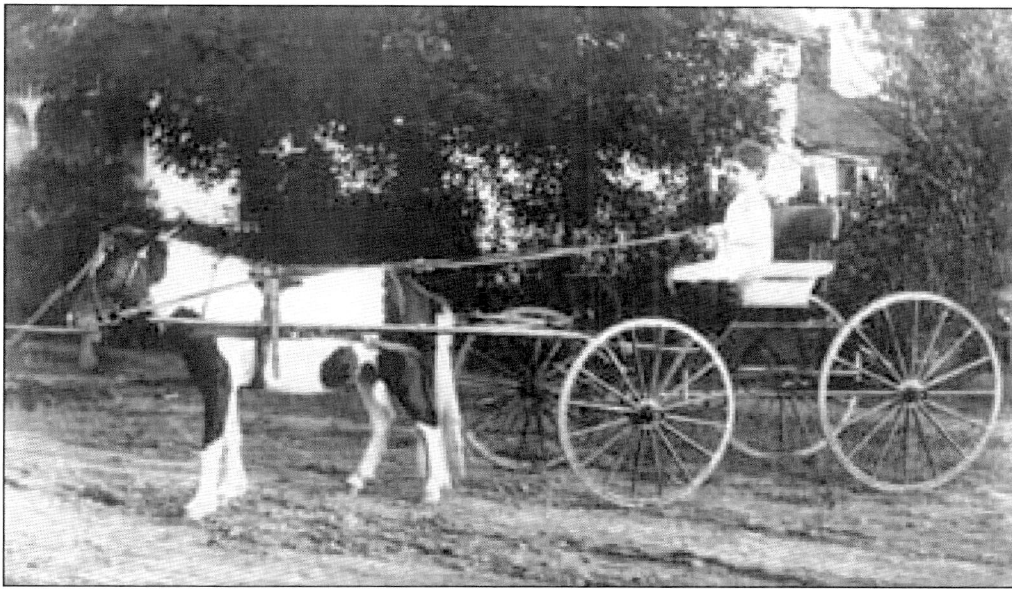

PONY CART. As a boy, Johnnie Davis was often seen driving his cart to town, delivering goods from the boats up to his family's hotel on College Avenue. Pony carts, oxcarts, carriages, and surreys were everyday sights in Daphne. (OMCMD, Davis Collection.)

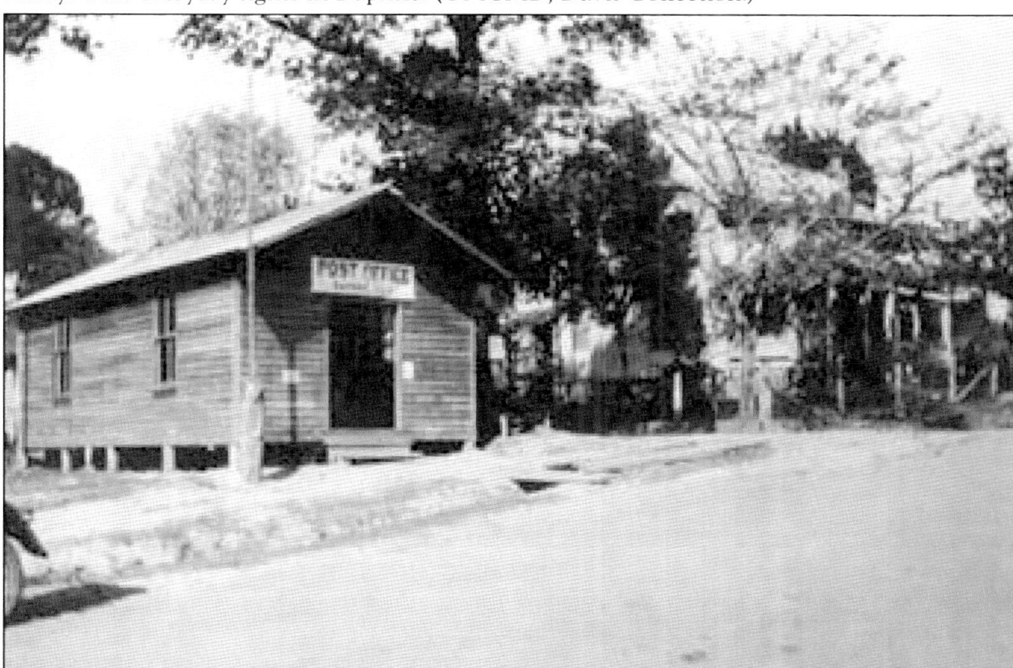

MAIL CALL ON THE BAY. The earliest post office operated out of the Howard Hotel and was run by postmaster William Howard. In 1874, Howard named the town "Daphne." This 1900 photograph is of the post office building located near the courthouse and bayfront hotels. As the population shifted away from the bayfront, the post office was moved to the Manci Building, next to Trione's Store on Main Street. (OMCMD.)

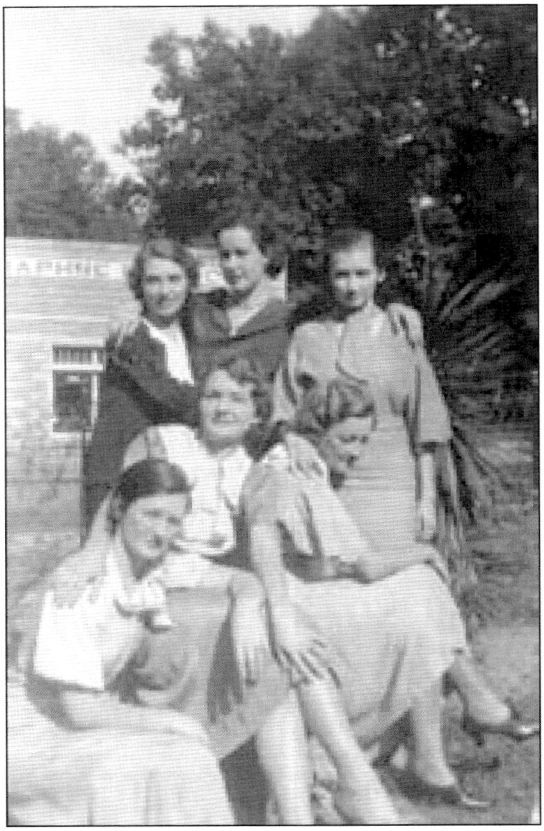

Meet Me at the Drugstore. One of the first businesses in town was the Daphne Drug Store, located on the corner of Captain O'Neal Drive and College Avenue, across the street from the courthouse (later the normal school). Here, girls from the normal school are sitting pretty in front of the drugstore. This business was later moved to Main Street. (OMCMD, Davis Collection.)

Downtown Starts to Grow. When automobiles became a major source of transportation and the courthouse was moved to Bay Minette, town life moved from the bay to Main Street. Framed houses face the dirt road, which is little more than a horse-and-buggy trail. Before the 1900s, the section east of the bayfront was owned and occupied primarily by African Americans, some of whom were former slaves. (OMCMD, Davis Collection.)

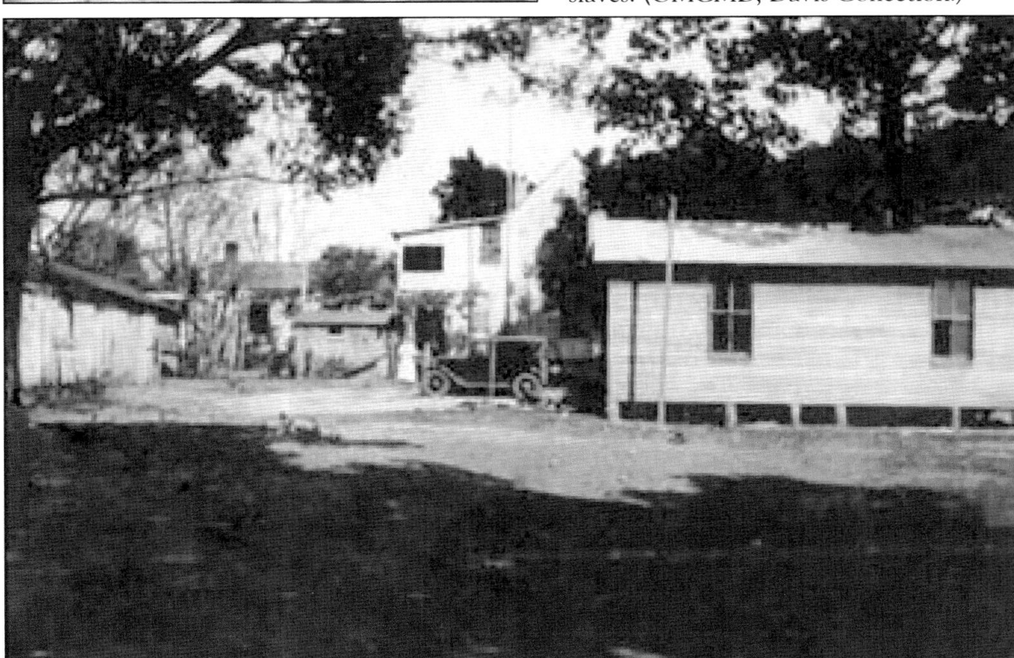

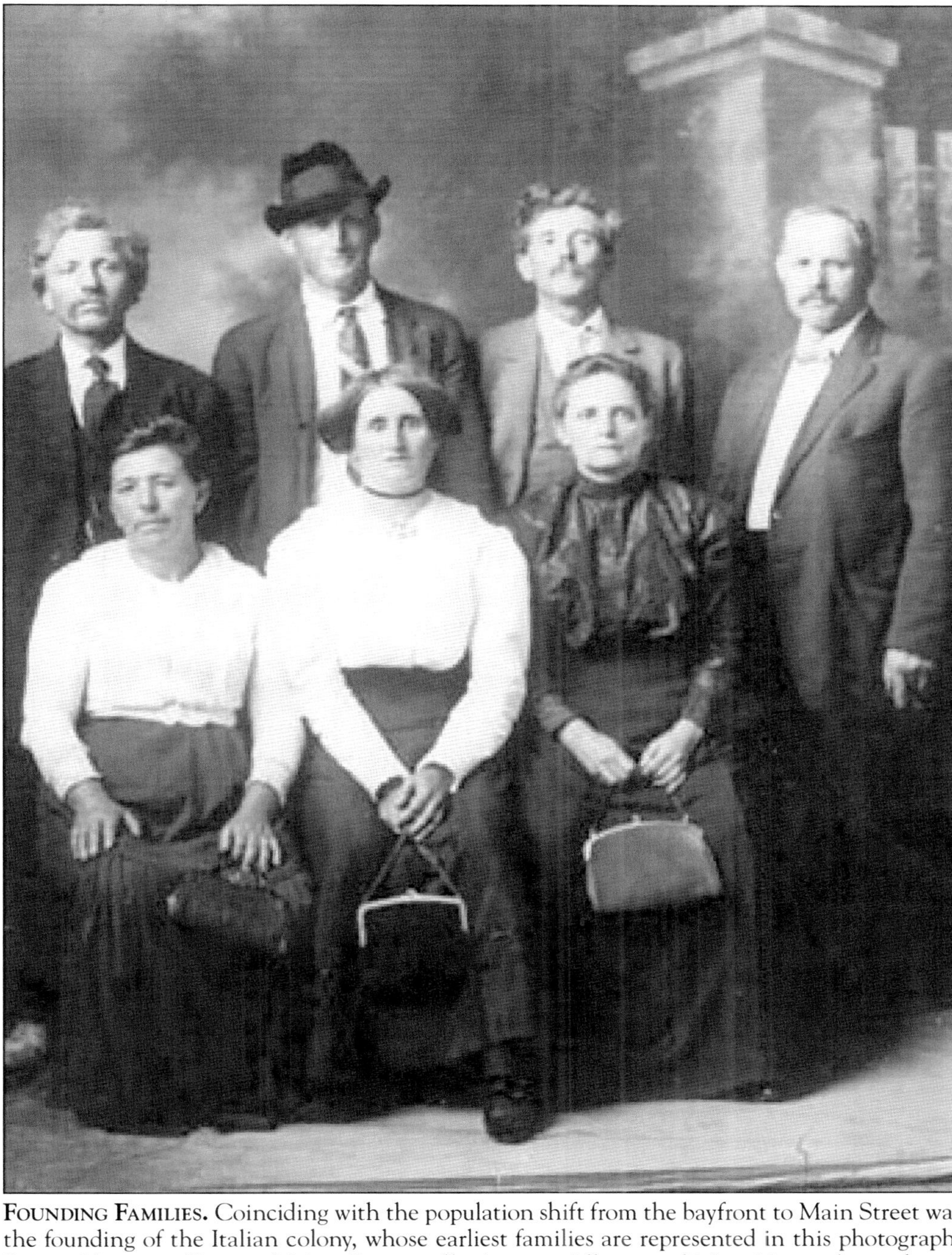

FOUNDING FAMILIES. Coinciding with the population shift from the bayfront to Main Street was the founding of the Italian colony, whose earliest families are represented in this photograph. Pictured here are (first row) Mary Bertagnolli, Assunta Allegri, and Mary Manci; (second row) Constante Bertagnolli, Frank Manci, Carlo Bruno, and Cipriano Allegri. (OMCMD.)

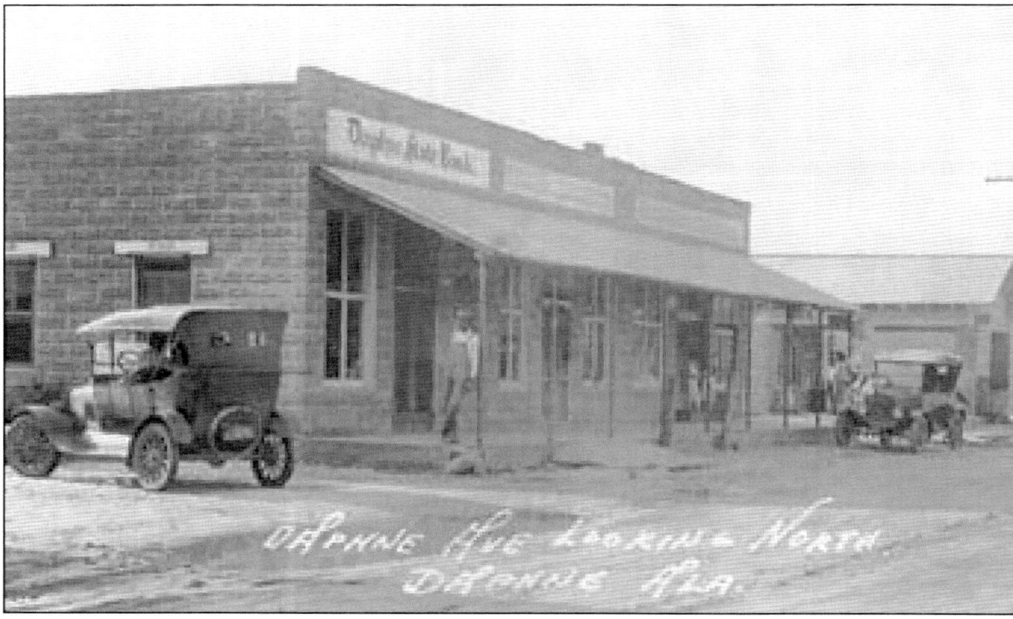

MAIN STREET. At 1715 Main Street is the symbol of Old Towne Daphne. Built in 1900 by Frank Manci and Angelo Trione, these storefronts have been home to various businesses. The Daphne State Bank closed during the Great Depression without penalizing its customers. Later, the post office was moved to this location. (John Lewis, The Gallery.)

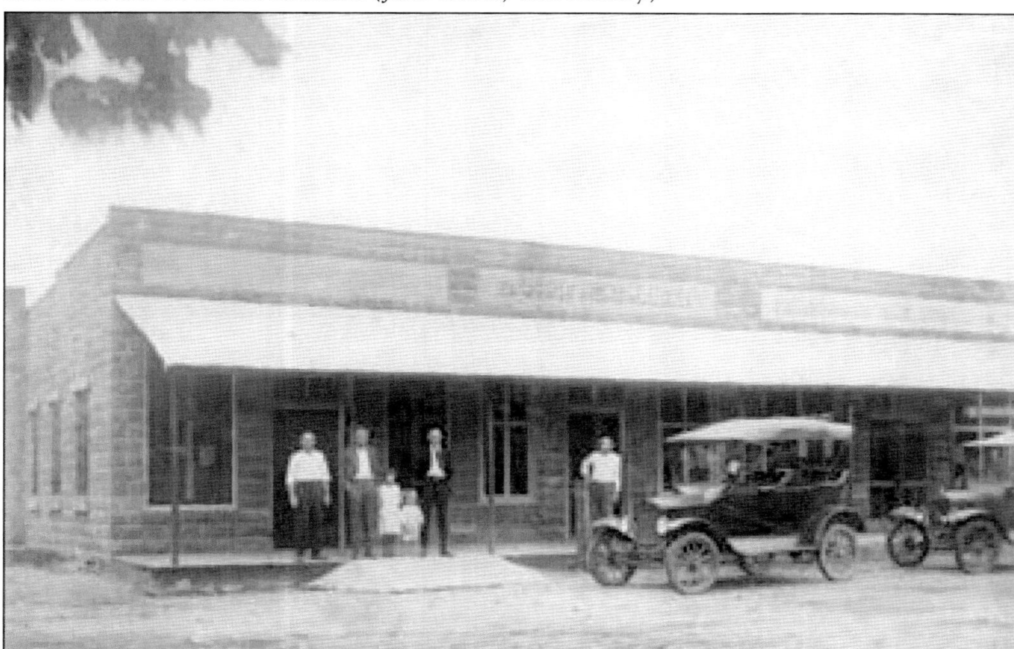

MANCI'S DOWNTOWN BUILDINGS. The middle section included Daphne Meat Market as part of Trione's Store. The building farthest to the north was a gas station until it became Manci's Antique Club, in which Arthur Manci displayed a wonderful collection of memorabilia. (Manci family.)

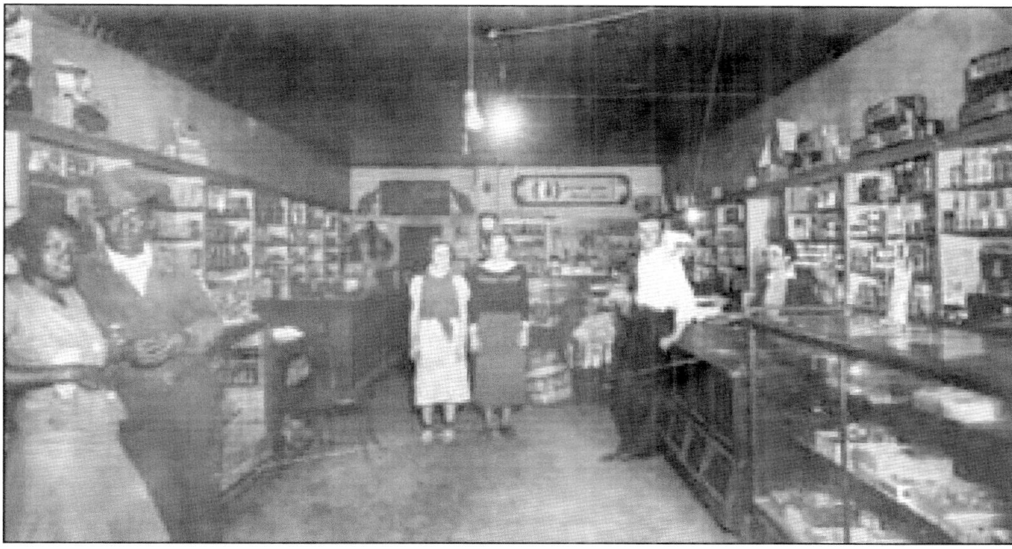

TRIONE'S STORE AND BUS STATION. Alvira Manci Trione and her husband, Angelo A. Trione, opened Trione's Store in 1903. Their son Leonard "Red" ran it until its 1984 closing. Trione's was the hub of activity in the small town. The couple at left is awaiting the Greyhound bus. Daphne's African American residents provided overnight board for traveling musicians, who knew they could find accommodations with families here during the days of segregation. (OMCMD.)

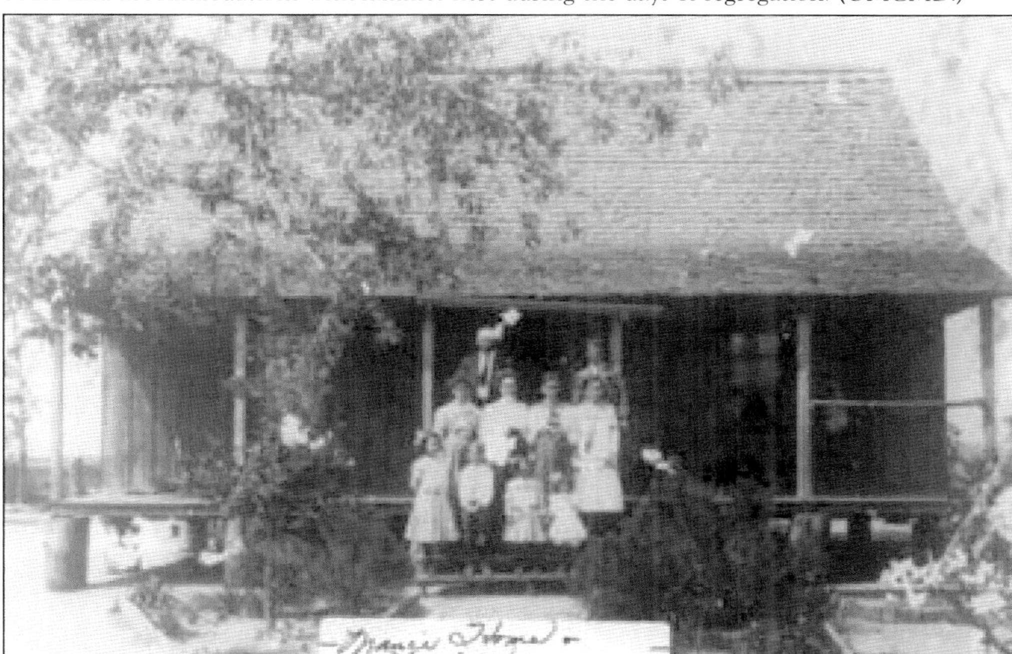

MANCI FAMILY HOME. One of the original Italian colonists, Francesco Manci, used his business acumen and talents to create many of the successful enterprises in Daphne. His homestead farm, pictured here, included a cotton gin and a sawmill. In 1902, Manci was one of the first farmers to plant and ship potatoes, which rapidly became the main cash crop throughout the county. (Manci family.)

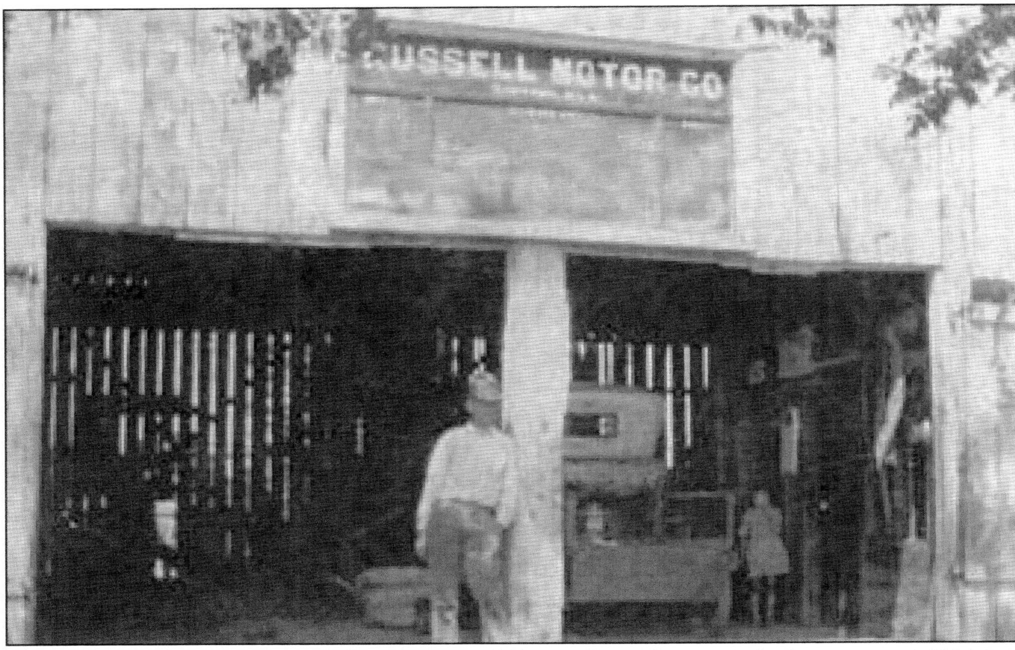

Russell's Filling Station. William John and Emma Russell started the business at 1408 Main Street in 1920 as the Bicycle and Buggy Shop; it evolved into an automobile dealership and garage by 1925. By 1940, the building was used as a factory for beautiful concrete masonry bricks used in many buildings in town, including the old Christ the King Church. (Russell family.)

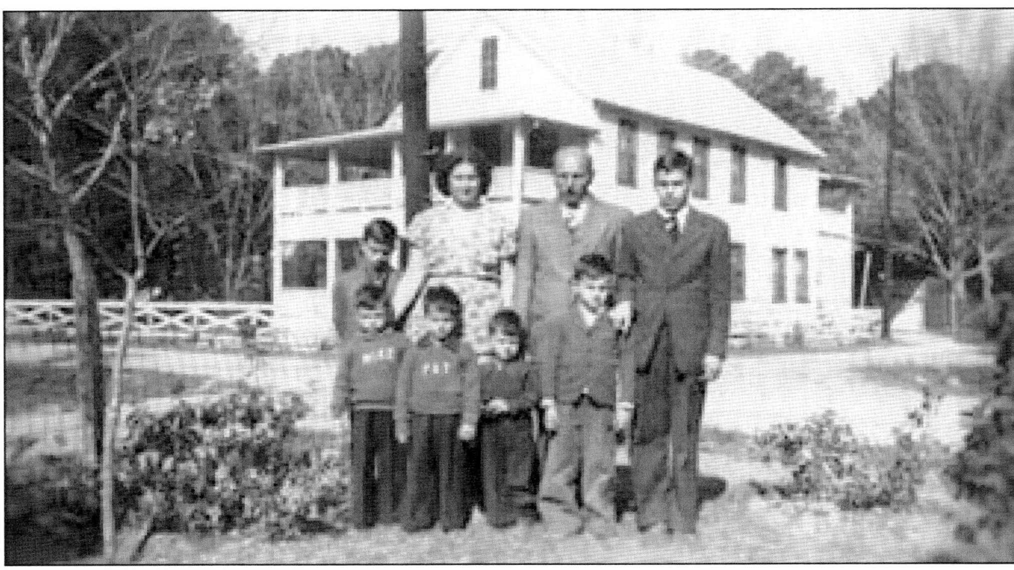

Bertagnolli's Store. This home, located at Sixth Street and Dryer Avenue, contained the first Bertagnolli's Store. Posing in front of the store are, from left to right, (first row) twins Mike and Pat, Tommy, and Henry; (second row) Gerald, Genevra, Henry, and Joe. The store made deliveries throughout town by wagon. The Bertagnollis later built a concrete brick factory and store at 1401 South Main Street. (Donald Bertagnolli.)

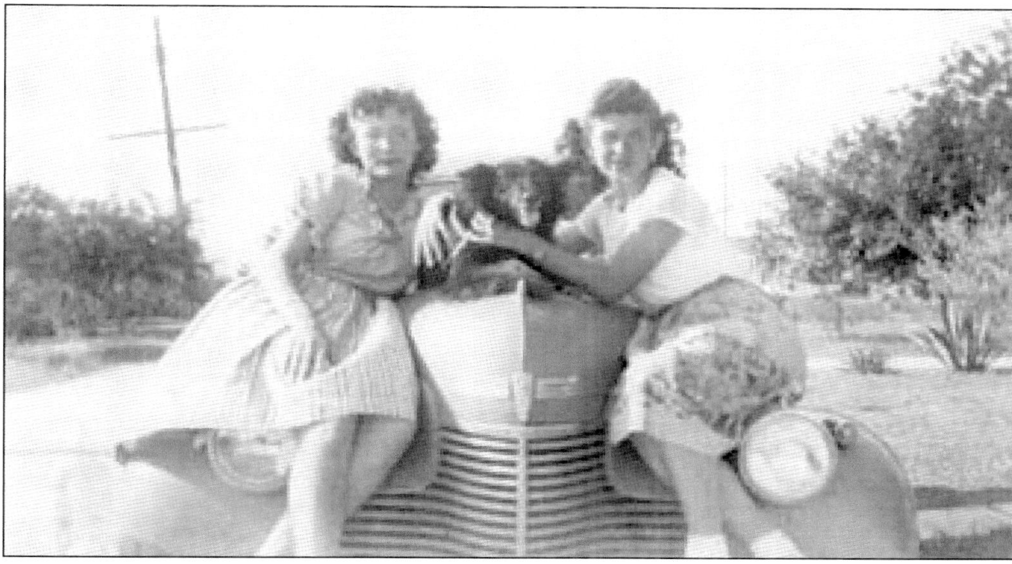

Nelda Bertagnolli and Mary Green. Best friends Nelda Bertagnolli (left) and Mary Green sit on the hood of a brand-new automobile. Nelda was the daughter of Frank Bertagnolli and granddaughter of original colonist Constante Bertagnolli. Nelda married Green's brother, William Pat Green, and they lived on Randall Avenue for their entire lives. (Donald Bertagnolli.)

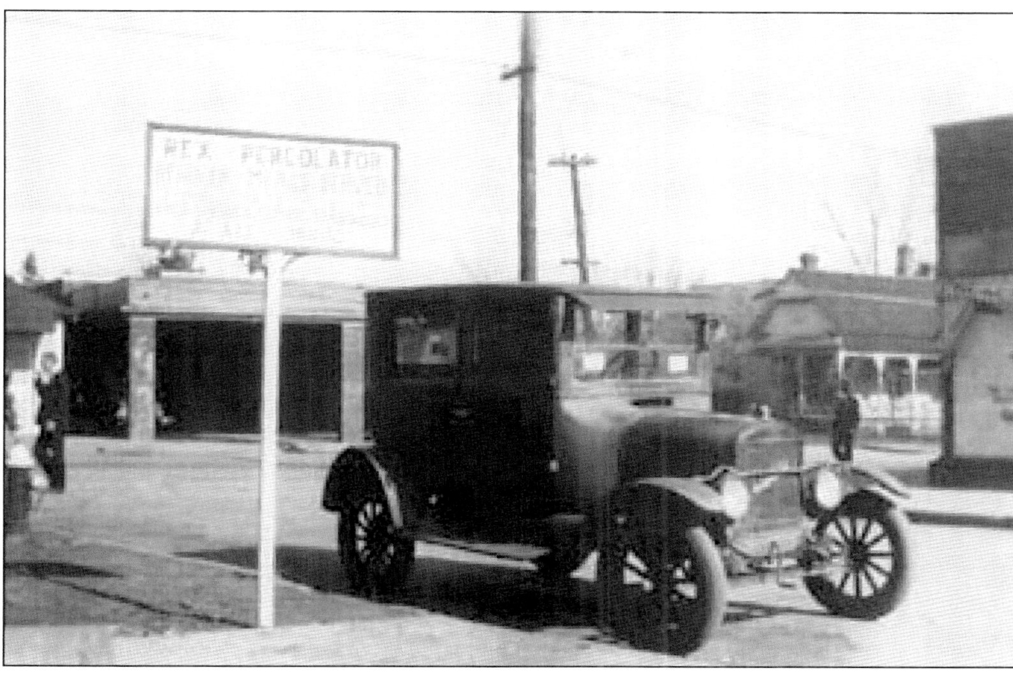

Automobiles Come to Town. This early Main Street restaurant sign says, "Rex Percolator, Regular Meals Served. Cold Drinks, Coffee, Sandwiches At All Hours". The Coster house, visible in the background at right, was used as a school for a while and is currently a café. (OMCMD, Davis Collection.)

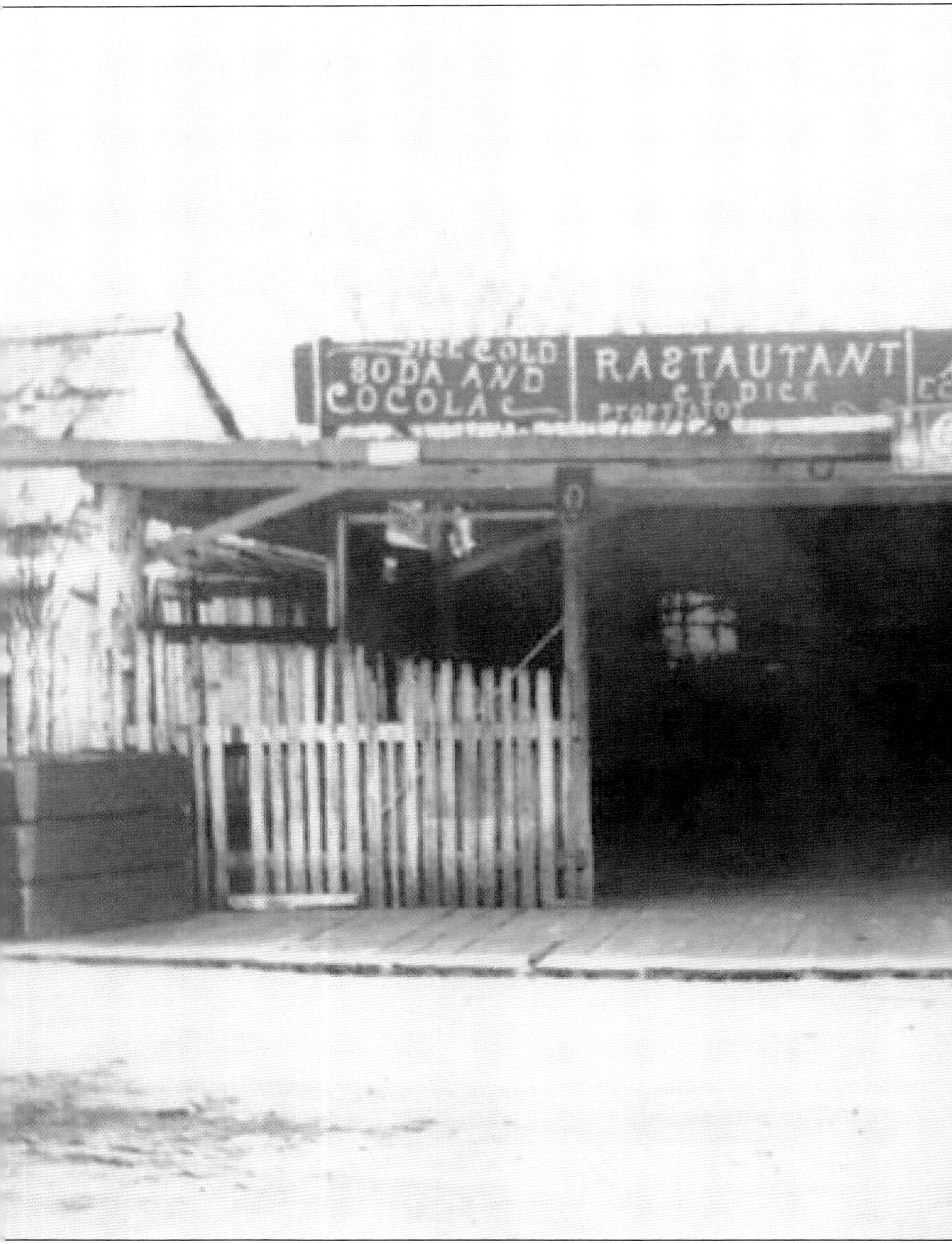
COLD
SODA AND
COCOLA
RASTAUTANT

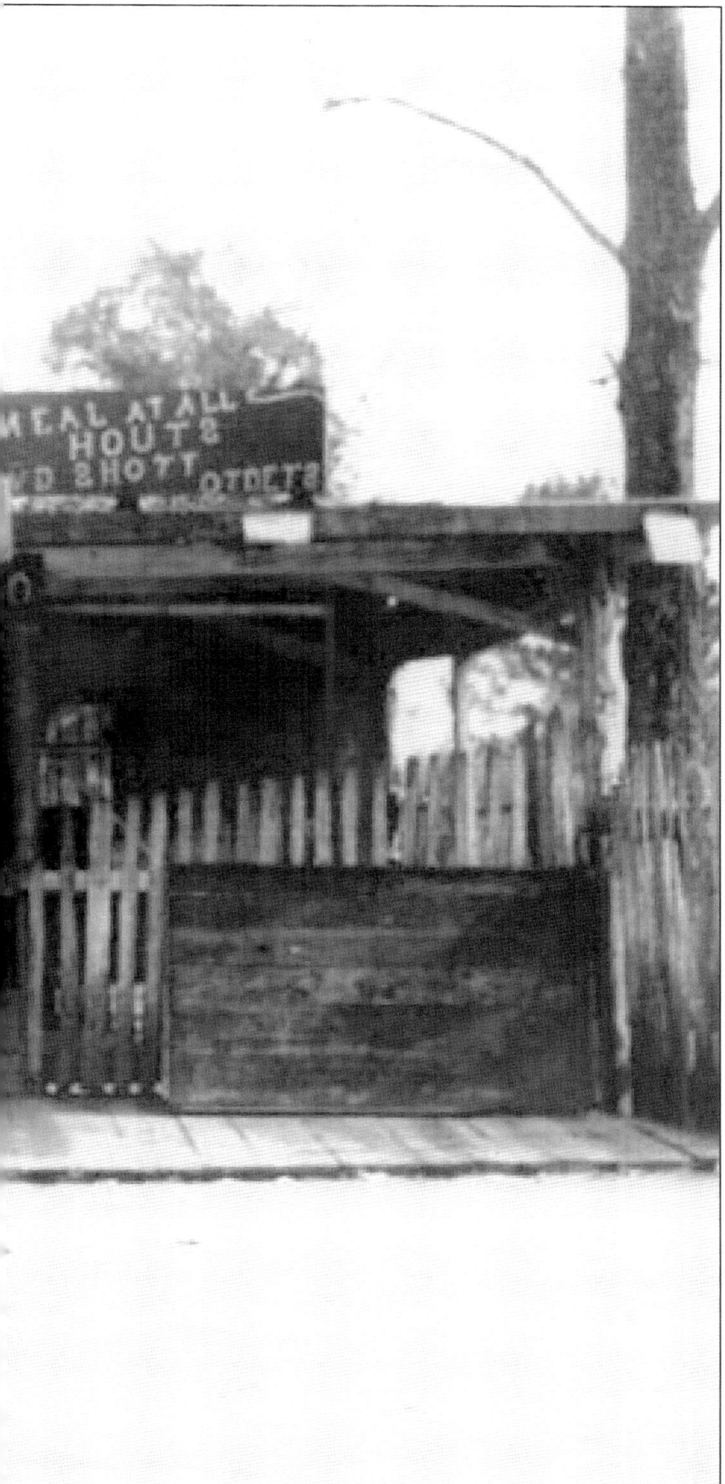

CUF DICK'S STORE AND RESTAURANT. Old-timers remember the colorful Cuf Dick, who ran this restaurant and dance floor at the corner of County Road 64 and Main Street on property acquired by his father, Russell Dick. Many famous black jazz and blues musicians played here before integration. The food was famous as well—especially the barbecue. (Dick Scott.)

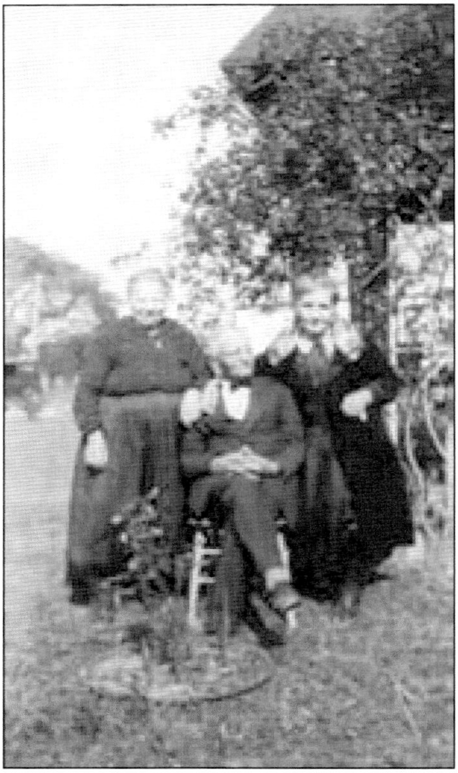

Bertagnolli Family. Three Bertagnolli siblings left Italy to join their parents, who were working in an Illinois coal mine. After marriage, all three couples moved to the Daphne Italian colony after seeing a newspaper advertisement. Pictured here, from left to right, are Theresa (married Vitorio Lazzeri), Constante, and Angelina (married John Predazzer), all of whom are among the patriarchs and matriarchs of the Italian community. (Al Guarisco.)

Guarisco Home. Mary Elizabeth Lazzeri married Agostino Guarisco, who had come to visit friends in the Italian community and stayed to work as a builder. He was building his family this lovely home on Randall Avenue when the hurricane of 1916 struck. He was on the roof nailing down tin when the storm hit, and Mary took their two children and fled to the barn. (Al Guarisco.)

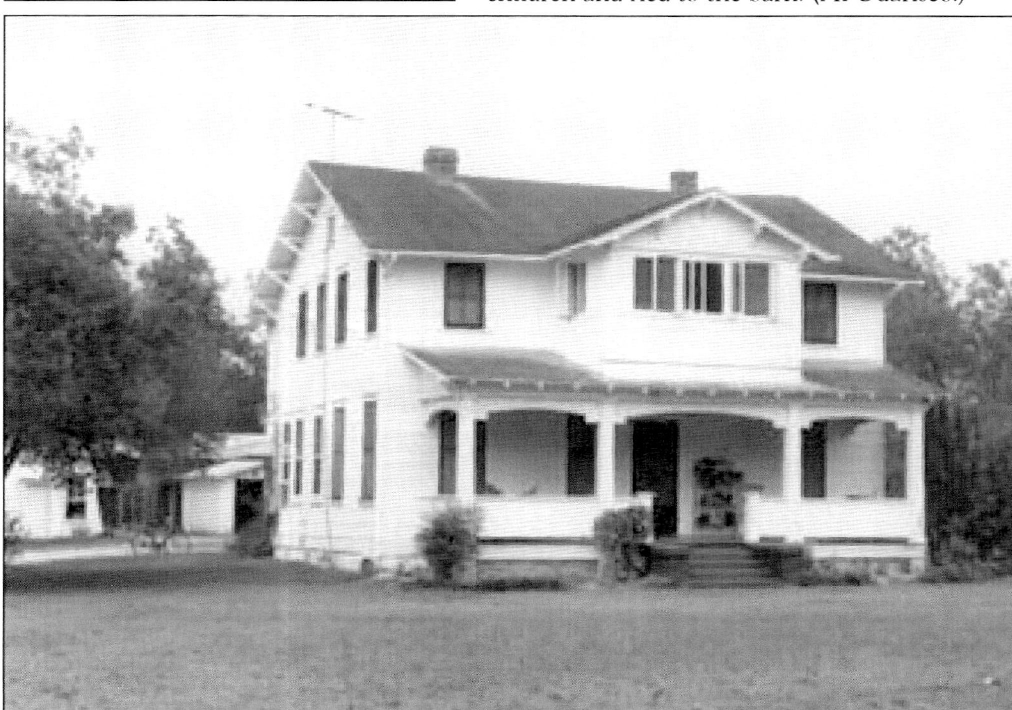

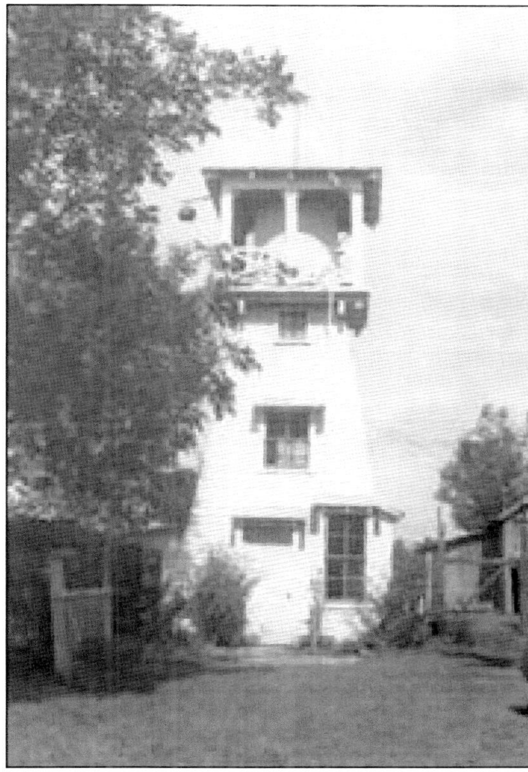

Water Tower. At first, the water tower on the Guarisco family homesite was a simple tank, built about 1930. Agostino Guarisco and his sons enclosed the structure to add a laundry room and storage facility. While the boys were busy working on the tower, a radio program was interrupted with news of the D-Day Invasion and cheers erupted on the worksite. (Al Guarisco.)

Lazzeri Grandchildren. On the steps of the Guarisco family home, grandparents pose with 38 of their 40 grandchildren in 1934. Alfred Guarisco is the third boy from the left on the front row. He is standing next to his grandmother Theresa. Grandfather Vitorio Lazzeri, the patriarch of this fine family, is seated in the front. (Al Guarisco.)

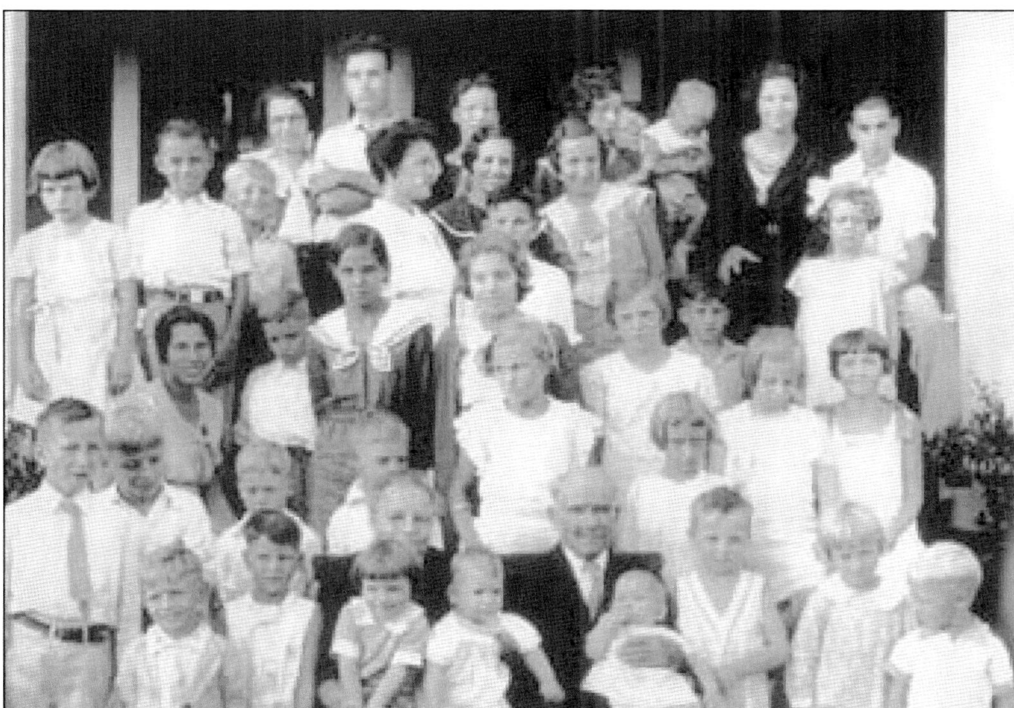

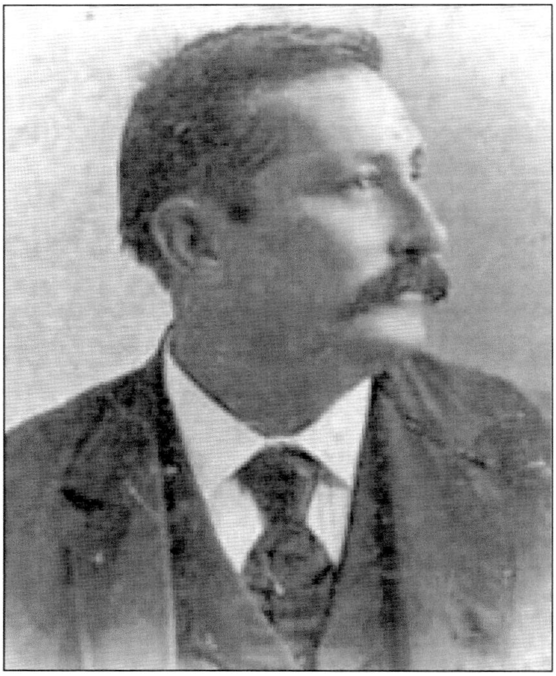

Capt. William O'Neal. "Billy" grew up in Daphne under the guidance of his colorful father, Capt. James O'Neal. James raised Billy on the water, teaching him the skills of a successful boat captain. While still a child, Billy suffered a serious facial injury caused by a fishhook, thus his standard pose in profile. Billy also founded and operated one of the first potteries in Daphne, making the bricks for Fort Morgan. (OMCMD.)

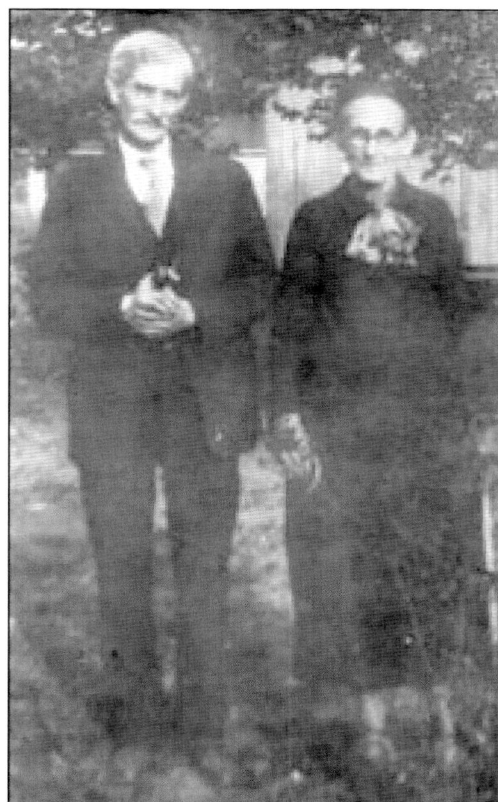

McAdams Potters. Potteries were one of the main industries in Daphne from 1850 to 1950. Peter and Florence McAdams were part of the famous McAdams Pottery industry founded by Peter's parents, James and Janet, in 1875. Florence's brother William O'Neal was also operating a pottery in Daphne, and the two joined resources in business. Peter created the altar for St. Paul's Episcopal Church. (OMCMD.)

Ed Grace, Potter. Ed Grace, one of the most skilled potters in the business, first worked at the O'Neal Pottery, becoming famous for his earthenware charcoal braziers. He was lured to the Daphne Pottery, which was housed in the remodeled cotton gin on the Dryer property, near the Dryer Hotel. The Daphne Pottery operated from 1907 through 1950. (OMCMD.)

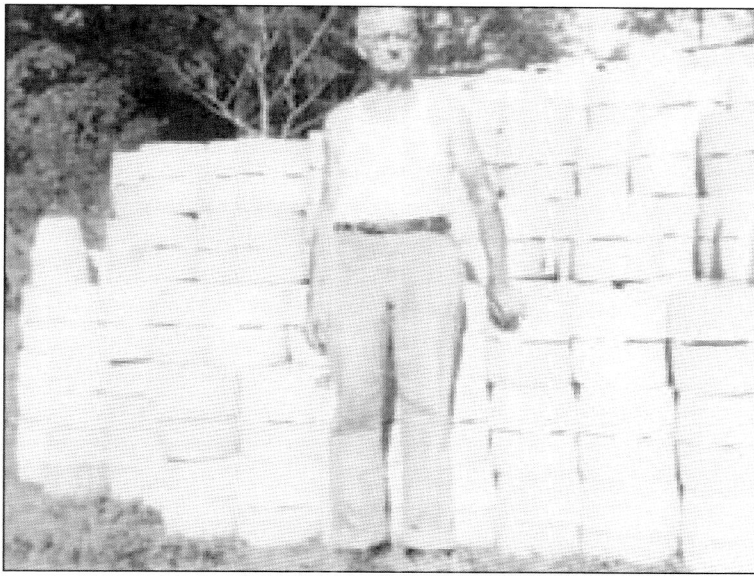

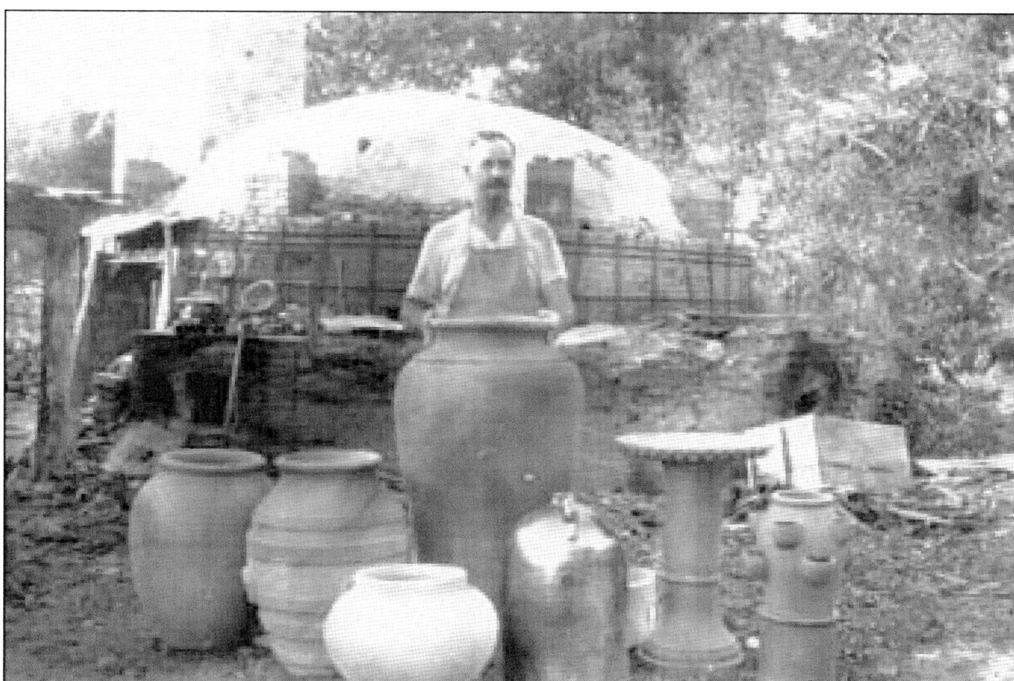

Daphne Pottery Kiln. Pictured at the Daphne Pottery is Calvin Carpenter. Ed Grace and Peter McAdams also both worked at the Daphne Pottery when it was one of the foremost industries in Daphne. Dan Johnson, William Johnson, David Sylvester, Herman Thompson, and William Valrie also worked there. Pots like those pictured were hauled to the bayfront by wagon and loaded at Dryer's Wharf. Daphne Pottery advertised jugs, jars, churns, and flowerpots. (OMCMD.)

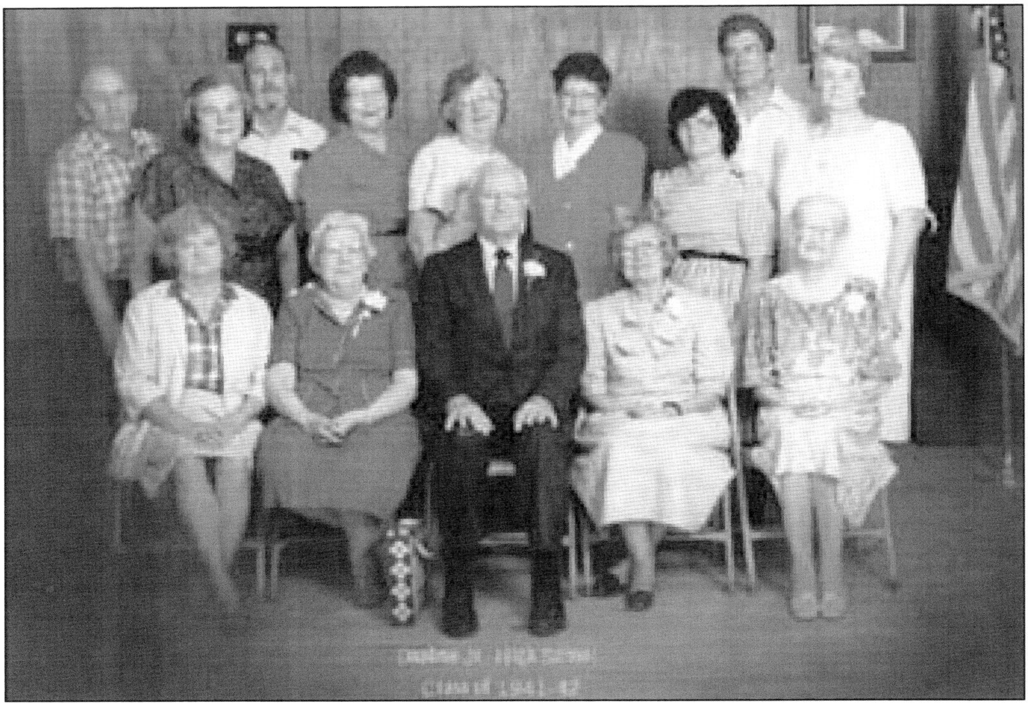

CLASS REUNION. A reunion of the 1941 Daphne Junior High School class shows Aubrey McVay, the first principal of the school, seated in the center of the front row. At far right is Elodia Van Iderstine, daughter of Elodia Hall Van Iderstine. By 1896, Elodia Hall was riding a mule from the Hall family homestead in Loxley to teach in Belforest. After marrying Dr. Reginold Van Iderstine in 1899 and moving to Daphne, she became a charter member of the Daphne Study Club. (Al Guarisco.)

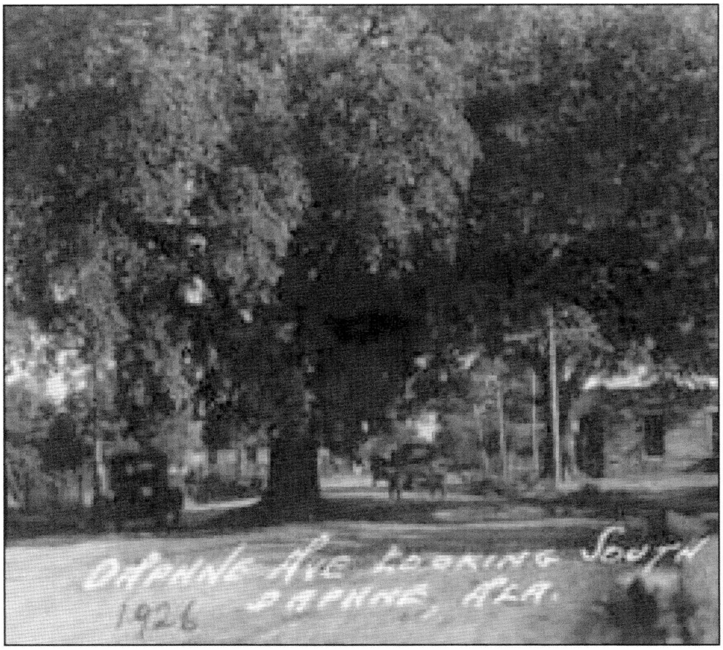

DOWNTOWN OAK TREE. A lovely oak tree in the center of town was a gathering place for many visitors to the town elders and housewives. When state highway improvements threatened the tree, Elodia Hall Van Iderstine and other members of the Daphne Study Club stood in front of the tree armed with pitchforks, forcing the operator off the dozer. Despite these efforts, the government prevailed and the tree was cut down. (OMCMD.)

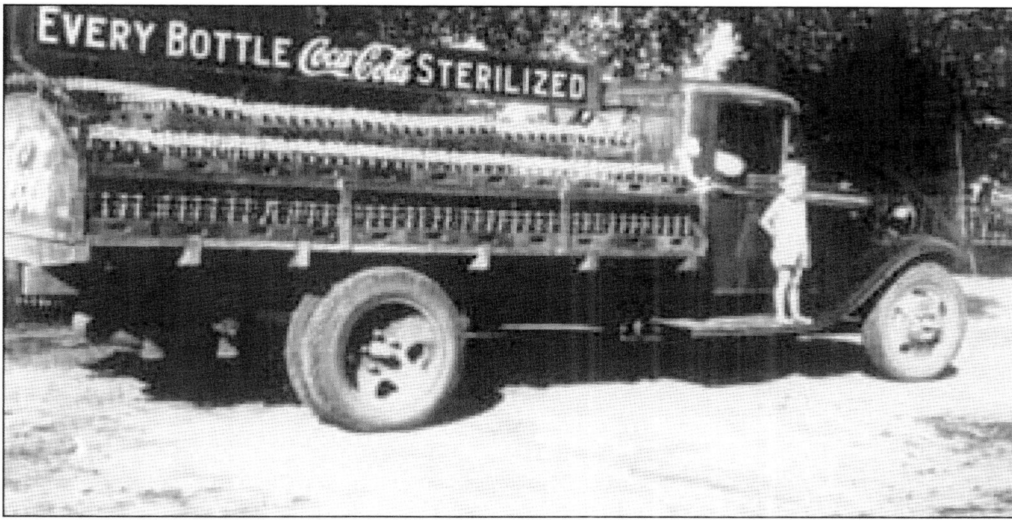

THINGS GO BETTER WITH COKE. As the 20th century progressed and moved into Daphne, Coca-Cola became as popular here as anywhere. Route driver Leslie Lowell photographed his son Carol "Doodlebug" Lowell standing on the running board. The route assistant, John Mims, later became the first African American elected to public office in Baldwin County. (John Lewis.)

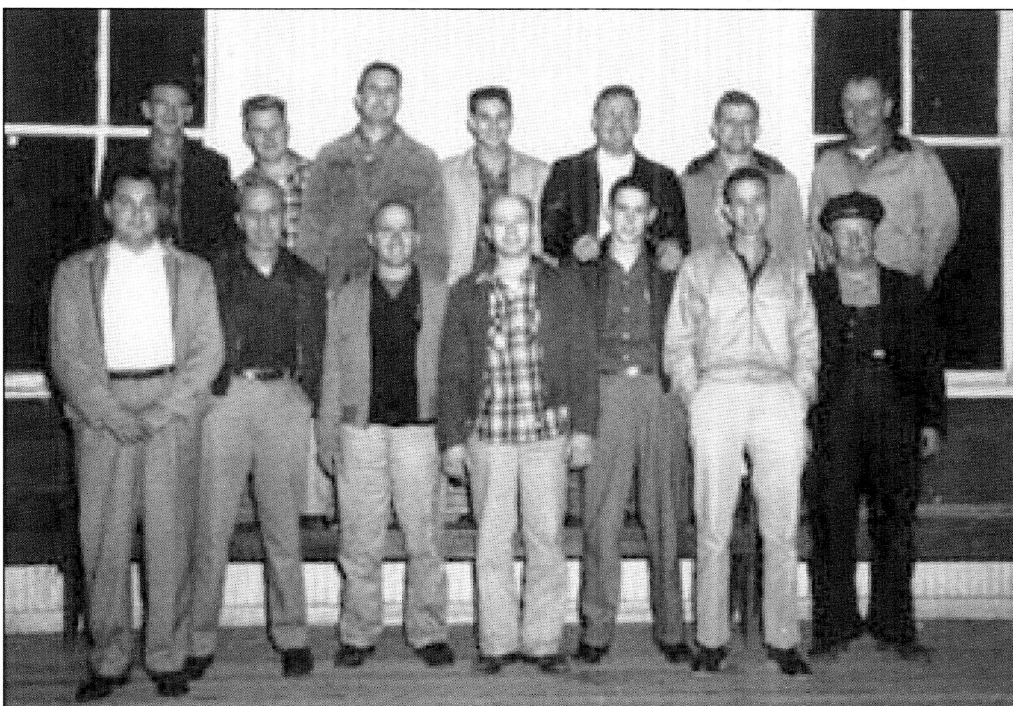

FIRE DEPARTMENT VOLUNTEERS. Stewart Foster captured this photograph at a 1954 meeting of the volunteer fire department. Pictured here are, from left to right, (first row) Edgar Brantley, Bruce Stuart, Thumpsie Trione, Red Trione, Manon Johnson, Donald Pruett, and Danny Smallwood; (second row) Felix Bigby, Ted Bertagnolli, Jesse Andrews, Al Guarisco, George Rains, Jesse Denman, and Adam Crestman. (OMCMD.)

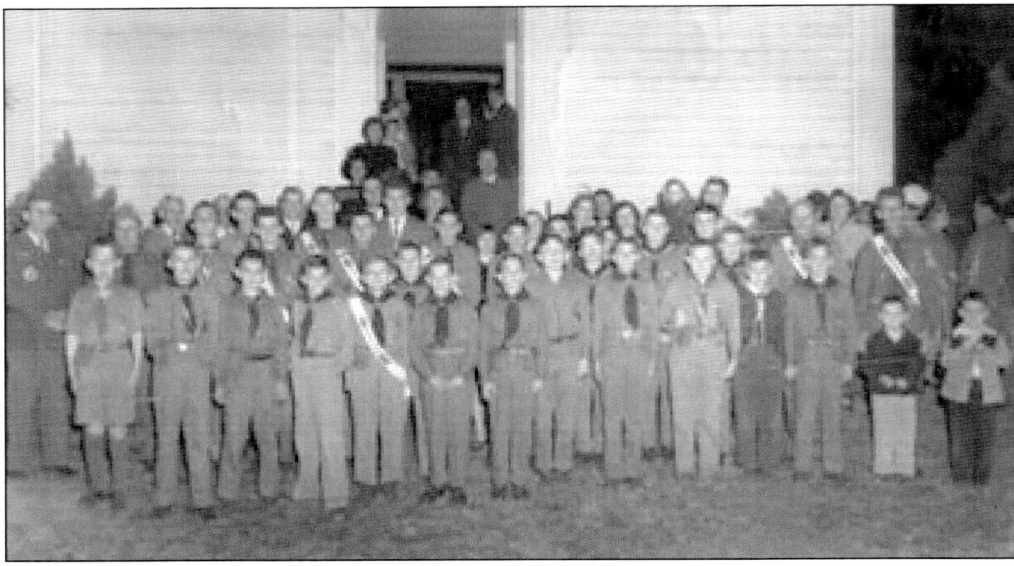

Boy Scouts. Local organizations consistently provided community service projects. Here, the Boy Scouts pose after an awards ceremony at the Old Methodist Church; the boys had worked to clean the cemetery. (OMCMD.)

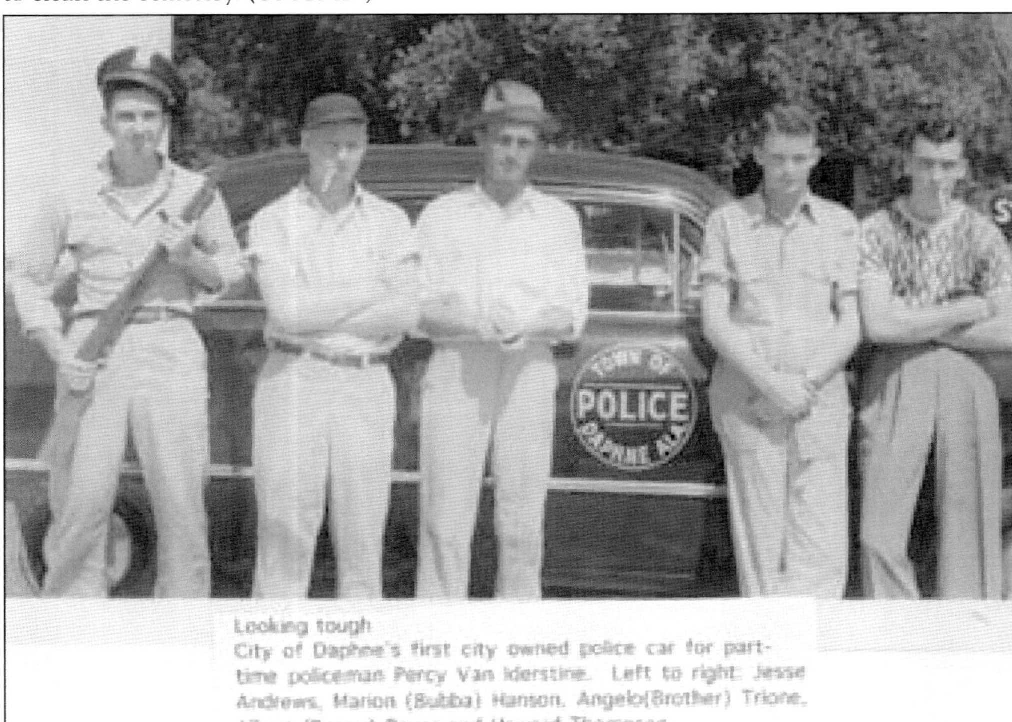

First Police Car. In 1955, an official police car was purchased for use by the only real policeman in town, Percy Van Iderstine (who actually worked part-time). Pictured here are, from left to right, Jesse Andrews, Marion "Bubba" Hanson, Angelo "Brother" Trione, Albert "Raney" Bauer, and Howard Thompson. (OMCMD.)

Four

A Grand Old Lady
Courthouse and Normal School

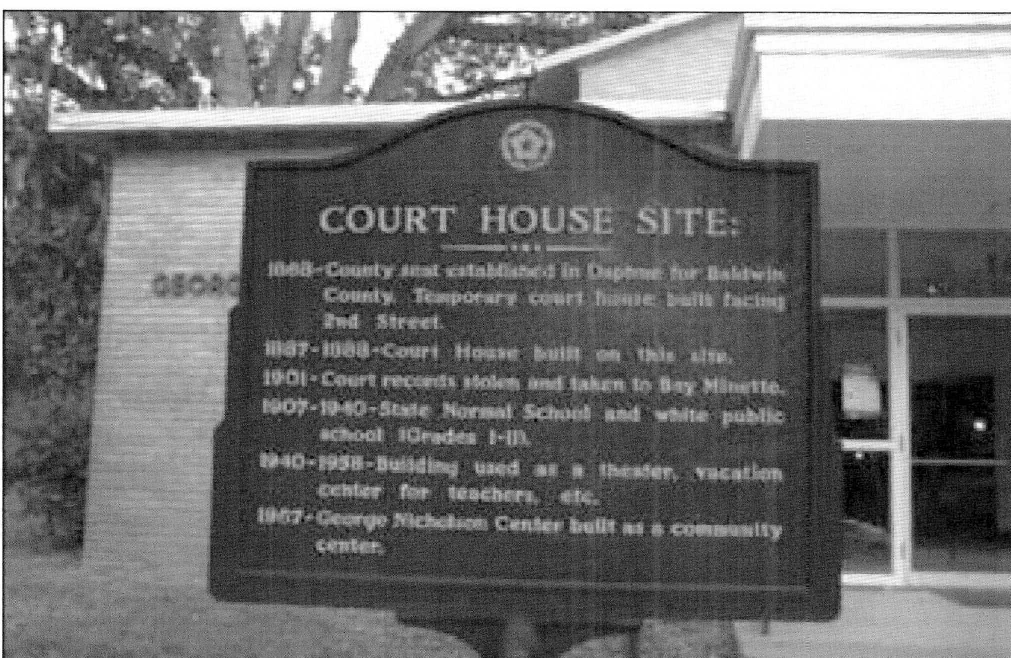

Historic Courthouse Marker. A historic marker on the site of the Baldwin County Courthouse lists the uses of the magnificent building that once stood there. The courthouse story evokes strong emotions among locals who tell of the relocation of official court records to Bay Minette in 1901. Of course, this marker uses the term "stolen" when referring to the night the relocation took place. (Photograph by Harriet Outlaw.)

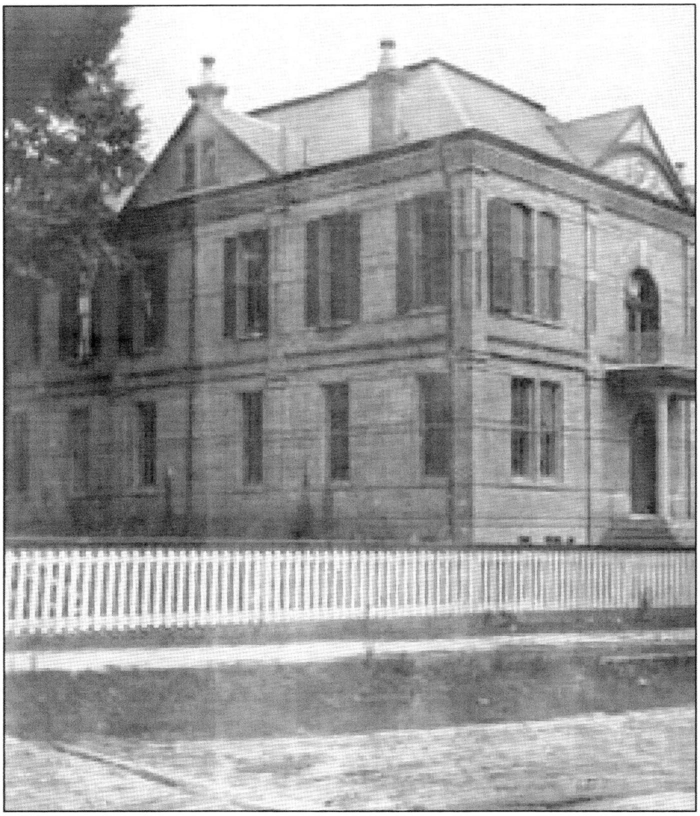

Courthouse Structure. In 1868, the Alabama legislature approved the move of the county seat from Blakeley to Daphne, which had become the primary water access to Mobile. While the courthouse (pictured here) was being constructed, court sessions were held under the "Jury Oak" on the Howard Hotel grounds. (OMCMD.)

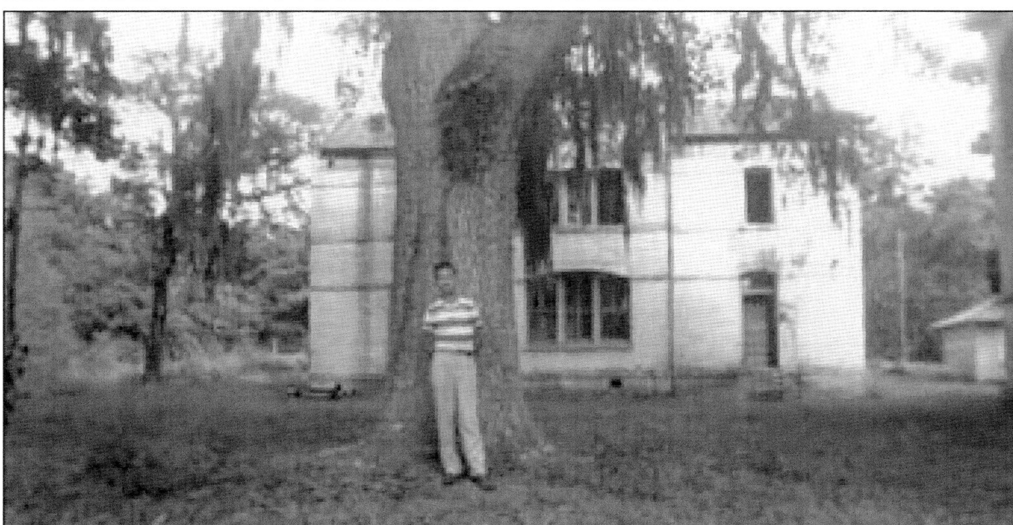

Jailhouse. A two-story jail was built next to the courthouse. On the night the courthouse records were removed, a prisoner was released and made to help transfer the boxes of records to Bay Minette, where he was once again locked up. Marshall Carney stands in front of the building shortly before it was demolished. Both the jail and the courthouse were demolished by 1958. (Dick Scott, Carney Collection.)

JUDGE GASQUE. William H. Gasque, born in St. Stephens, Alabama, in 1811, was the first judge of probate in Daphne. He was reputed to be a dyed-in-the-wool Democrat. He was a Mason and entered the Mobile Lodge No. 40 in 1944. Judge Gasque never married, but lived in Daphne most of his life and is buried in the Old Methodist Church Cemetery. (OMCMD.)

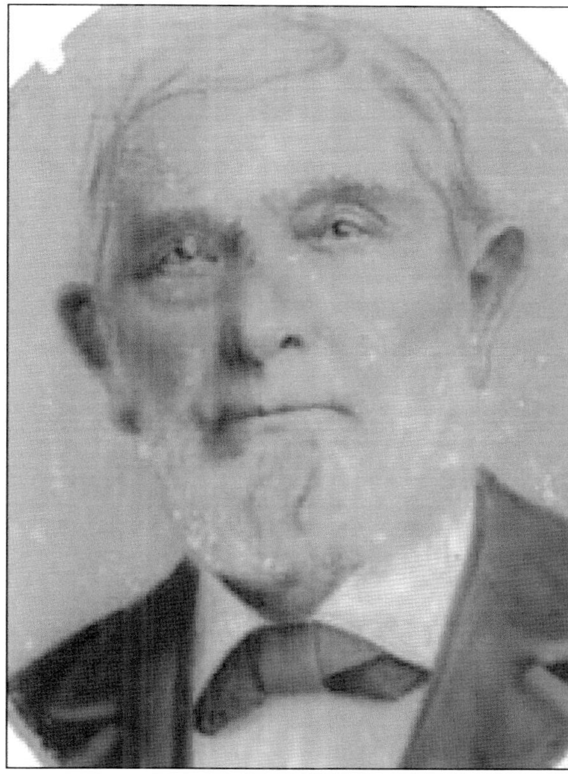

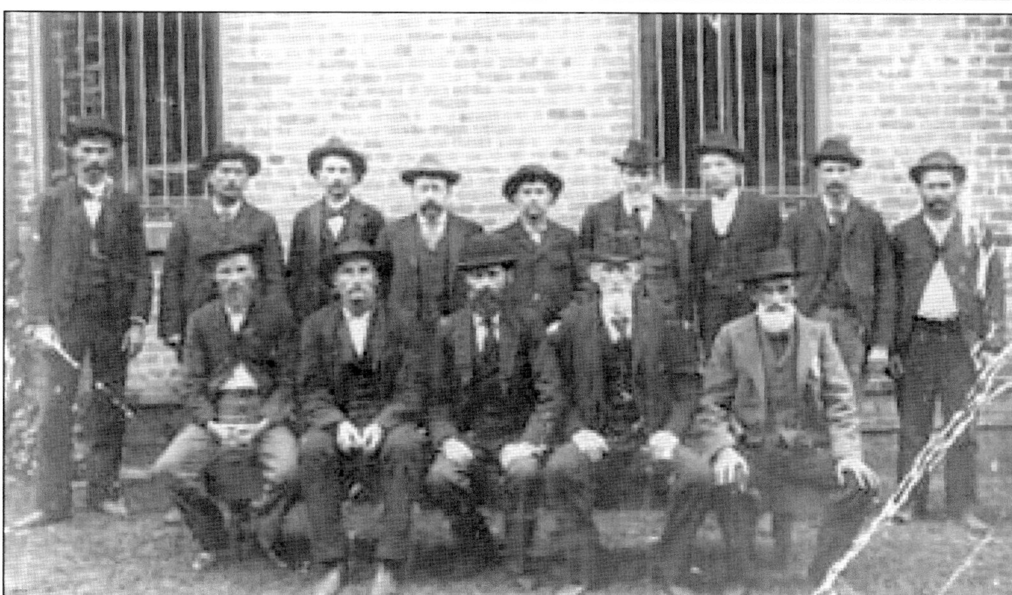

TWELVE MEN PLUS TWO ALTERNATES. An 1897 grand jury posed for a photograph outside the jailhouse. The court provided lodging and meals in Daphne hotels for jury members. Travel to Daphne from outlying areas of the county meant a horse-and-wagon ride on rough dirt roads. The county seat was moved to Bay Minette in 1901. (John Lewis.)

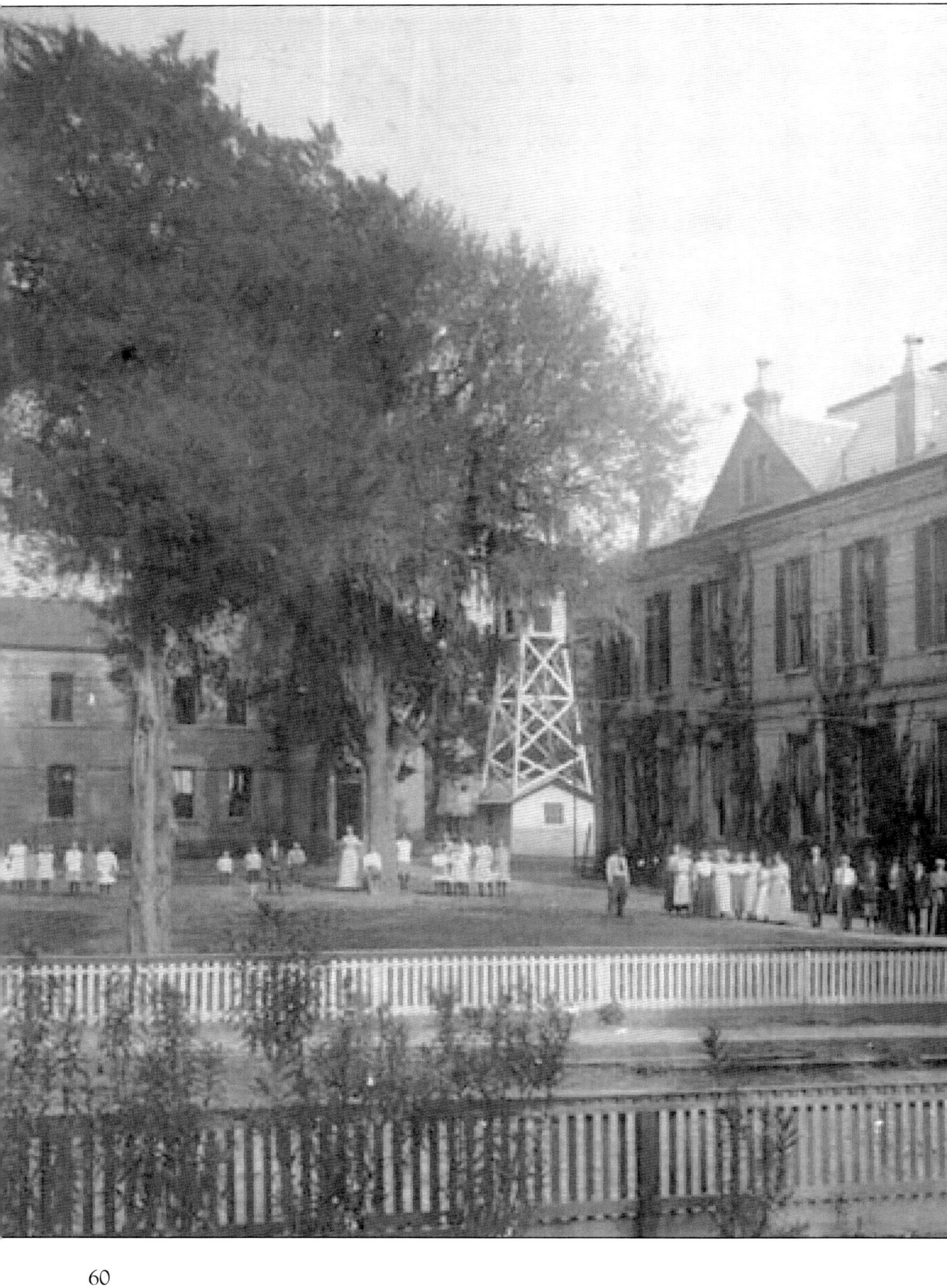

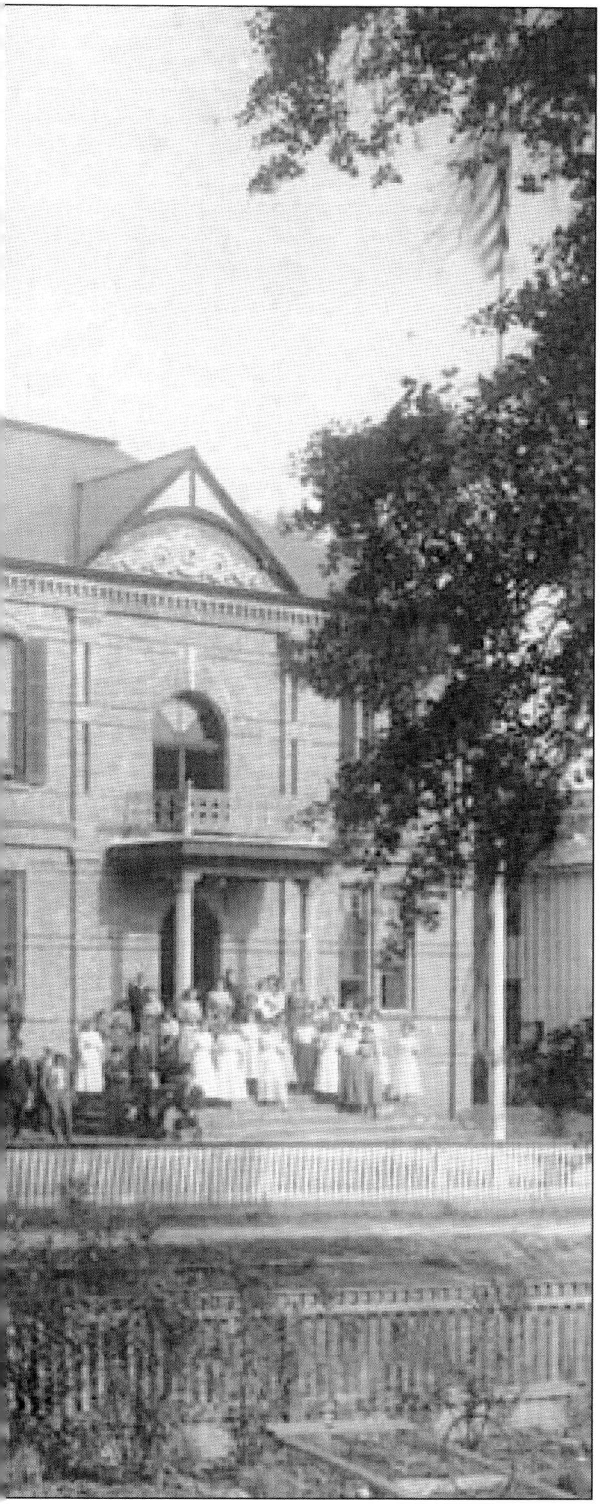

NORMAL SCHOOL OPENING. The former courthouse in Daphne became the Alabama State Teacher College on Mobile Bay and the normal school for grades one through twelve in 1907. The grade school became the public school for the city and teachers in training taught classes under leadership of experienced teachers provided by the Baldwin County Board of Education. A single-engine pump that transported the water to the wooden water tower filled the school's water tank. Former students tell of the numerous times that squirrels got caught in the tank, only to be discovered when the water became too putrid to drink. Classes were mainly in the building that once served as the county jail. Former students remember the floor often flooding. One esteemed educational professional remembers sitting outside the window to listen in on Dr. Aubrey McVay's class, hungry for his knowledge of maps and geography. (OMCMD.)

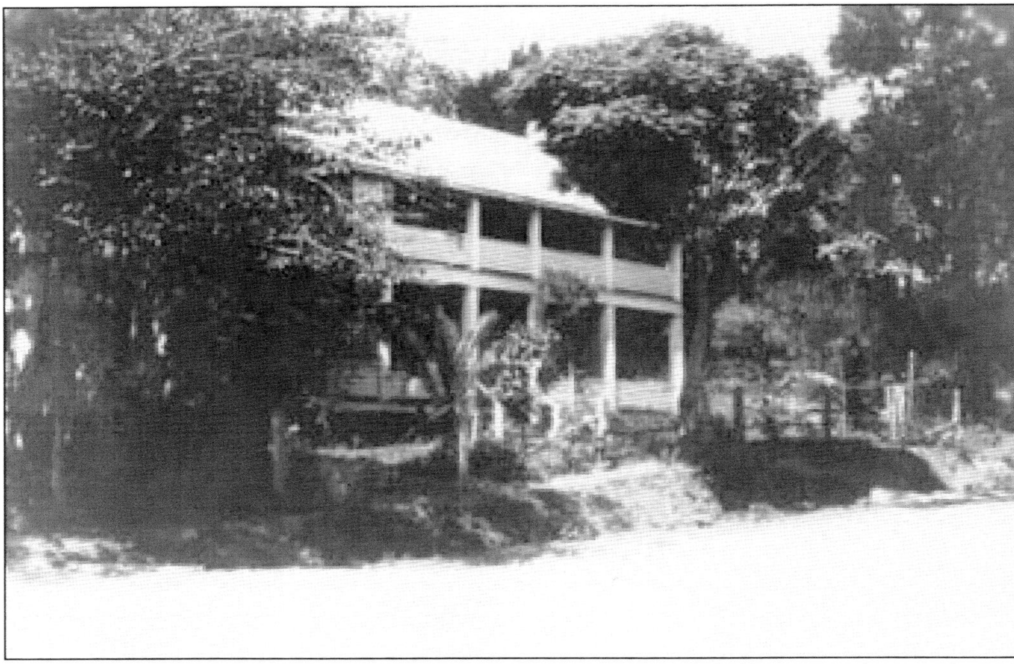

Boardinghouses. The normal school provided education for local children in grades one through twelve, but students in the two-year teacher training program often traveled great distances to enroll in classes. Nearby boardinghouses accommodated the future teachers. This is one of the homes that provided room and board. (OMCMD, Davis Collection.)

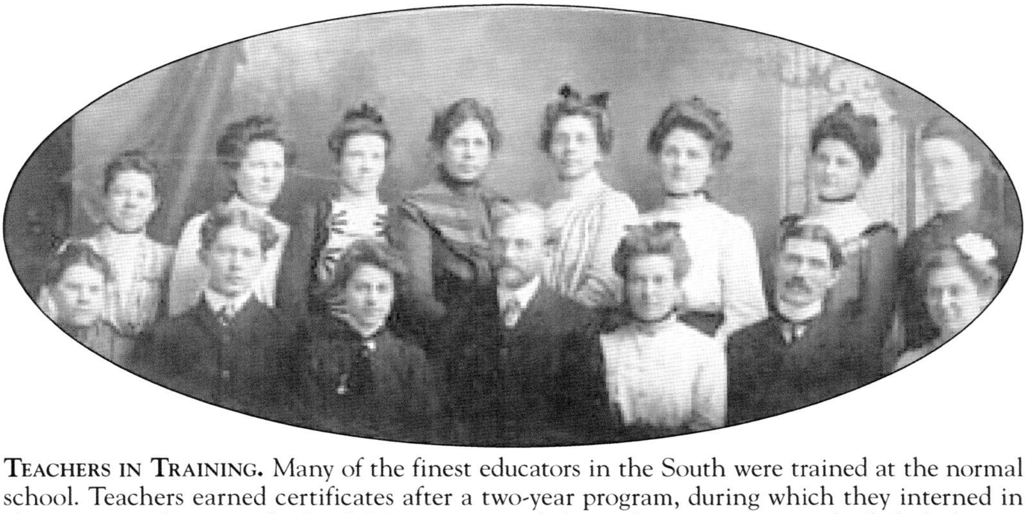

Teachers in Training. Many of the finest educators in the South were trained at the normal school. Teachers earned certificates after a two-year program, during which they interned in classrooms at the normal school. Many continued their educations, earning bachelor's degrees at Montevallo or Livingston Teacher College. (OMCMD, Davis Collection.)

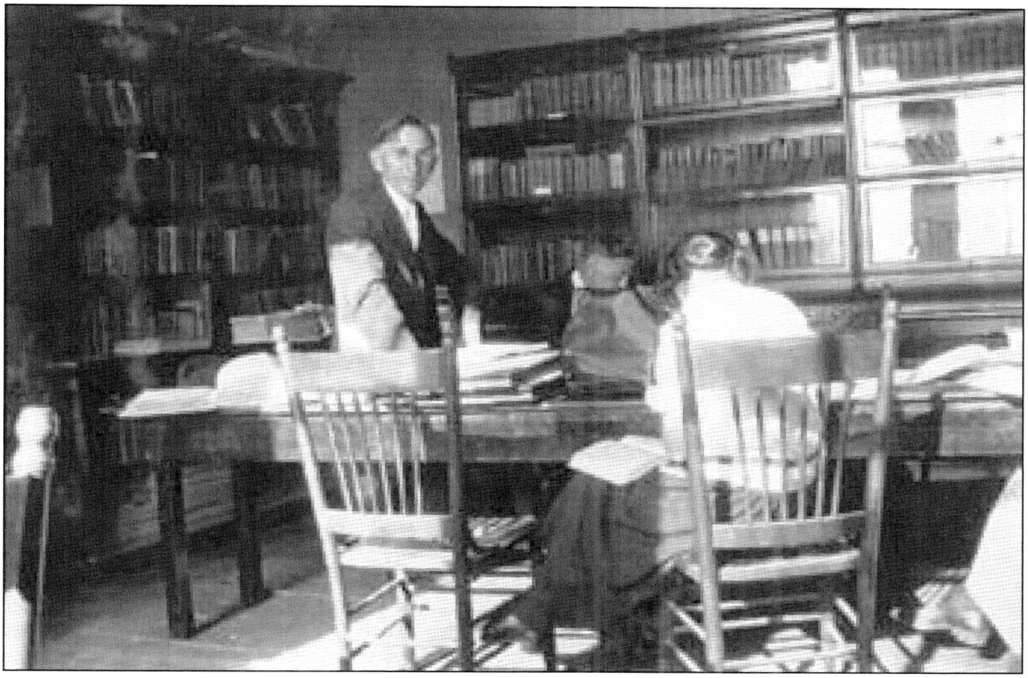

REVERED TEACHER. Prof. Frank J. Frelich is pictured here in a photograph taken by Johnnie Davis for the *Nymph*, the yearbook of the normal school. The 1924 *Nymph* was dedicated to Frelich in recognition of his outstanding dedication to the students and improvement of the school. His science class inspired Davis to continue in engineering and physics. Frelich was chairman of the faculty of Daphne Normal School. (OMCMD, Davis Collection.)

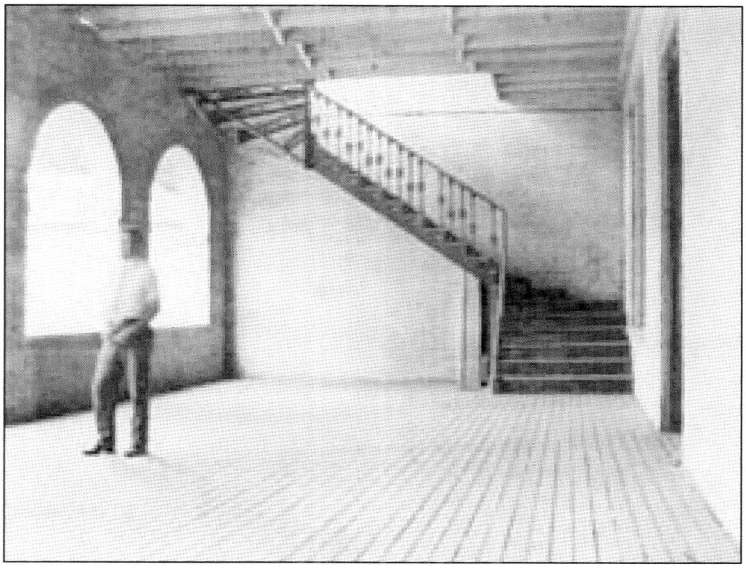

THE GRAND STAIRCASE. The back of the courthouse building had external staircases leading to the upstairs courtrooms. However, 1917 renovations at the normal school included enclosing the east-side rear porch and creating a large reception room. (OMCMD, Davis Collection.)

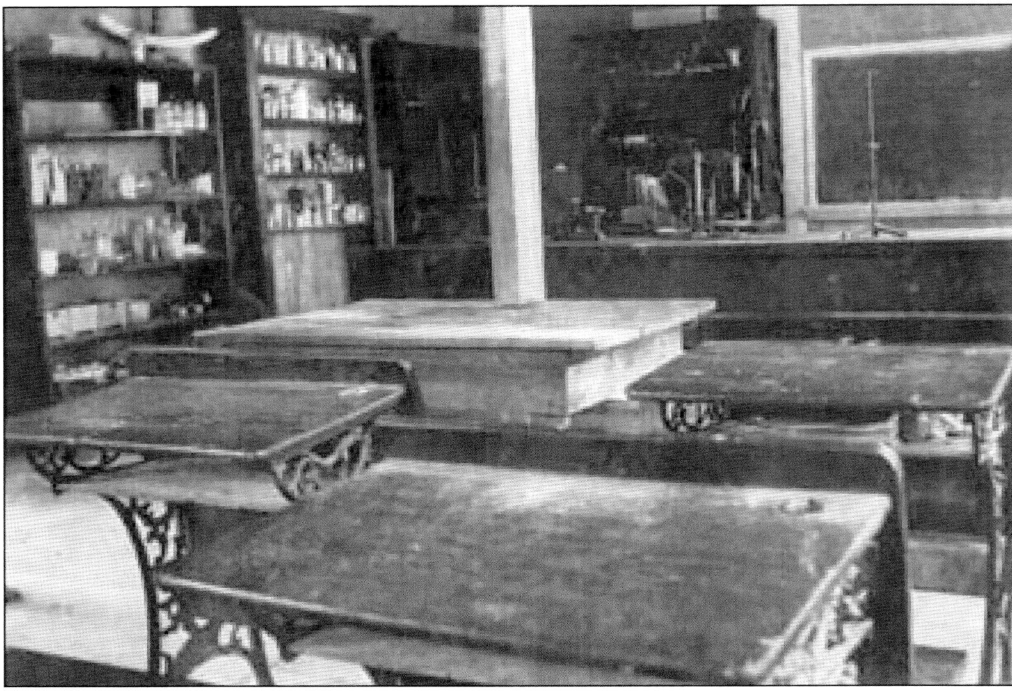

Science Laboratory. High school curriculum included the most up-to-date classes in science and chemistry. Classes for high school students were held in the main building on campus. The model teachers for the upper school were responsible for the high school curriculum, as well as for training would-be teachers. (OMCMD, Davis Collection.)

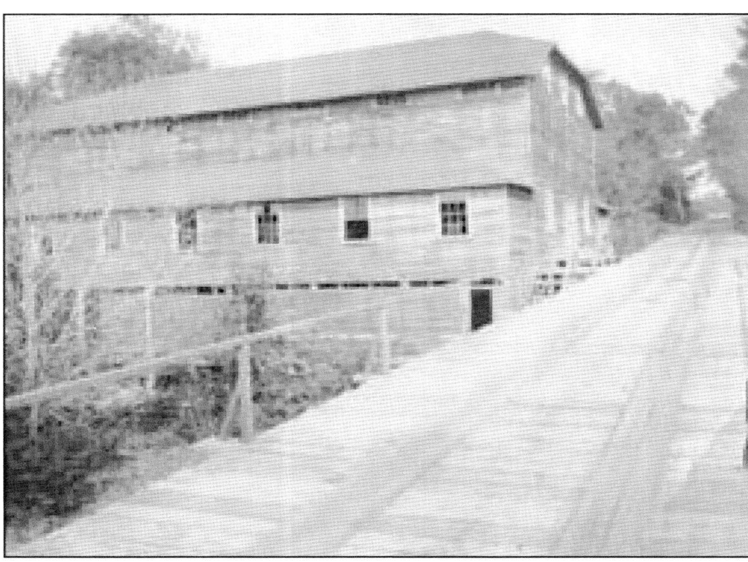

Gymnasium on the Wharf. Funding was raised to build a gymnasium at the Wharf Street Pier for use by the school and the community. Students participated in indoor physical education classes here during the school day, and on weekends and evenings, the building became a gathering spot for athletic and social events. (OMCMD, Davis Collection.)

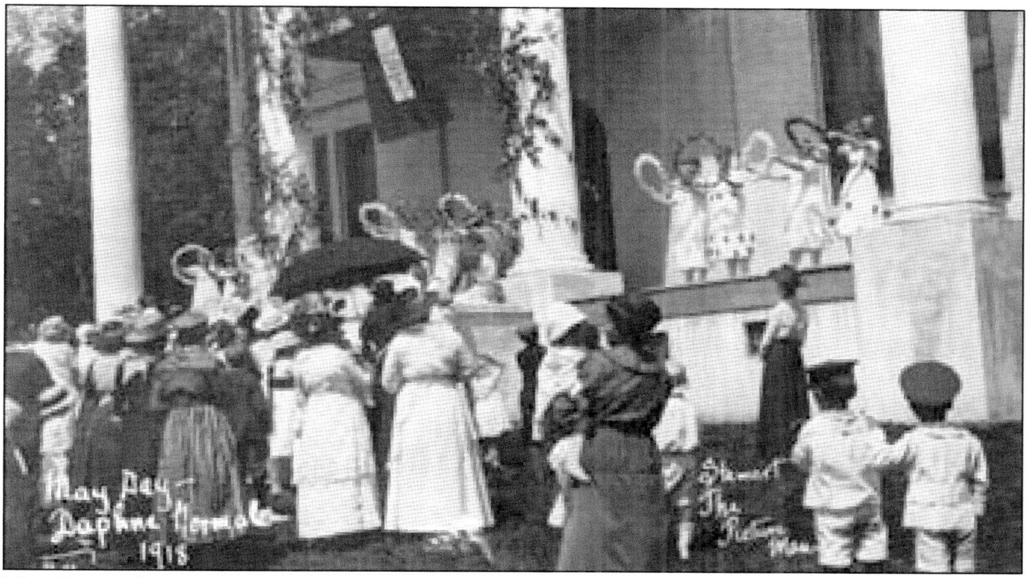

MAY DAY. The springtime rite of Daphne's May Day Festival was first instituted on the grounds of the normal school under the leadership of Bonnie Baker, wife of school president B.B. Baker. She patterned the celebration after the Daisy Chain event at her beloved Vassar. In 1911, the crowning of the first queen, Isabel Goldsby, began an annual event that lasted for more than 50 years. This image shows the 1918 program, which was held on the veranda of the newly remodeled building. (OMCMD.)

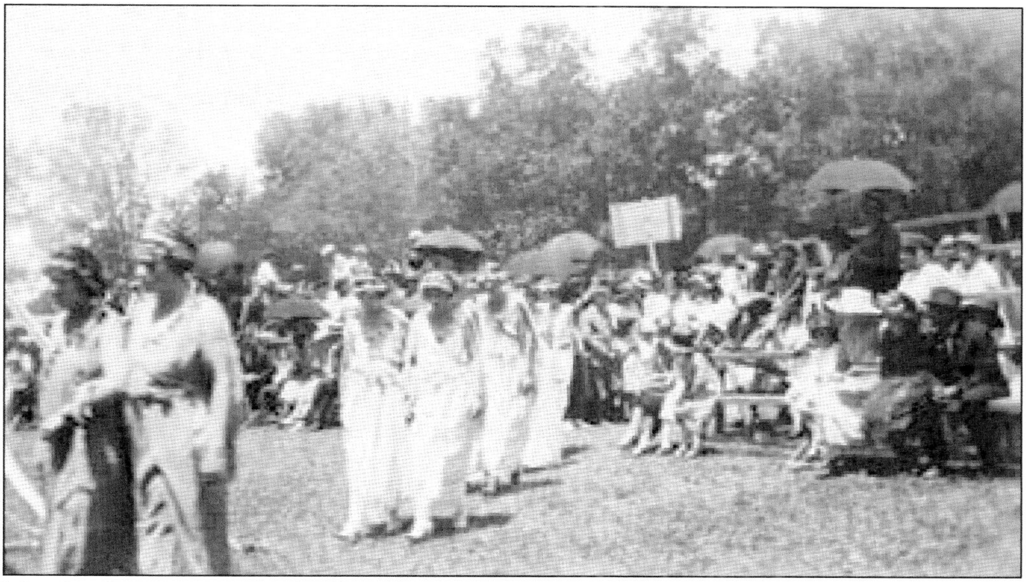

MAY DAY PROCESSIONAL. The day of festivities followed a pattern typical throughout the country during this era. The court processed to a stage area—first pages and flower girls, then knights and ladies-in-waiting. The king crowned the queen of May, who was always from the Daphne area. The event grew to include representatives from other high schools in Baldwin County, each with its own court in the processional. (OMCMD.)

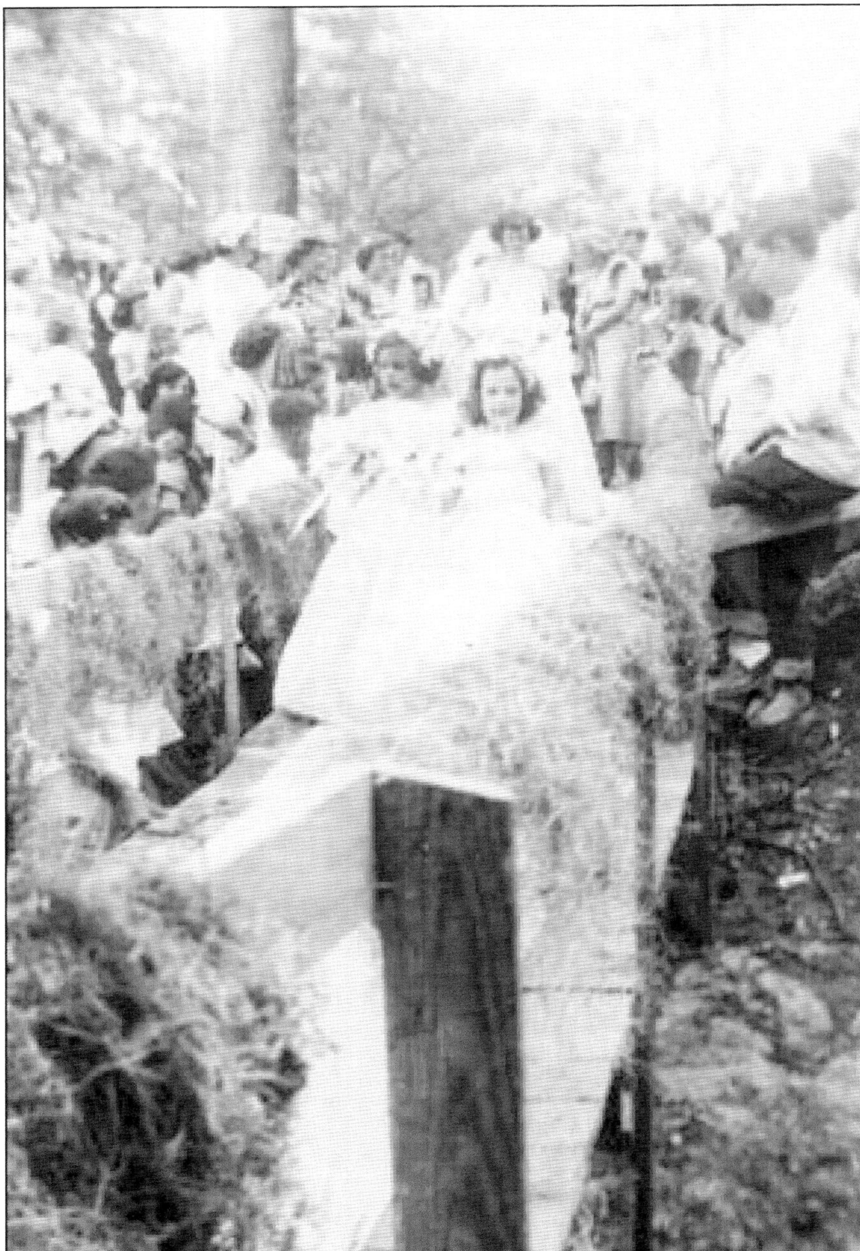

On the Bayfront Trail. Many springtime festivals took place across the road from the normal school, an area now called May Day Park in commemoration of the festivities held there. Here, a flower girl makes her way to the stage across a bridge decorated with Spanish moss and springtime flowers. When the decision was made to discontinue the Alabama State Teacher College in 1937, students were moved to temporary classrooms in the Woodman's Hall, the Baptist church, and the Lowell home while the new school was under construction. May Day continued to be held through the 1960s at the site on the bayfront; today, the concrete stage is used for events, and a new boat ramp enhances public access to the bay. (OMCMD, Davis Collection.)

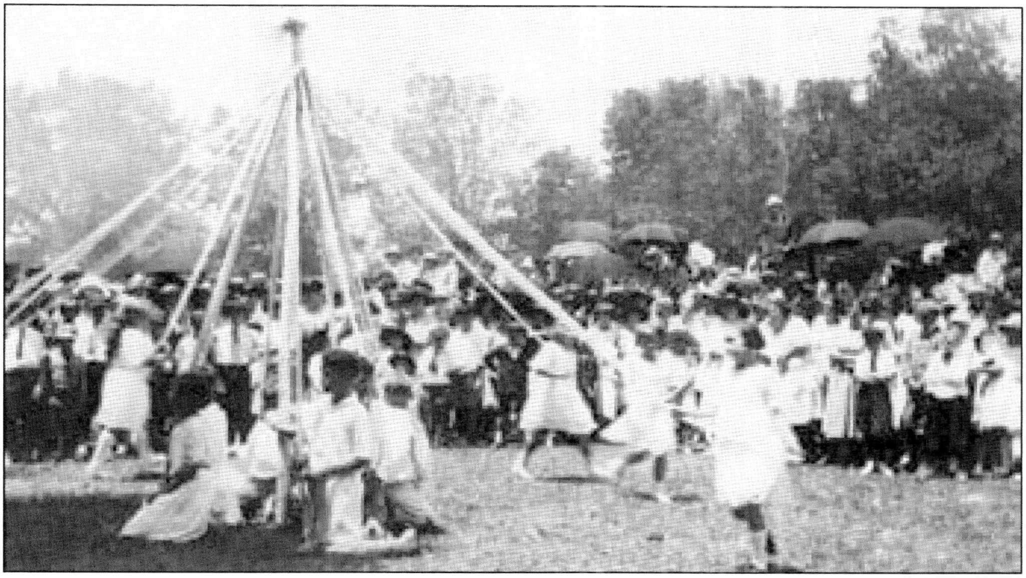

DANCING THE MAYPOLE. Following old European customs, the maypole is wound with ribbons. Dancers stand in two circles facing opposite directions. As the music plays, the dancers weave under and over each other, creating the braid that ends up covering the pole. The final Daphne May Day celebration was held in 1969, and the maypole is preserved at the Daphne Museum. (OMCMD.)

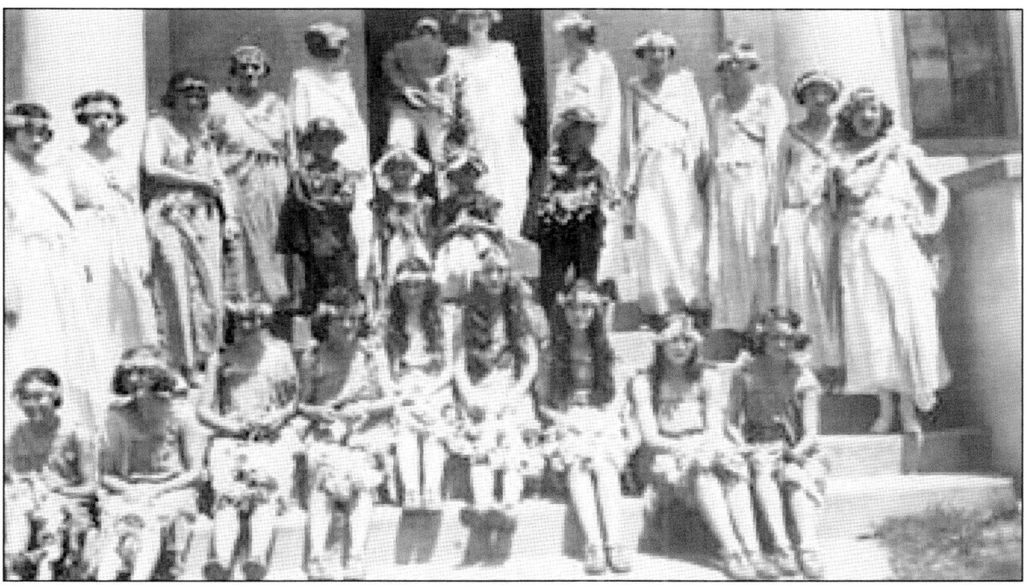

PAGEANTS AND TABLEAUX. As was the rage of the era, every event was highlighted with a pageant or tableau enacted by students and other community members. The earliest festivals had themes and portrayed stories, usually from classic literature. The court was bedecked in costumes appropriate to the theme. This tradition is still observed in most Mardi Gras society tableaux. (OMCMD.)

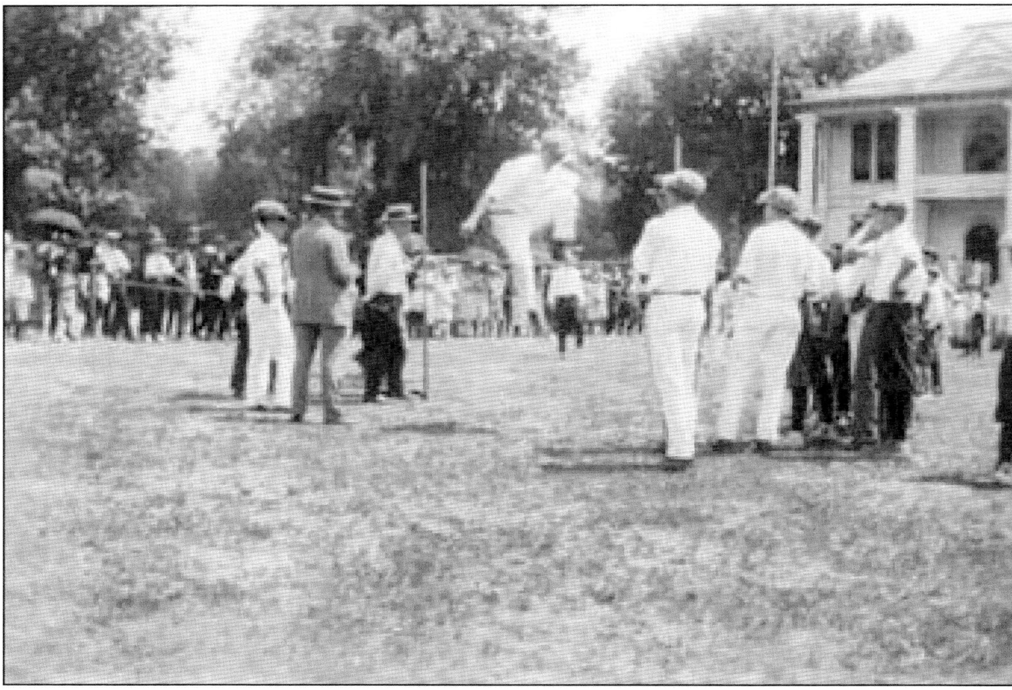

May Day Games. Following the coronation processional, many dances and skits were performed for the court, with each school class responsible for a performance. The processional was followed by games, some of which were competitive for prizes, such as this high jump competition. Some years, the festival included a baseball game against Bay Minette. (OMCMD.)

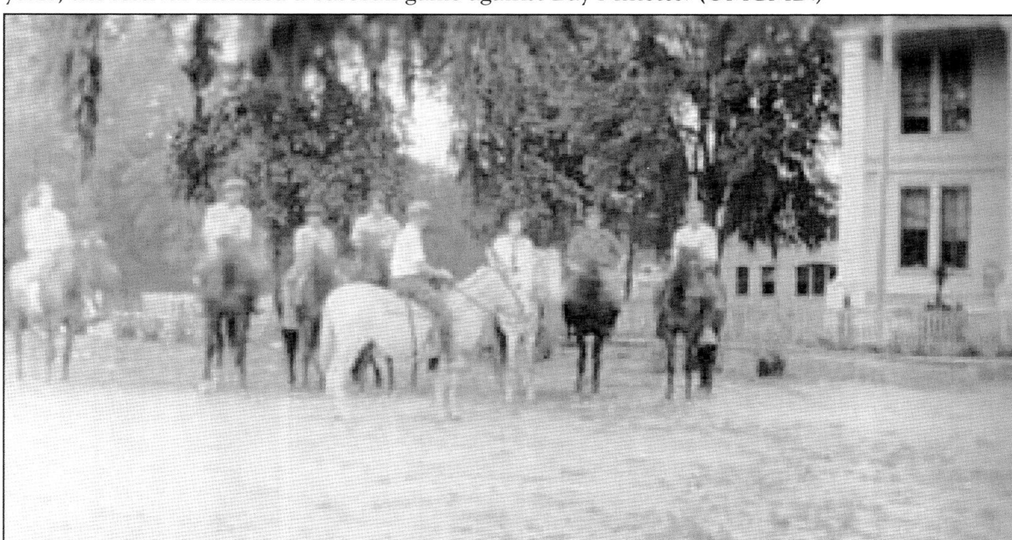

Horseback Excursion. Horses were regularly ridden throughout town until 1940s. Here, a boy riding the pet donkey Blanquita, who belonged to the Hammet girls, entertains a gathering of the Horseback Riding Club in front of the normal school. The Hammet home, located north of May Day Pier, became Villa Mercy, a rehabilitation facility. Today, the original Hammet home's stone wall is visible on the grounds of Mercy Medical. (OMCMD.)

Five

Education Pioneers
Black Schooling

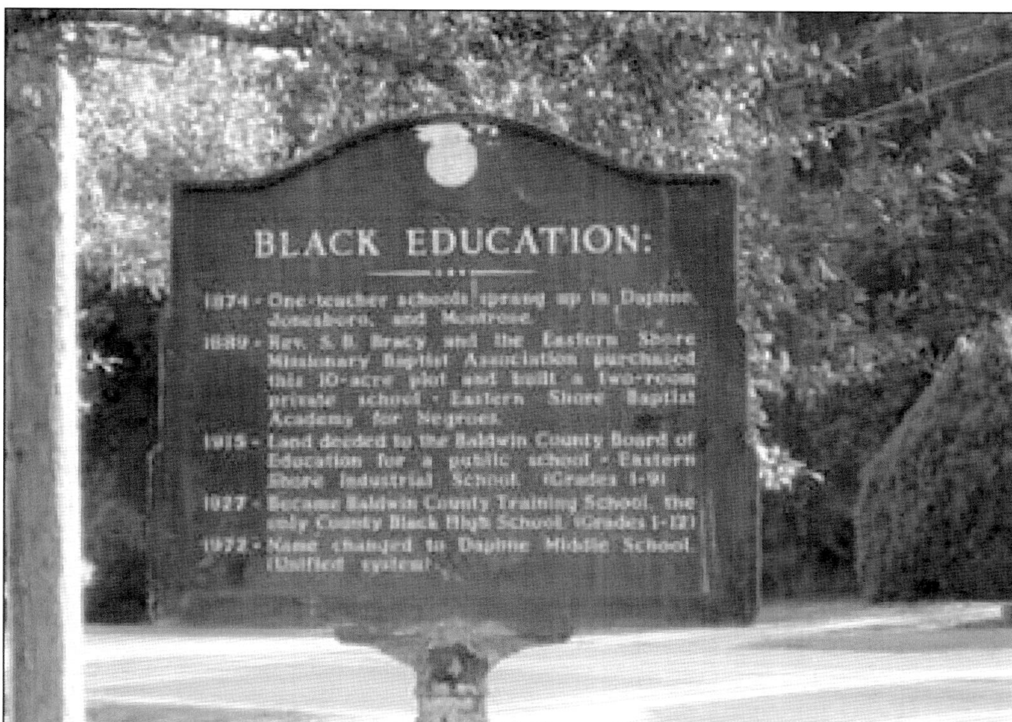

Black Education Historic Marker. In 1889, the journey to educate the black children of Baldwin County began when the Eastern Shore Missionary Baptist Association purchased 18 acres of land and built a one-room structure to train ministers and deacons. Under the leadership of S.B. Bracy, the Eastern Shore Missionary Baptist Association Colored School was founded in Daphne. (Photograph by Penny Taylor.)

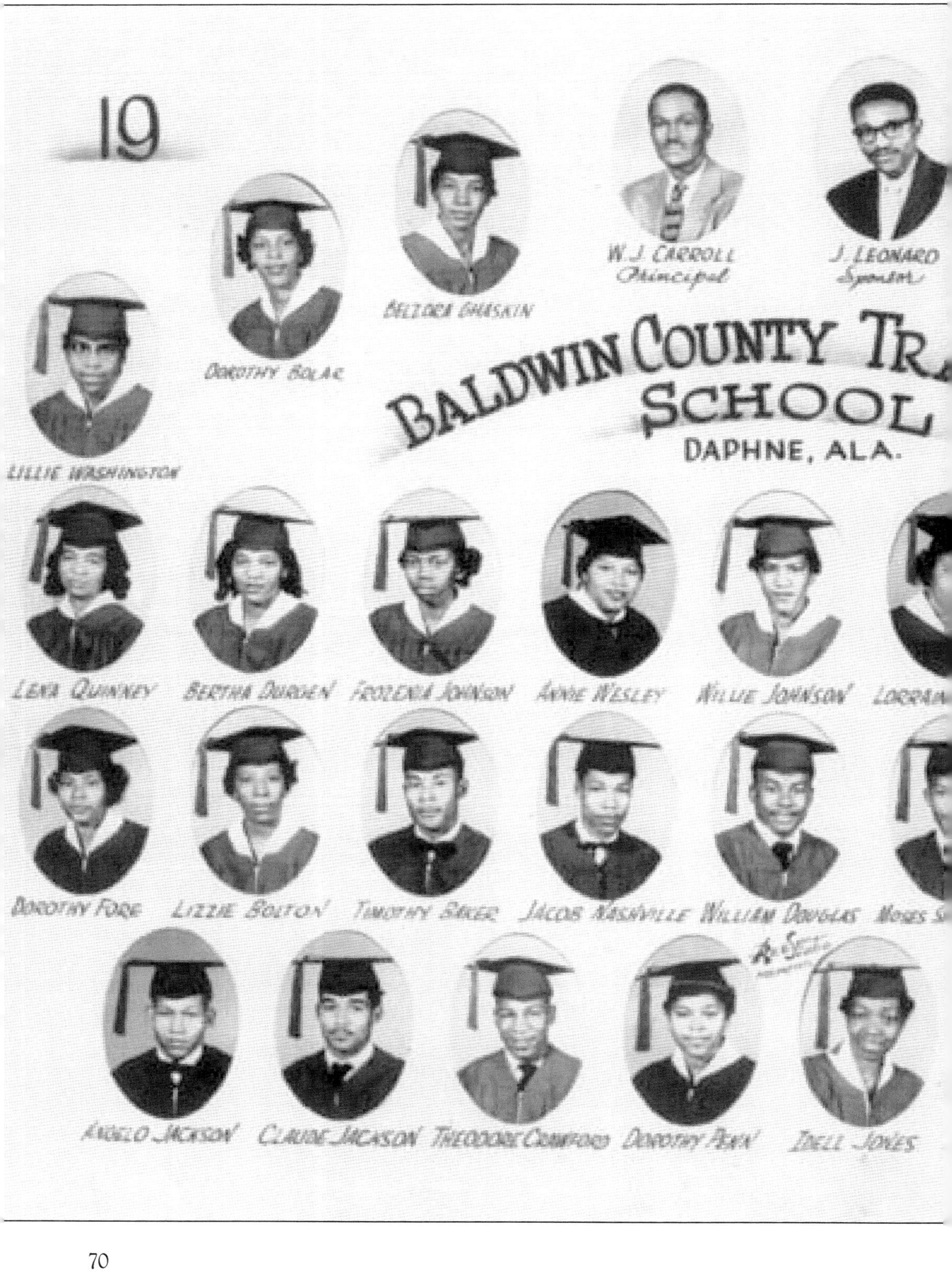
19
W. J. CARROLL
Principal
J. LEONARD
Sponsor
BELZORA GHASKIN
DOROTHY BOLAR
LILLIE WASHINGTON
BALDWIN COUNTY TR
SCHOOL
DAPHNE, ALA.
LENA QUINNEY
BERTHA DURGEN
FROLENIA JOHNSON
ANNIE WESLEY
WILLIE JOHNSON
DOROTHY FORE
LIZZIE BOLTON
TIMOTHY BAKER
JACOB NASHVILLE
WILLIAM DOUGLAS
ANGELO JACKSON
CLAUDE JACKSON
THEODORE CRAWFORD
DOROTHY PENN
IDELL JONES

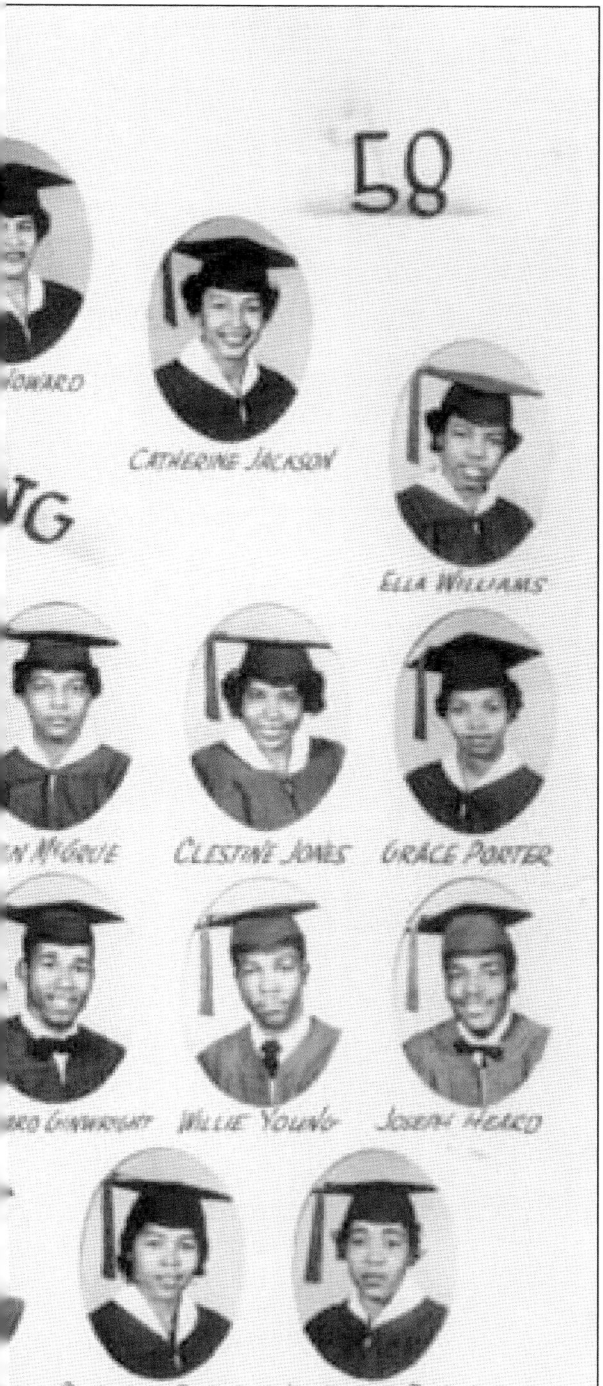

Class of 1958. High school curriculum was added under the principalship of E.S. Peeples, and the first graduating class consisted of four girls in 1936. Over the years, more than 1,500 students received diplomas. The last graduation was held in 1970, with 70 graduating seniors. More than 20 small community schools throughout the county had grades one through eight, but until two additional schools were constructed, students had to attend high school in Daphne to continue their education. Douglasville High School was built in Bay Minette in 1950. The Baldwin County Training School class of 1958 included students from the Foley area, as Aaronville High School had not yet been built. Dormitories were no longer in use at this time, and students from Foley came to Daphne in buses actually driven by students. (OMCMD.)

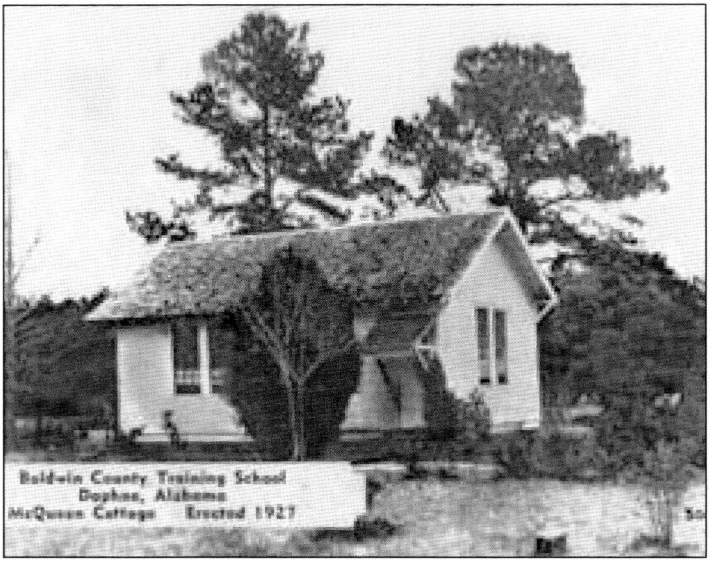

Daphne's Rosenwald Building. This building was constructed with Rosenwald funds, a national program established by Julius Rosenwald to build schools for African American children. This was used as the industrial arts building of Baldwin County Training School and was later attached to the back of the 1942 vocational building. (Black Education Museum, Daphne.)

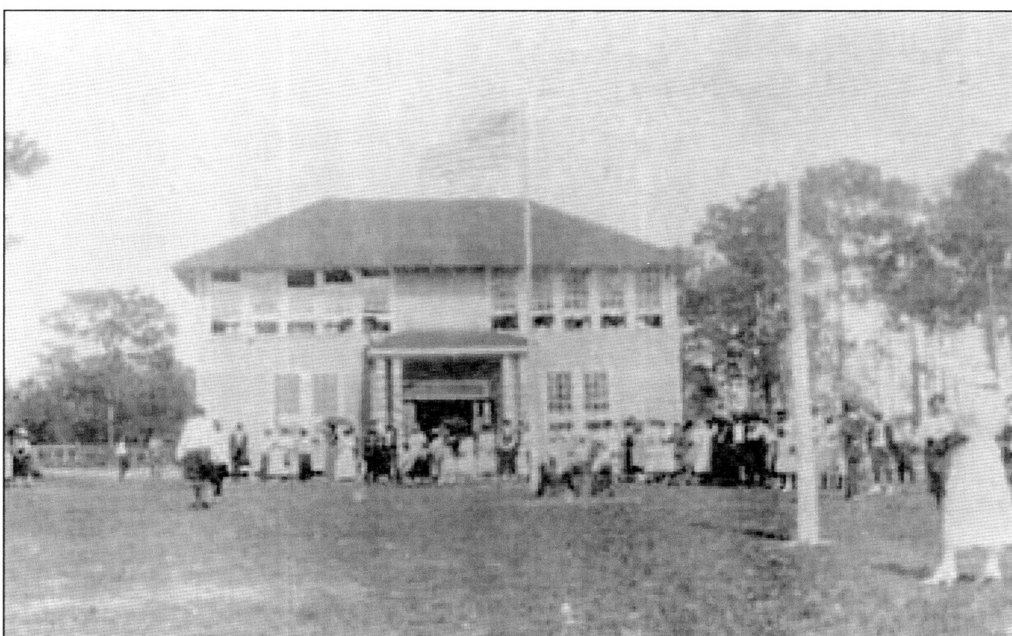

Eastern Shore Industrial School. In 1916, the school's board of trustees agreed to deed the 18 acres and the two one-room buildings to the board of education to "be used as a public school for the benefit of the colored race." Named the Eastern Shore Industrial School, it served students in grades one through ten. Pictured is the school's main building that was constructed in 1918. (Black Education Museum, Daphne.)

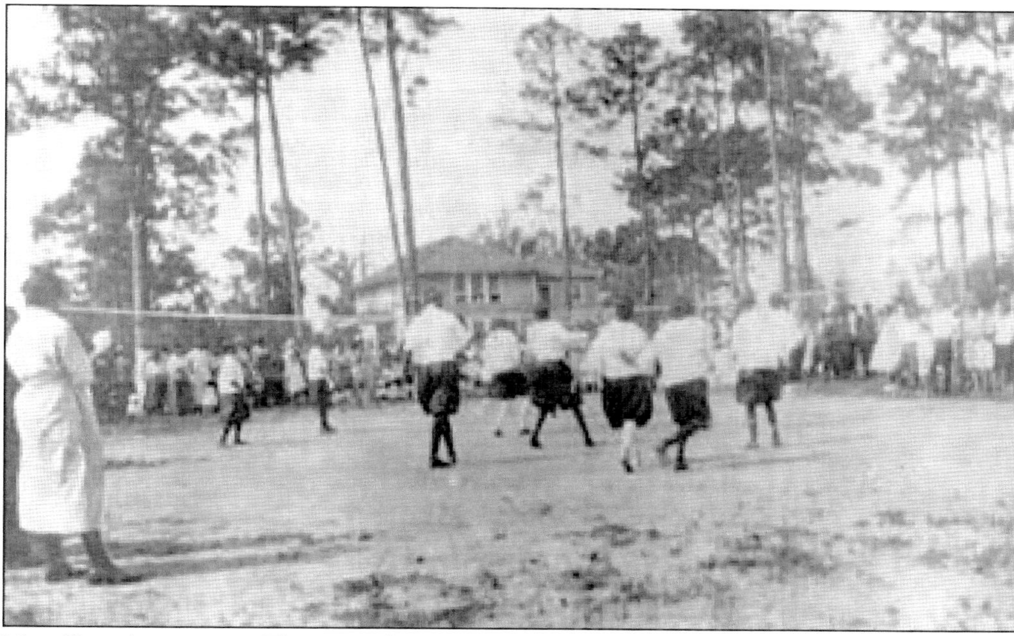

MAY DAY ACTIVITIES. The annual May Day was filled with two days of activities, parades, entertainment, and games for families and the entire community. Here, students play a ball game in front of the historic classroom building, which burned down in 1941. (Black Education Museum, Daphne.)

GIRLS' DORMITORY. The first principal of Baldwin County Training School, Ligon A. Wilson, secured board of education funding to assist in housing 40 students who had requested admission as boarding students in 1919. The two-story girls' dormitory also housed the domestic science classrooms and a kitchen. Students were charged $9 per month to board. (Black Education Museum, Daphne.)

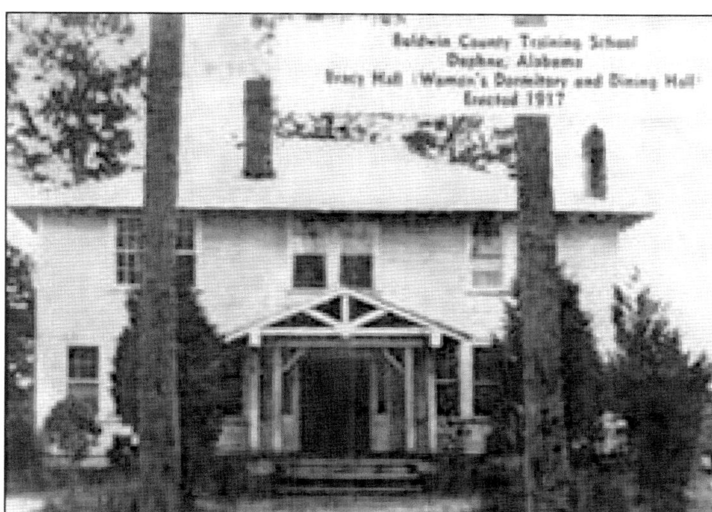

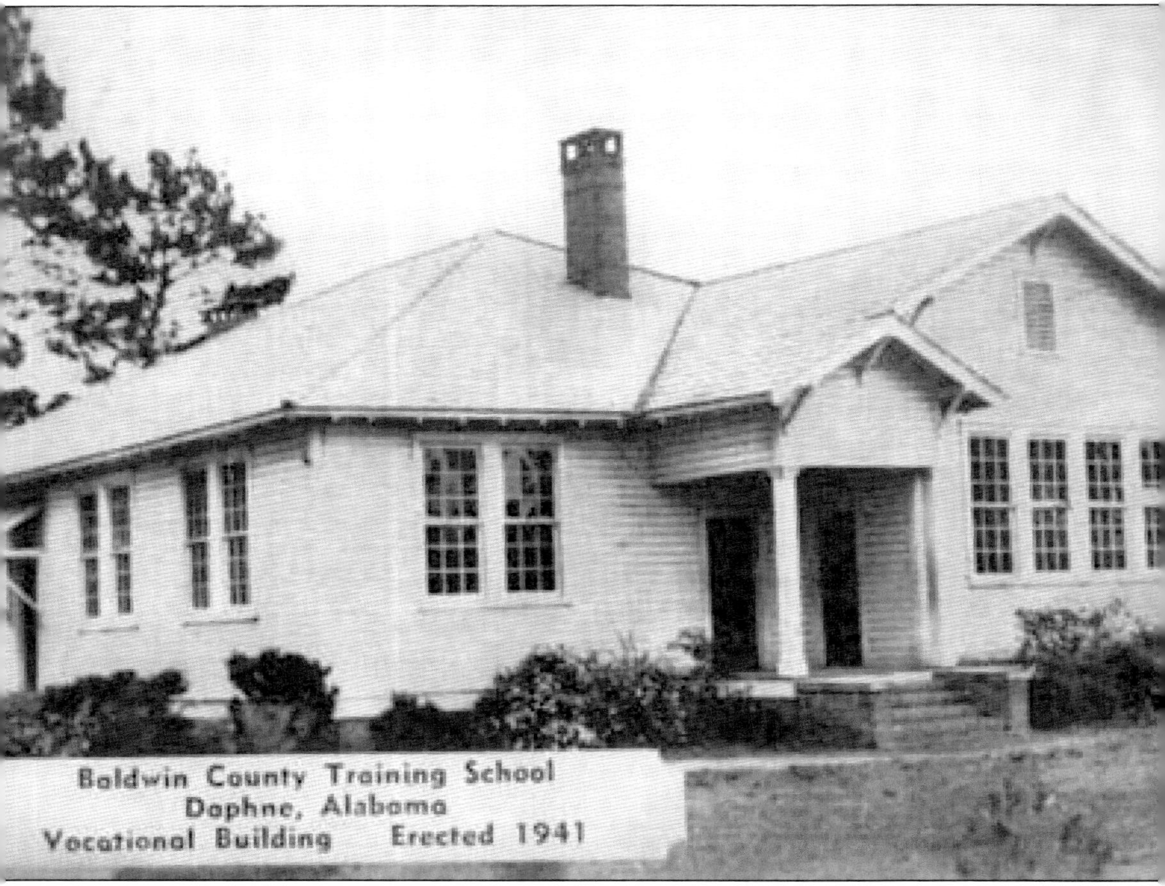

VOCATIONAL BUILDING. In 1941 and 1942, a vocational studies building was constructed with student labor under the direction of Agostino Guarisco. W.O. Jones, the shop and agriculture teacher, was an outstanding mentor for the young men in the school. This building now houses the Black Education Museum. It is located on the campus of W.J. Carroll School on Main Street. (Black Education Museum, Daphne.)

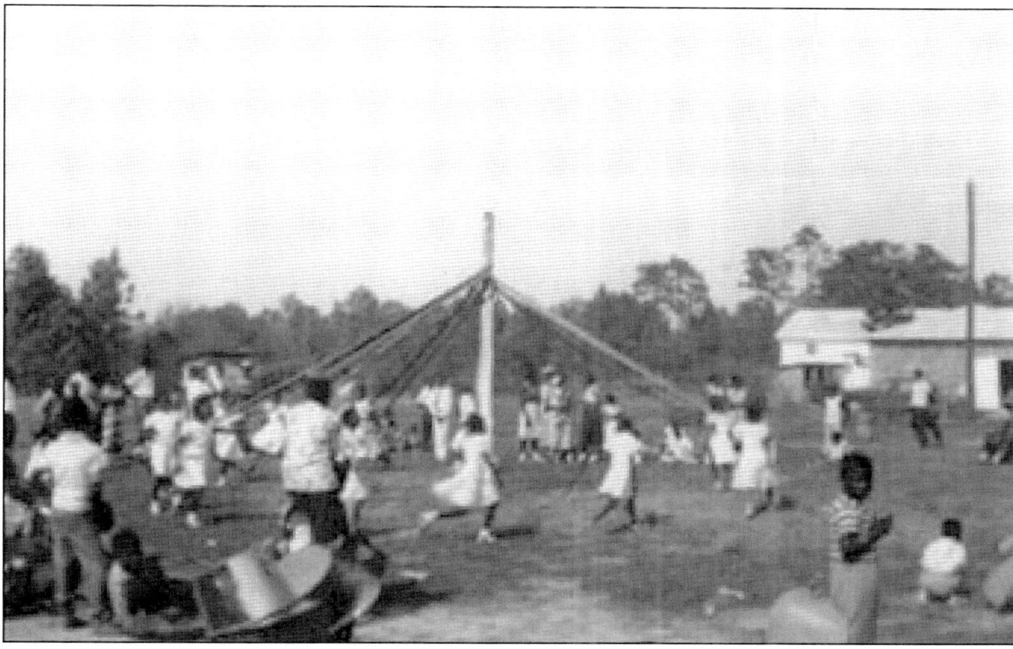

May Day Finery. The entire community turned out for the two-day festival of May Day. Students dressed in their best springtime outfits were chosen to weave the ribbons around the maypole. (Black Education Museum, Daphne.)

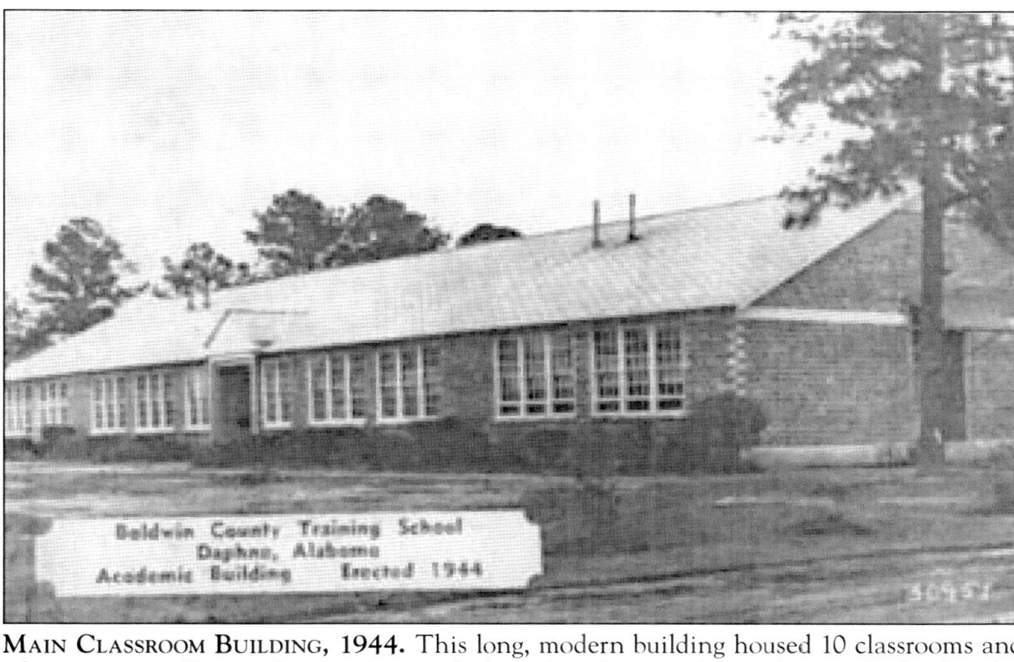

Main Classroom Building, 1944. This long, modern building housed 10 classrooms and administrative offices and was constructed of red clay tiles manufactured in nearby brickworks. The installation of an electric water pump made modern plumbing possible. A cafeteria, added in 1955, was the site of that year's graduation. (Black Education Museum, Daphne.)

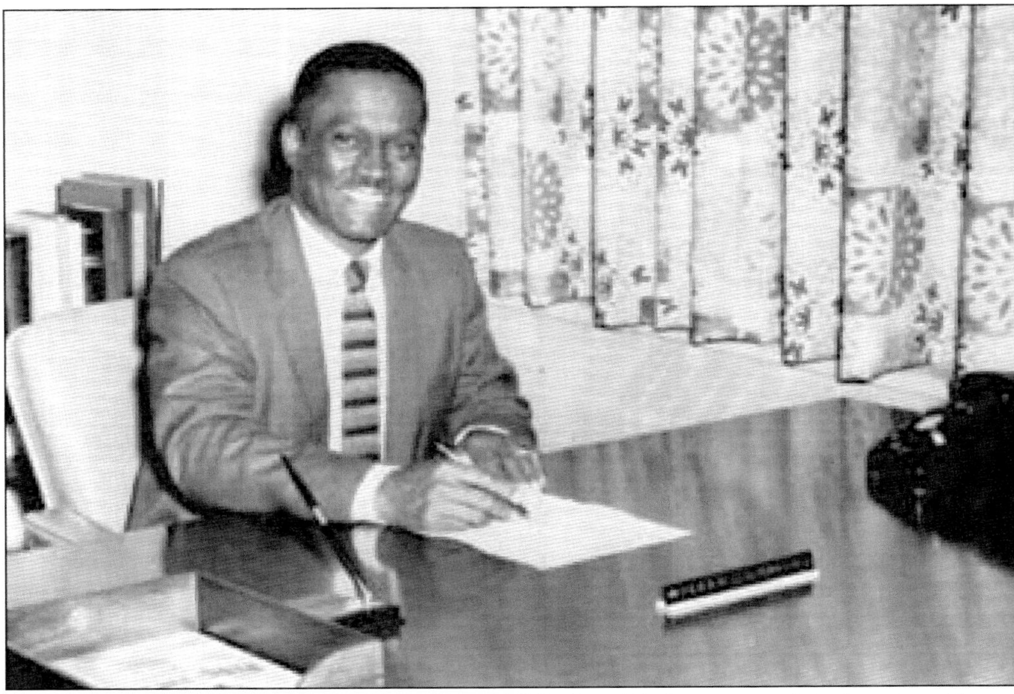

Walker J. Carroll. As principal from 1938 to 1970, Carroll left an unequaled educational legacy. A new elementary school is named in his memory, and the institution continues a long tradition of excellence. (Black Education Museum, Daphne)

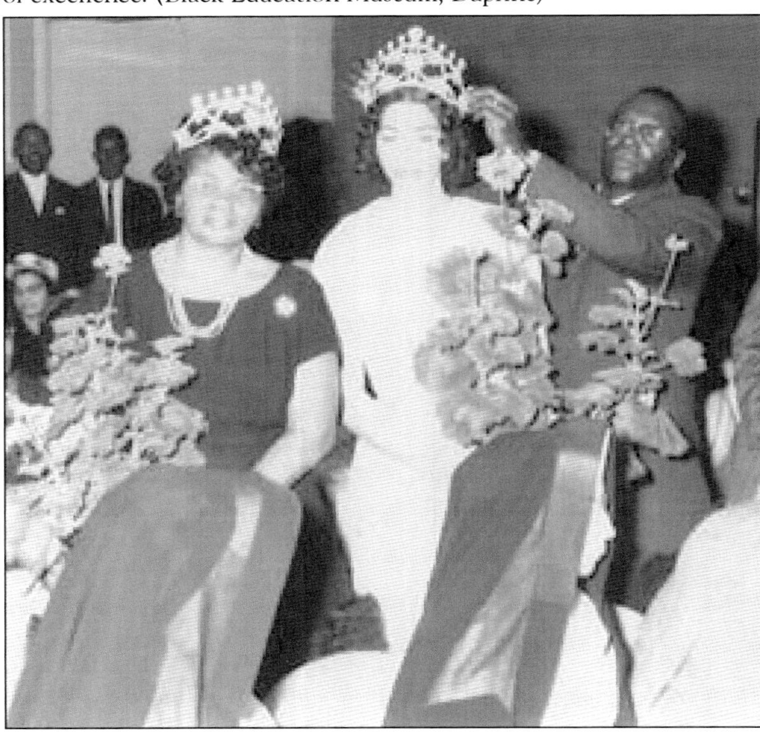

Green Tea. Parents, teachers, and other members of the community enthusiastically embraced the task of raising funds to provide books and supplies to the school. One of the most loved events was the annual Green Tea, during which one woman was crowned queen for a day. (Black Education Museum, Daphne.)

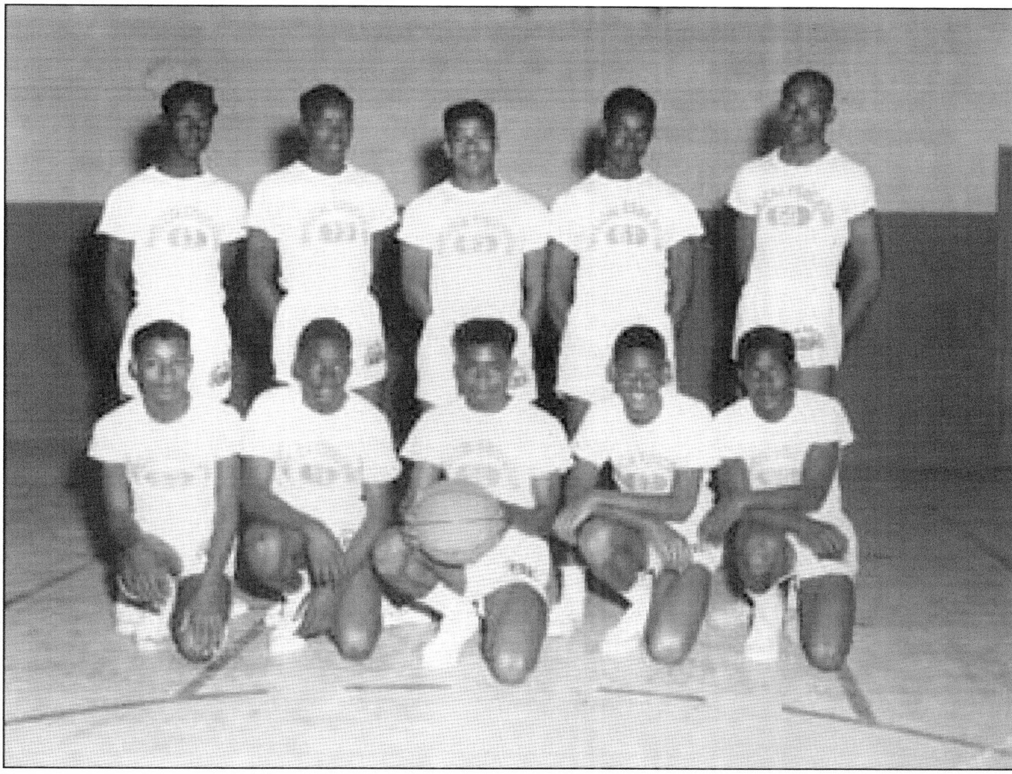

Basketball Team. Baldwin County Training School played its first athletic event, a football game, against Snow Hill Institute in 1946. Pictured here is one of the many outstanding BCTS Wolverine basketball teams, which won numerous state championships. (Black Education Museum, Daphne.)

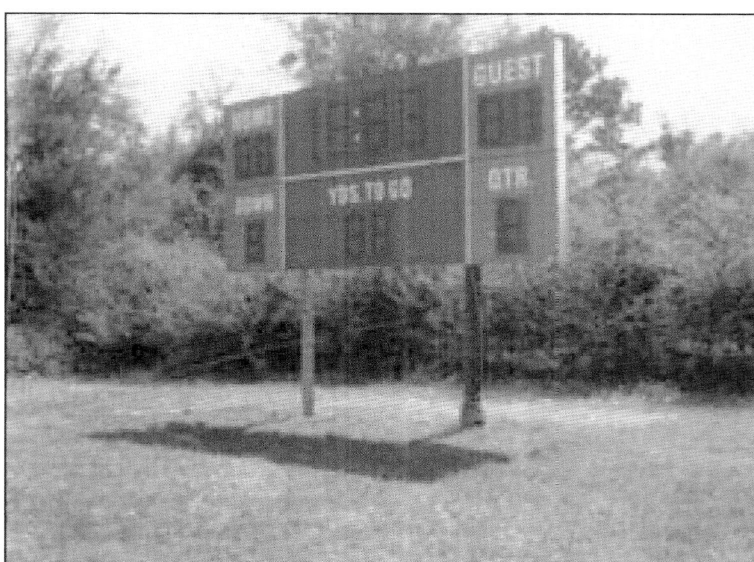

Scoreboard. In 1959, a football field was built on the BCTS campus. The snack bar was located under the concrete bleachers. Lights were added, and night games upped the excitement for many outstanding athletes. (Black Education Museum, Daphne.)

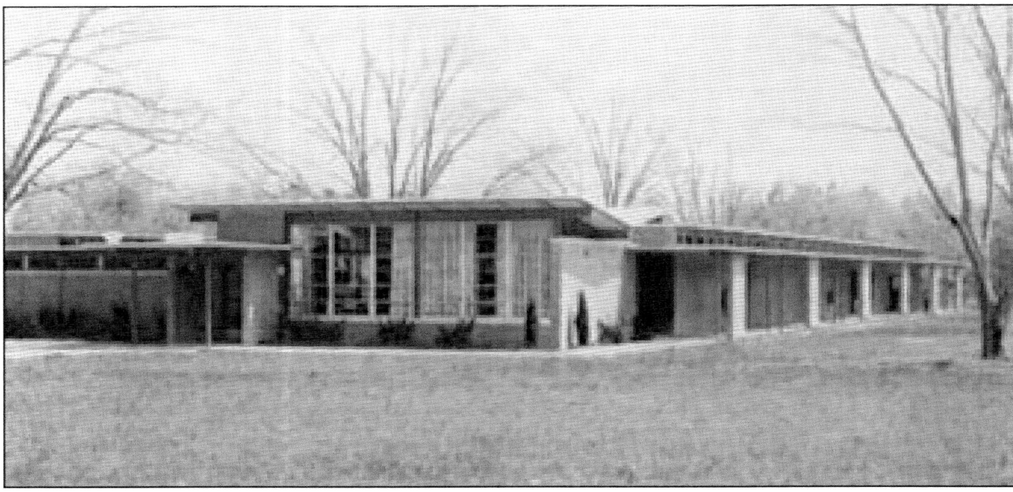

New School Building. An elementary complex of classrooms and office space was built in 1960 and 1961. The flagpole was mounted in a brick base, which was designed and constructed by masonry classes at Baldwin County Training School. The 1911 cornerstone was embedded in the new base, dedicated in 1961. (Black Education Museum, Daphne.)

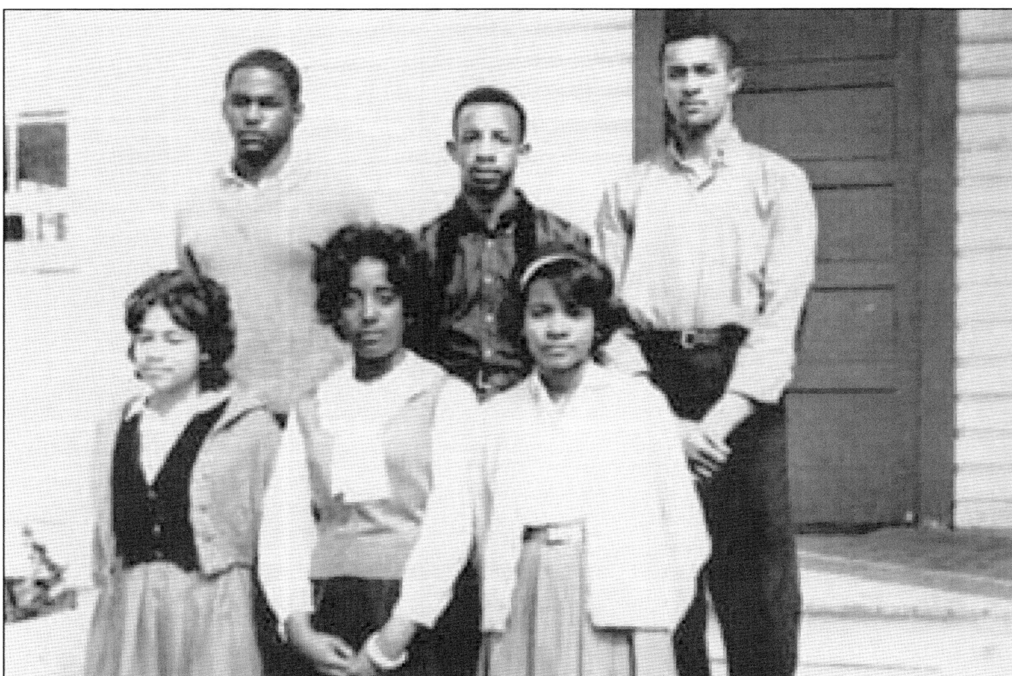

Class Officers. Students at Baldwin County Training School exhibited outstanding leadership qualities. These class officers of 1964 later helped organize an alumni association, the Baldwin County Training School Heritage Fest Foundation, which has preserved the history of the school for display at the Black Education Museum, located in the former vocational building on campus. Pictured are, from left to right, (first row) Rickey Nichols, Thelma Young, and Louise Yelding; (second row) Charles Larry, Charles Hall, and Andrew Bolar. (Black Education Museum, Daphne.)

Six

CHURCHES AND SCHOOLS

BACKBONES OF CITIZENRY

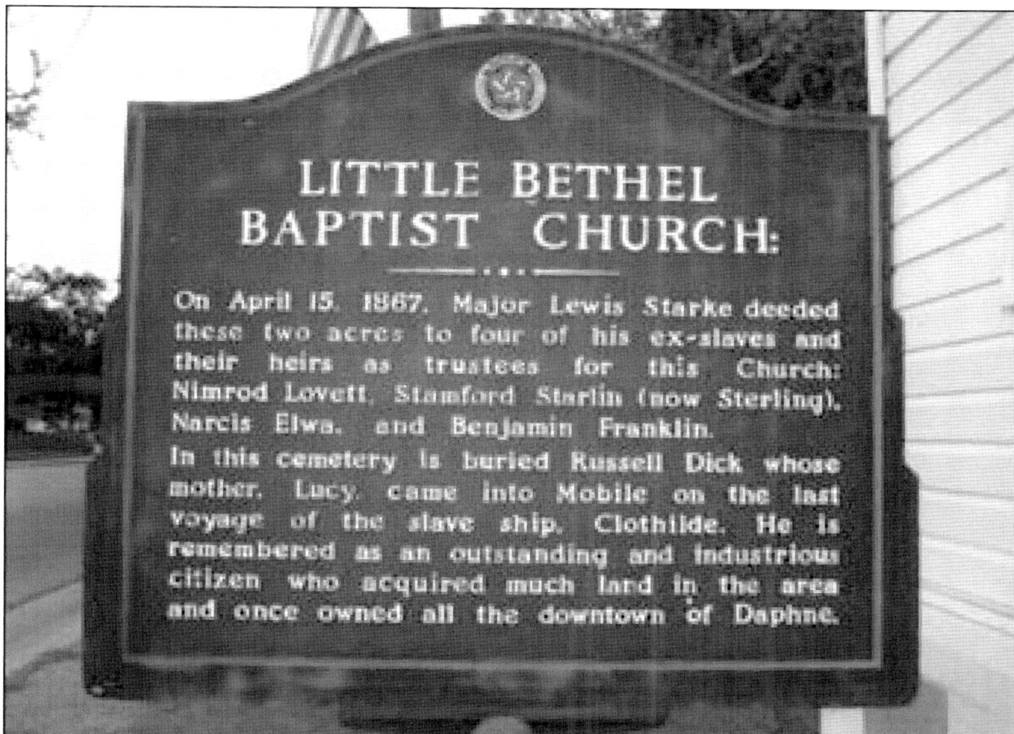

LITTLE BETHEL HISTORIC MARKER. This marker reads: "On April 15, 1867, Major Lewis Starke deeded these two acres to four of his ex-slaves and their heirs as trustees for this Church: Nimrod Lovett, Stamford Starlin (now Sterling), Narcis Elwa, and Benjamin Franklin." (Photograph by Harriet Outlaw.)

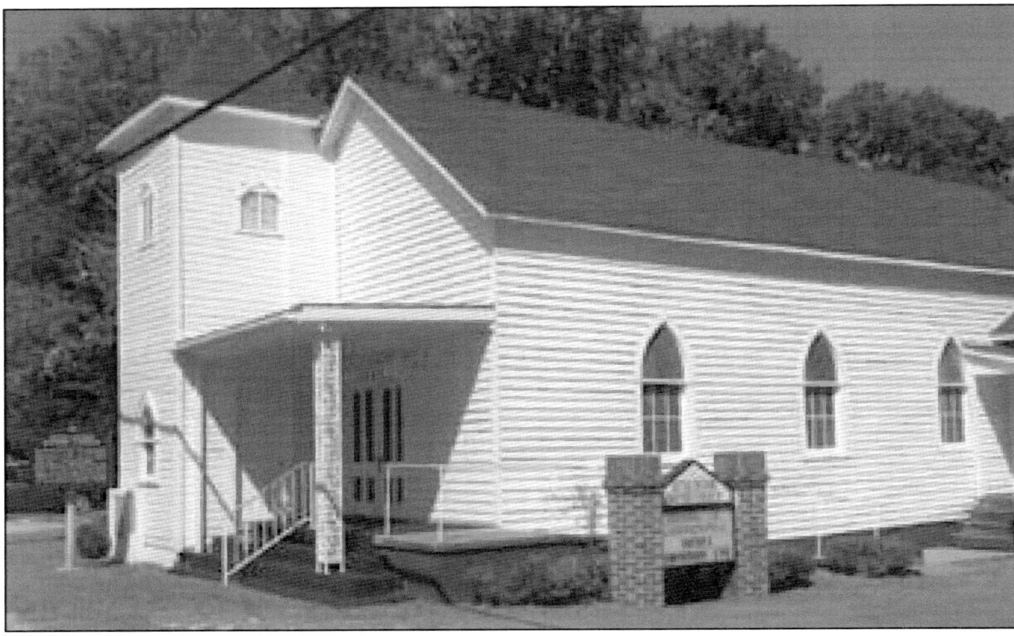

Little Bethel Baptist Church. One prominent church member was Russell Dick, a successful businessman in Daphne. Dick was a cook during the Civil War, a sexton of the Methodist church, custodian for the courthouse, cook for the jail, and eventually became the owner of most of downtown Daphne. His mother, Lucy, came to America on the last voyage of the slave ship Clotilde. Dick is buried in the Little Bethel Cemetery behind the church. (John Lewis.)

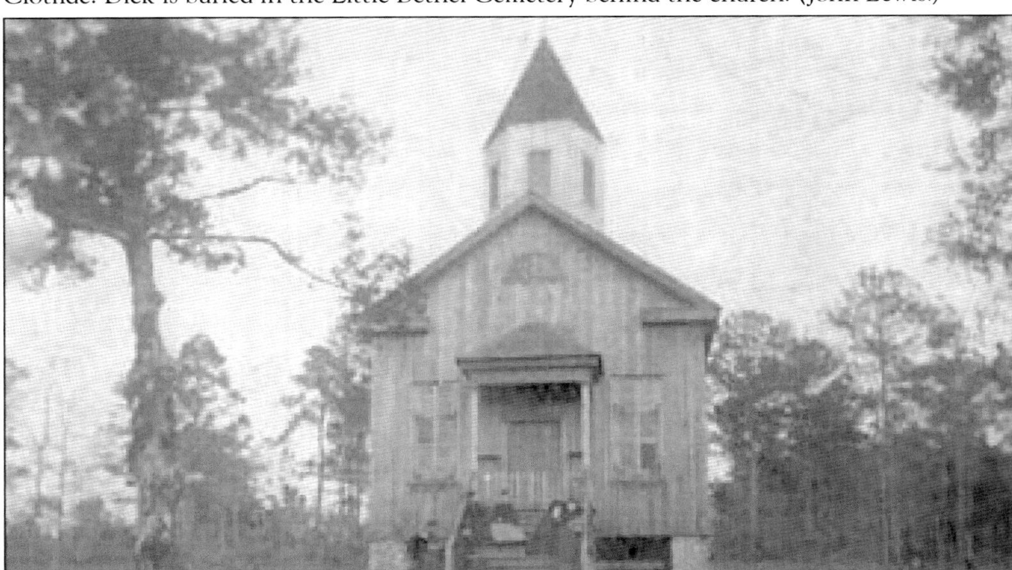

Bayshore Baptist. The original Protestant congregation, founded by itinerate preacher Lorenzo Dow, built this wooden structure. The Bayshore Baptist cemetery, on land donated by Anne and Larkin Edmondson in 1890, remains at its original location on Old County Road, but the congregation moved into a new wooden building on land donated by Russell Dick, then into the current brick church, which is on land donated by William and Clarence Dryer. (OMCMD.)

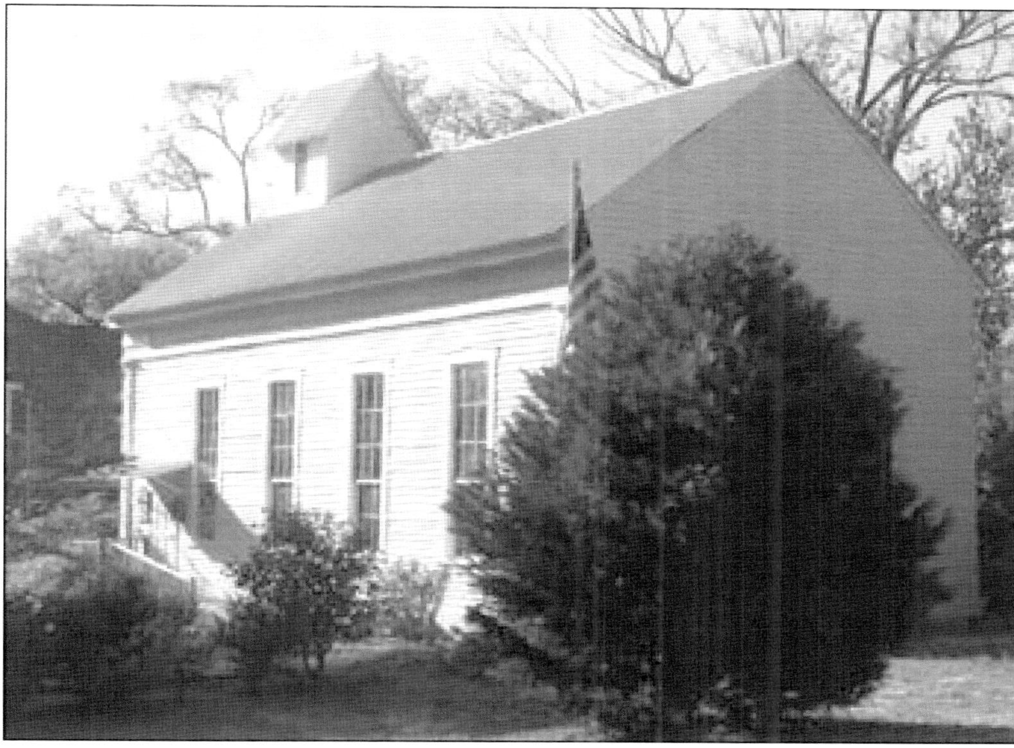

Methodist Church. Built in 1858, the stately clapboard Methodist Episcopal Church served all Protestant groups, much like its predecessor, the Union Church. Capt. William and Elizabeth Howard donated the land and oversaw construction of the Greek Revival building, made of pine logs and put together with wooden pegs. The church was built with a slave gallery and a side entrance for African Americans who joined in the worship services. The original pews and light fixture have been preserved. (Photograph by Penny Taylor.)

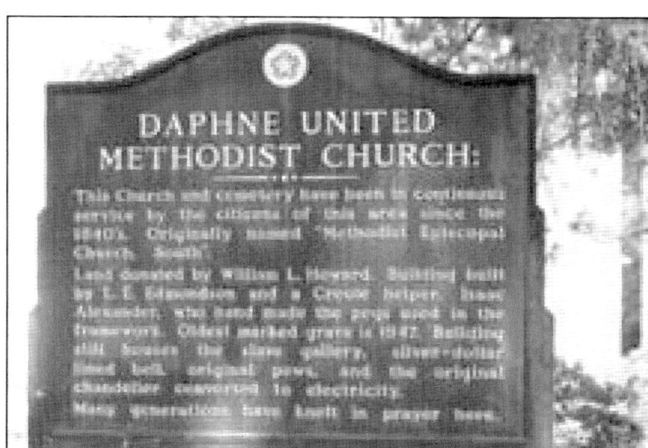

Historic Church and Cemetery. A historic marker placed during the US bicentennial in 1976 tells the story of the historic Daphne United Methodist Church, which currently serves as the Old Methodist Church Museum of Daphne. During the Civil War, the Union army occupied the building and grounds as they prepared to attack Spanish Fort and Blakeley to the north. The oldest grave in the cemetery dates to 1847. (Photograph by Penny Taylor.)

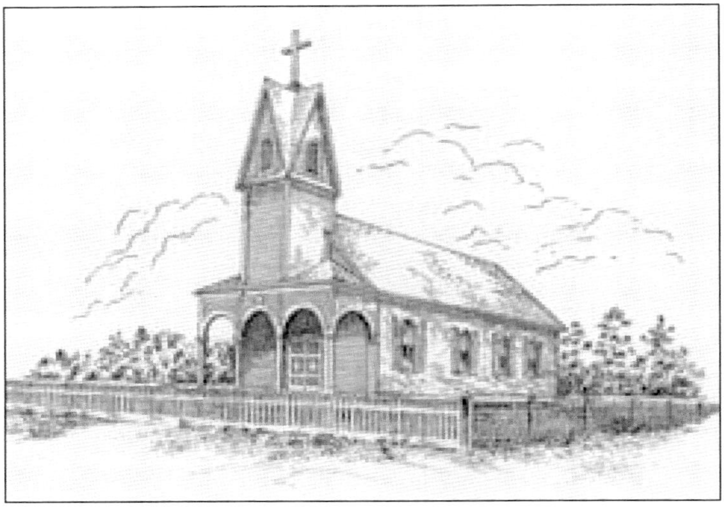

CHURCH OF THE ASSUMPTION. When the first Italian colonists settled in the Daphne area, Rev. Angelo Chiariglione was assigned as the resident Catholic priest. Known as "Father Angelo," he served the community faithfully until his death in 1908. The first Catholic church was named the Assumption and was built by the colonists. (Dick Scott, sketch by Richard Scott.)

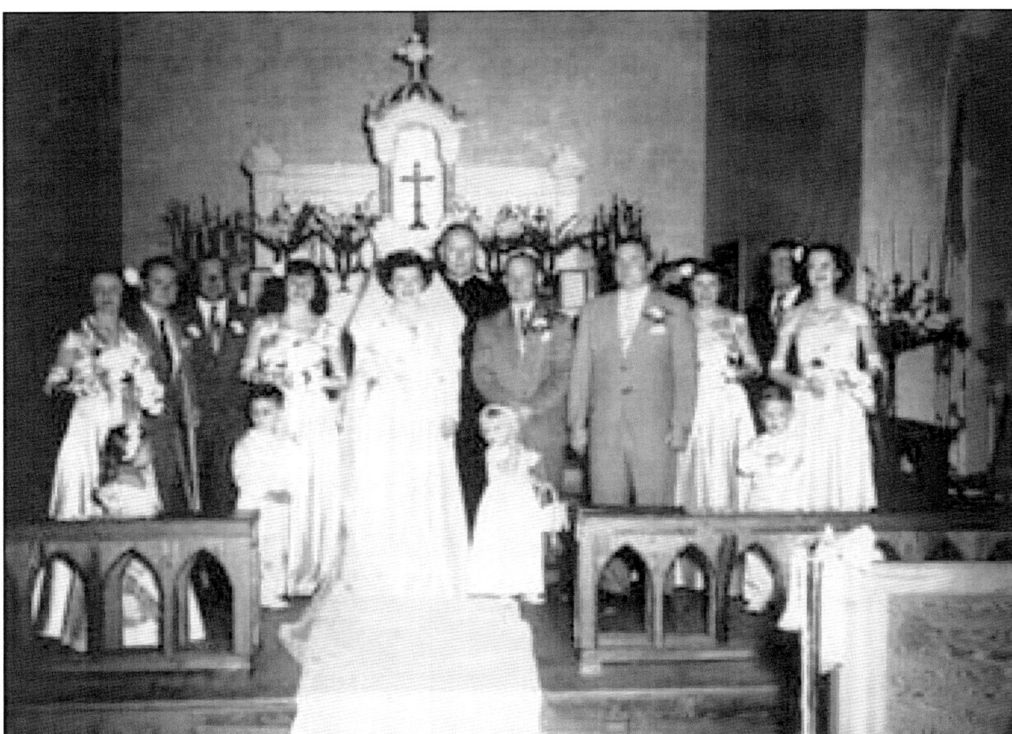

CHRIST THE KING CHURCH. A cement church built on Main Street was named Christ the King Church. A parochial school was started in 1949 under the administration of the Sisters of Loretta. In 1993, the newest church building was erected on the site, displaying the names of the founding families in marble at the entrance. The picture depicts the 1950 wedding of Roy and Alice Simms. (Mildred Simms Foster.)

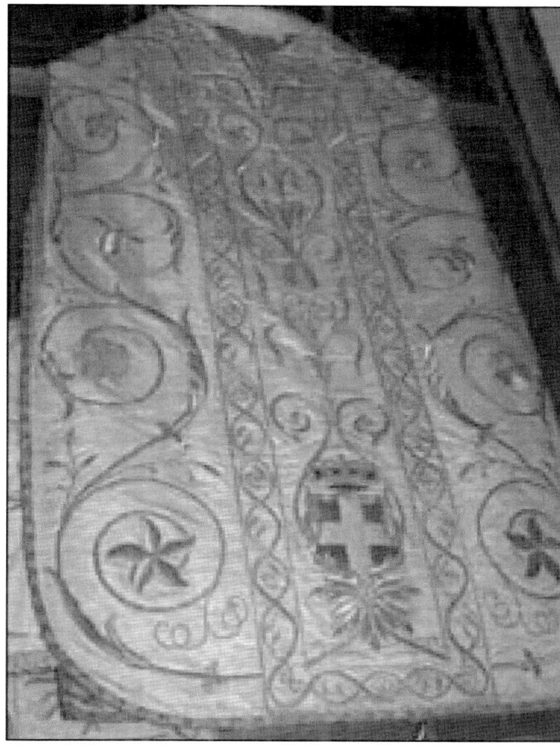

HOLY VESTMENTS. When Margherita of Savoy, queen of Italy, heard about the Italian colony at Daphne, she signaled her endorsement and support of the church in the form of extravagant gifts. She sent vestments with rich embroidered panels, an elaborately illuminated Bible, and two boxes of books. The gifts were presented to the colonists at the Feast of Corpus Christi on June 9, 1898. The vestments, called "chasuble," are on display in the church's museum. The embroidery reads as follows: "Presented to the Rt. Rev. Bishop of Mobile, by Her Majesty, Queen Margaret of Italy, for use among the Italian Catholics at Daphne, Ala. Feast of Corpus Christi, June 9, 1898." (Photograph by Penny Taylor, courtesy of Christ the King Church.)

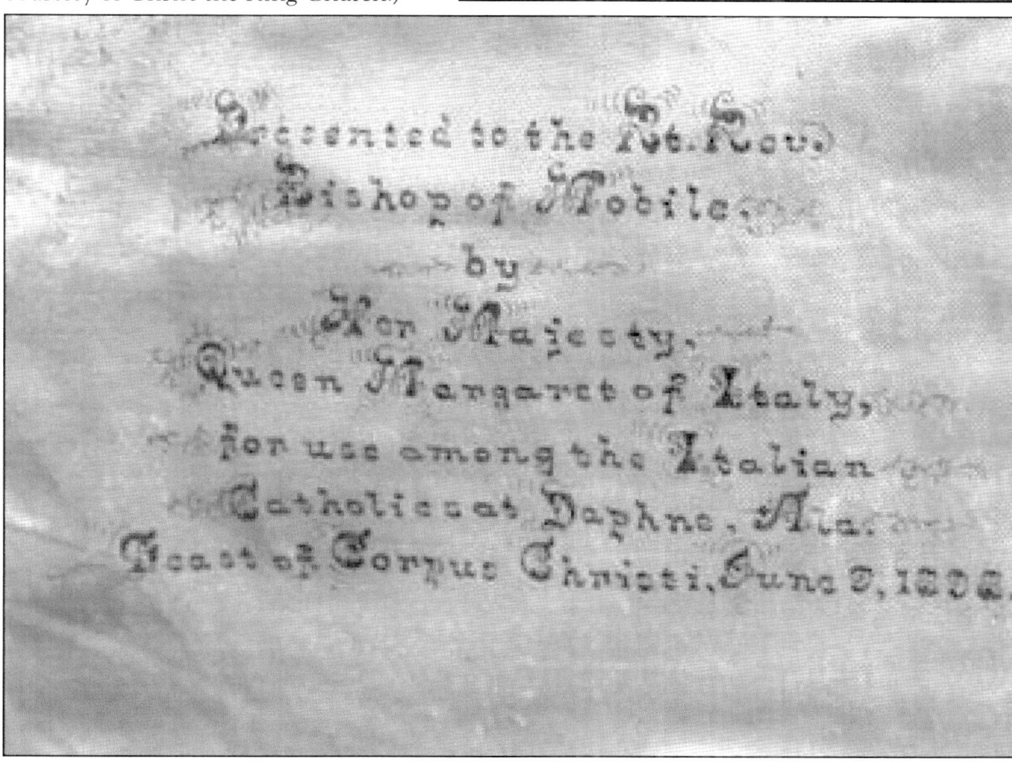

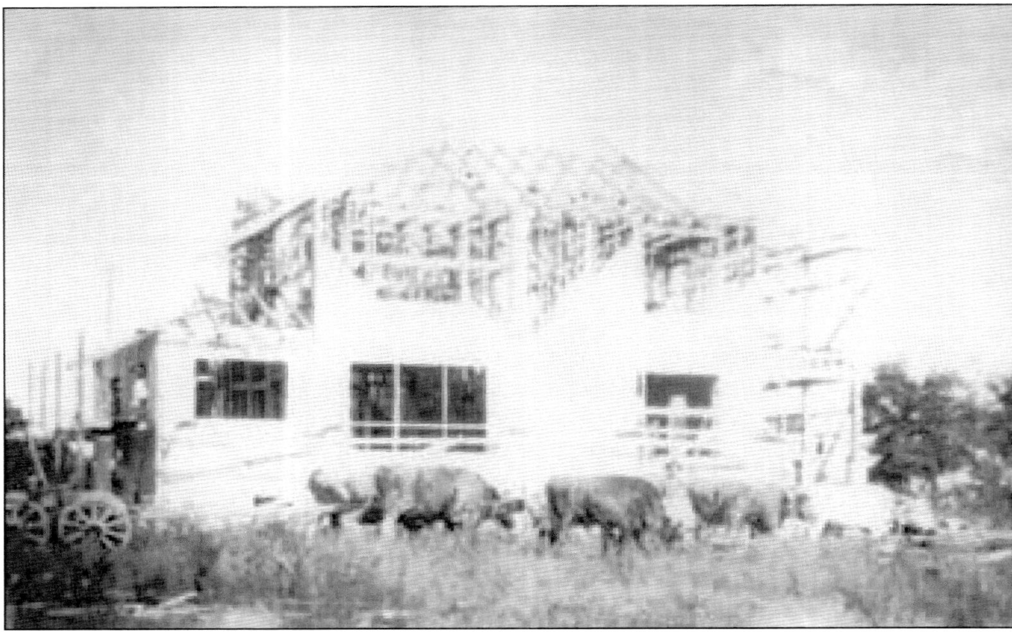

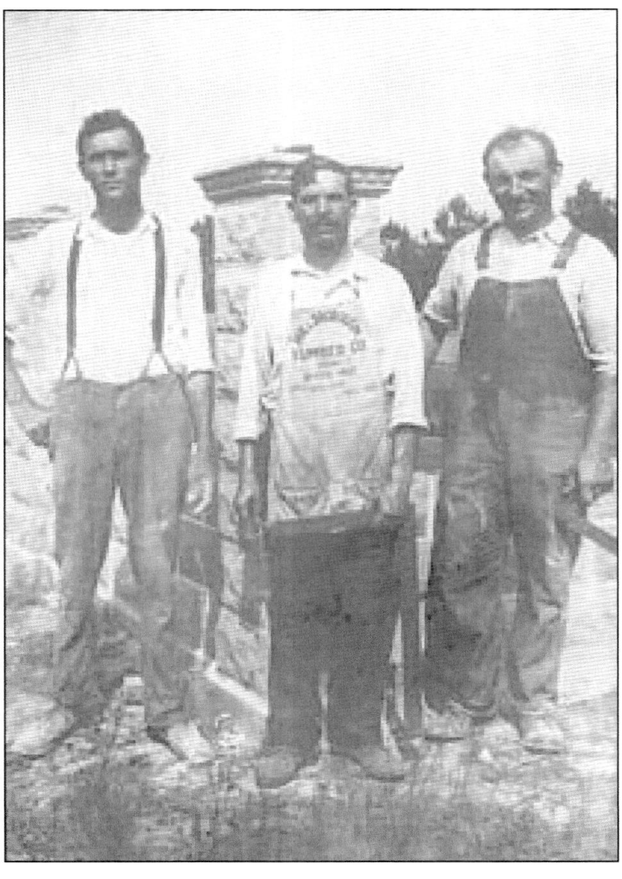

Building the Rectory. Agostino Guarisco came to Daphne in 1905, met his future wife, and went to work for Cipriano Allegri building a sawmill and cotton gin. He became a successful builder, and when the church was in need of a rectory, he answered the call. In the 1920s, ox teams were still the most efficient means of delivering lumber from his sawmill. (Al Guarisco.)

Proud Workmen. Agostino Guarisco stands between Frank (left) and Olivo Bertagnolli for a photograph during a break from building the rectory next to the Church of the Assumption. The rectory housed the priest and offices of the parish until it was demolished in 2011. The concrete post behind the workmen is a good example of the concrete blocks that were manufactured at Bertagnolli masonry. (Al Guarisco.)

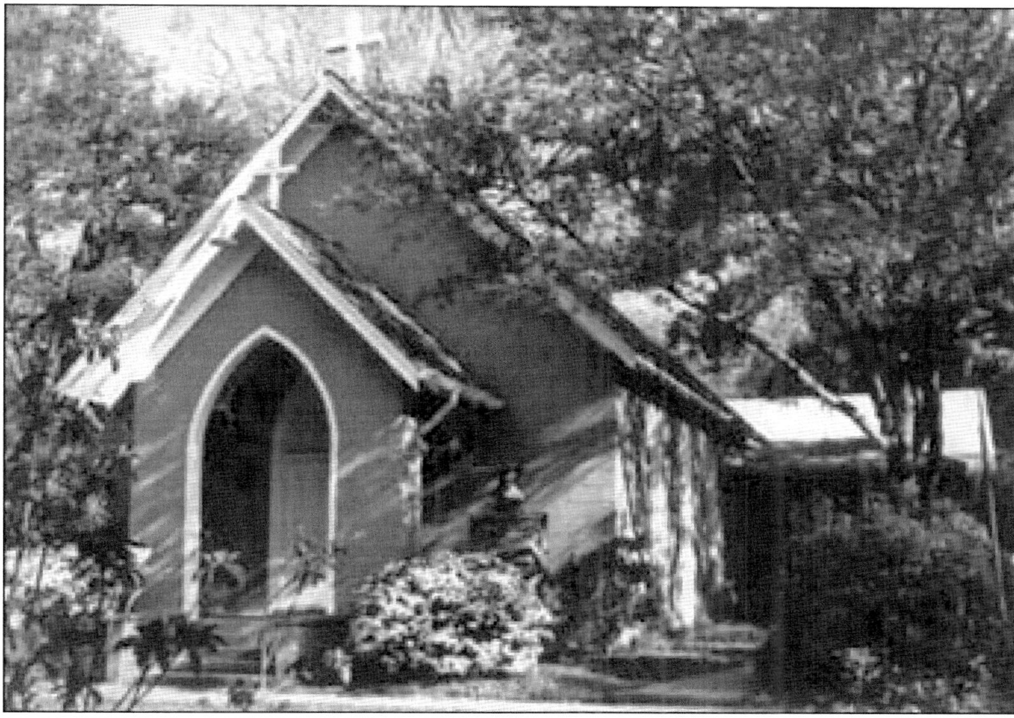

St. Paul's Episcopal. At 415 College Avenue, the Malone family built St. Paul's Episcopal to honor the memory of their son Gratz. Master potter Peter McAdams created a distinctive clay altar for the church. Tragically, McAdams's son, Peter, was killed in an accident, and the altar was dedicated to his memory. When the church moved to a new location, attempts to move the altar resulted in its destruction. (OMCMD.)

Macedonia Baptist. The original Macedonia Baptist was founded in 1878 by Rev. A.A. Williams and faced the community well. After several renovations and enlargements, the church now faces County Road 64 and is known for its steadfast congregation. (Dick Scott, sketch by Richard Scott.)

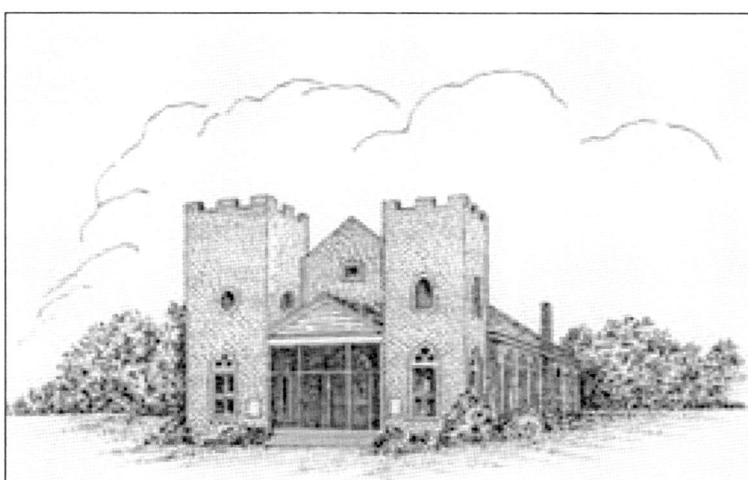

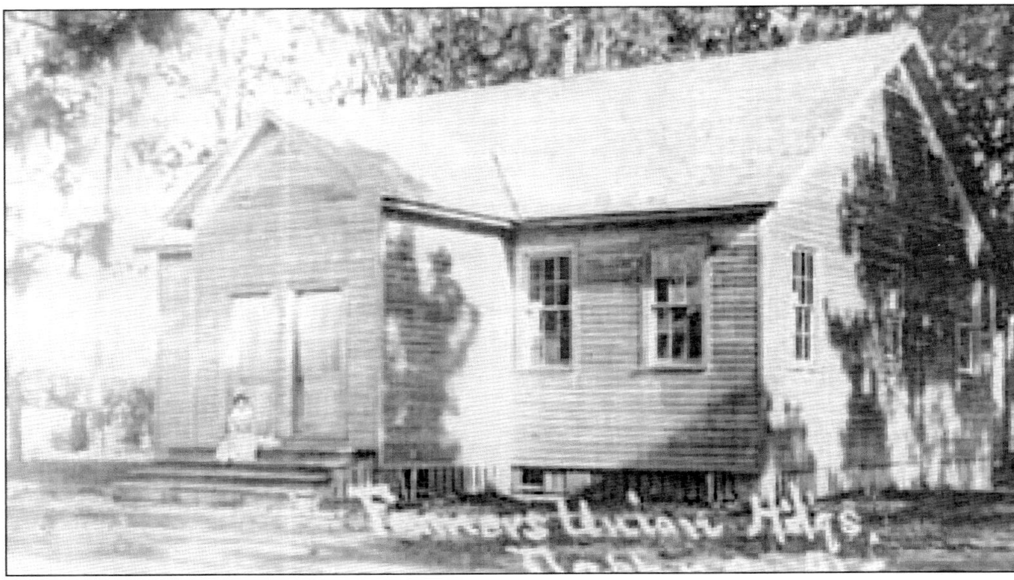

First Schoolhouse. One of the earliest schools on record operated at the Hollywood Hotel from 1867 to 1873. During the 1890s, the one-room wooden schoolhouse shown here was built on Randall Avenue; several families financed the venture and supported the teacher. (OMCMD.)

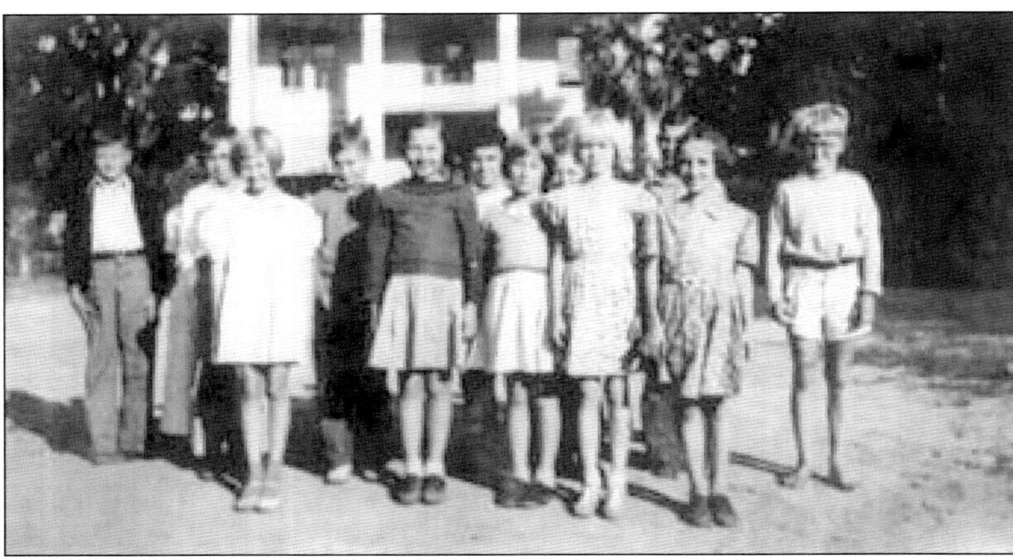

Jean Yuille's Class. Jean Yuille was the descendant of the Yuille family, which purchased land in 1845 and built the Magnolia Hill residence. Yuille attended the Daphne Normal School and earned her teaching certificate. Her first class in Daphne is pictured here. She later taught at Daphne Junior High School for many years. (OMCMD.)

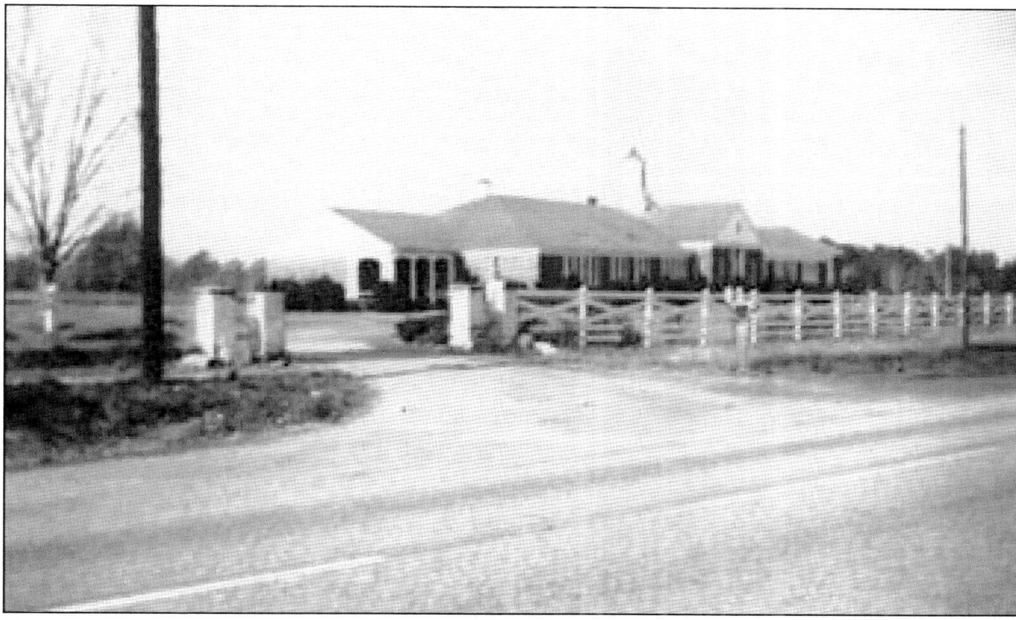

Daphne Junior High School. As compensation for the loss of the State Teacher School in Daphne, the Alabama legislature commissioned the building of a modern school, which opened its doors in 1938 for grades one through nine. The school had more conveniences than any other in the county, including an intercom system, indoor restrooms, and floors that were actually shellacked. (Dick Scott, Carney Collection.)

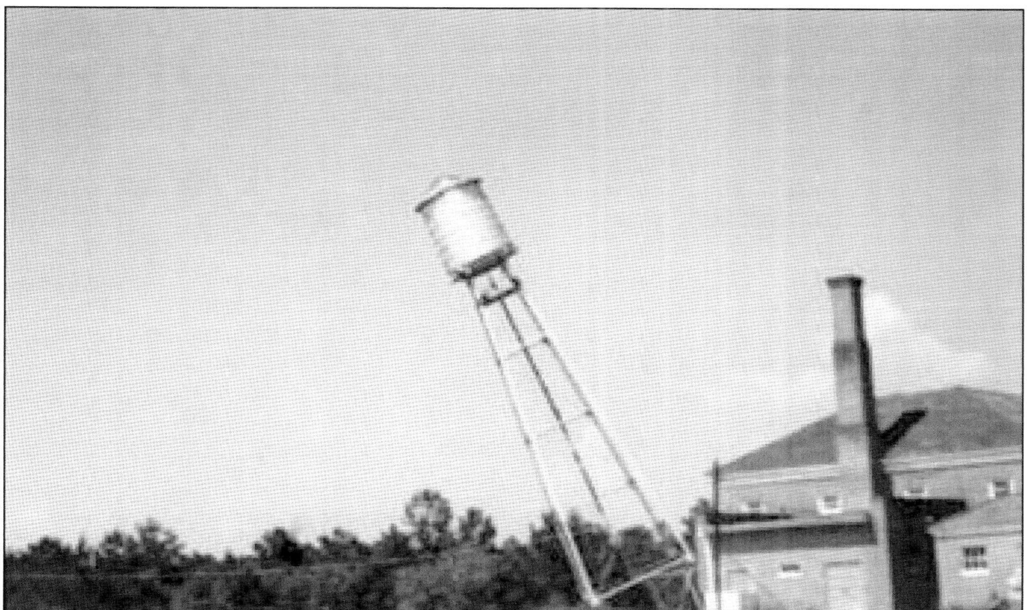

Water Tower Down. Former school superintendent Dr. R.L. Smith, of Latham, was a graduate of the Daphne Normal School. While serving as the buildings and transportation director, he supervised the demolition of the school's water tower, snapping three photographs of its fall. This is the middle photograph of the series, as the tower was on the way down. (Leslie Smith.)

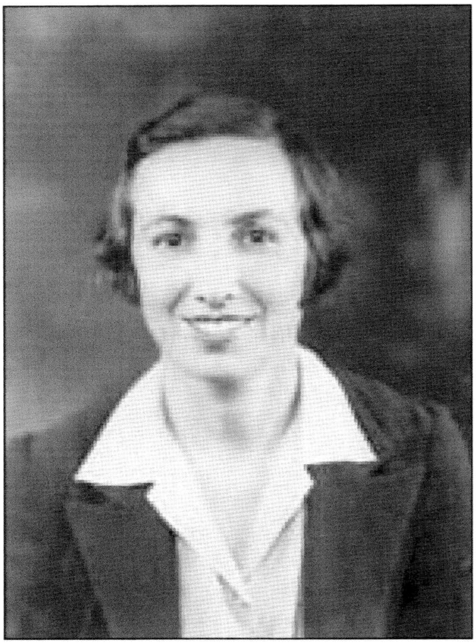

Mary Guarisco. The oldest daughter of Agostino Guarisco, Mary became an English teacher extraordinaire at Daphne Junior High. Students continuously gave her credit for their success. In the early 1970s, schools were redistricted and the building became an elementary school. Daphne Junior High was relocated to the former Baldwin County Training School, and Mary continued her career at Murphy High School in Mobile. (Al Guarisco.)

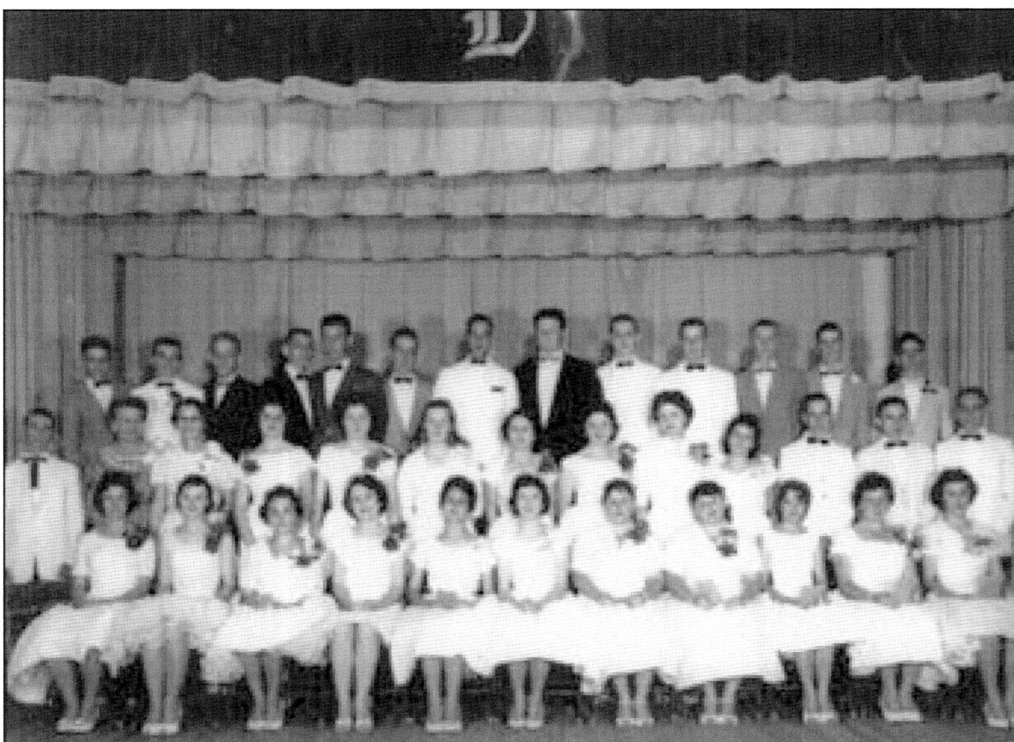

Class of 1959. Here, eighth-grade graduates pose on the stage, which was one of the finest facilities of its time and still serves students as Daphne Elementary School North. The girls and boys dressed formally for the ceremony celebrating their move to high school—which was Fairhope High School until Daphne High School was built in 1992. (OMCMD.)

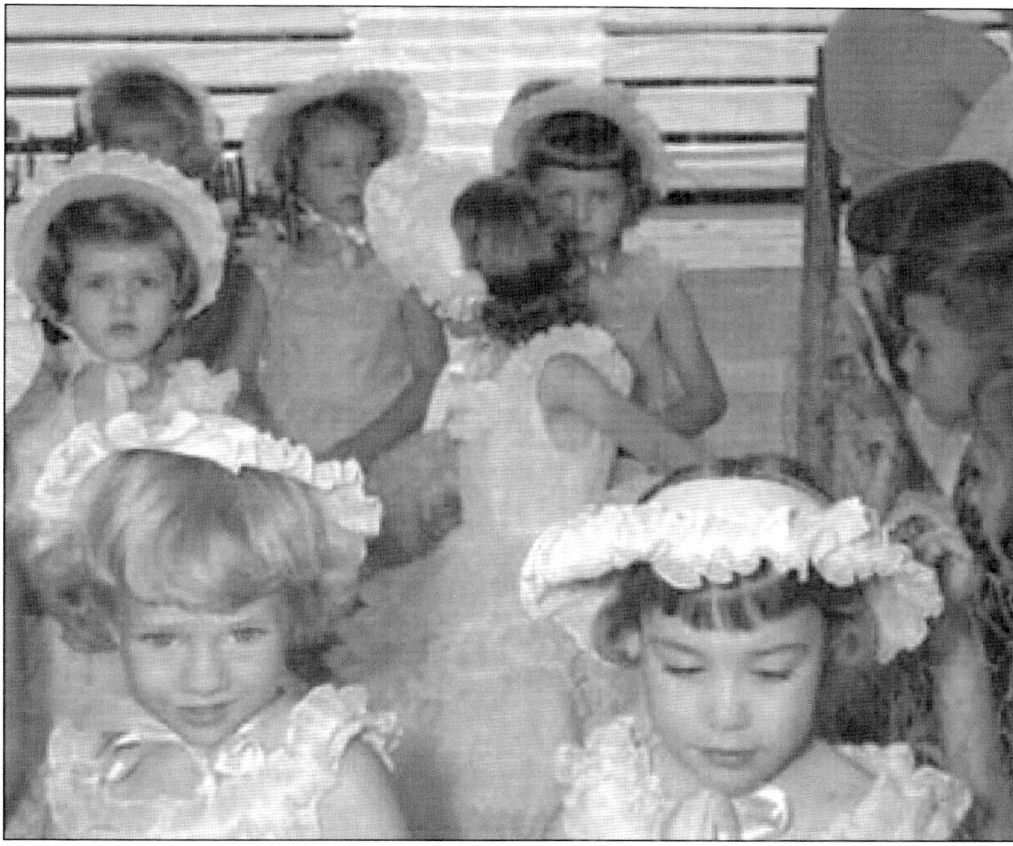

Flower Girls for May Day. May Day celebrations continued after the school was moved from the normal school campus to Daphne Junior High School. Each grade was represented by a flower girl and a page, who dressed in costumes and processed in the coronation. Pictured here, from left to right, are Stephanie Foster, Mary Jane Coxwell, Laura Gray, Linda DeFilipi, Melinda Lowell, and Mary Green. (Mildred Simms Foster.)

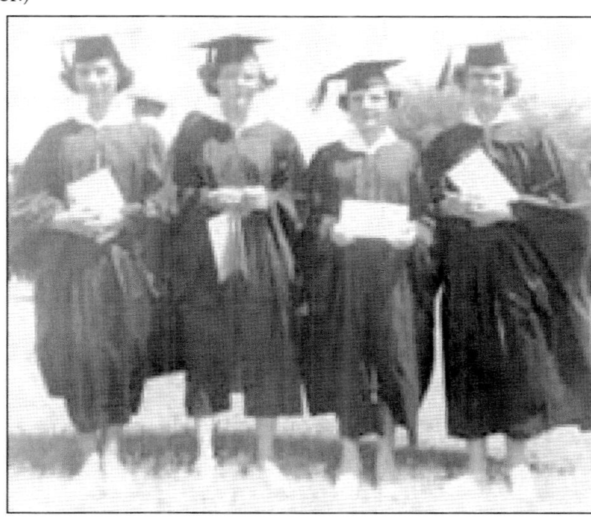

Graduation Day. Here, four young unidentified ladies pose for a 1958 graduation photograph. (Donald Bertagnolli.)

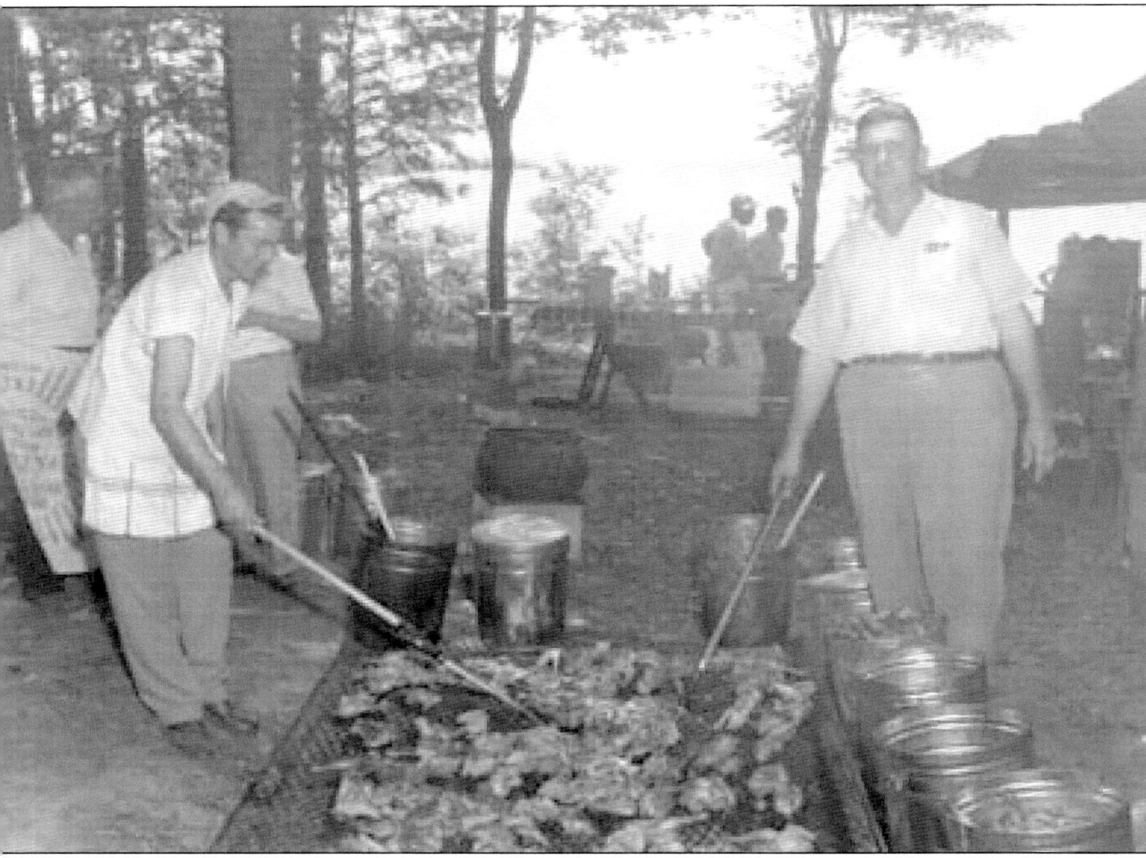

Cooking for a Cause. May Day not only included pageants and programs; parent organizations worked diligently at booths to help raise funds for the school. Here, men of the community grill chicken over a charcoal fire, tempting passersby with the smell. (OMCMD.)

Seven

To the North
Spanish Fort

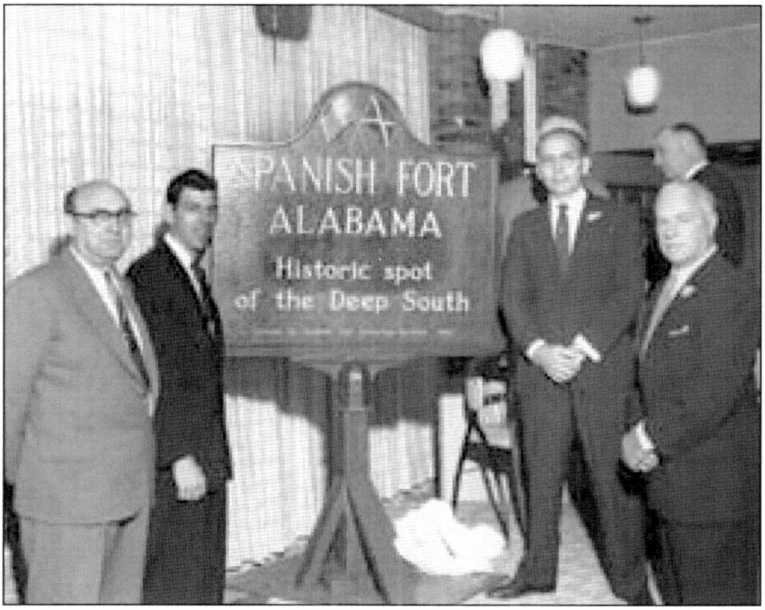

Historic Spot of the Deep South. The sign welcoming road traffic coming "Up the Hill" at Spanish Fort was placed by the Spanish Fort Historical Society under the leadership of the Fuller Brothers, who were instrumental in the development of the community. Here, George Fuller Jr. (far left) unveils the sign at the Spanish Fort Restaurant. (Charles "Chuck" Philipp.)

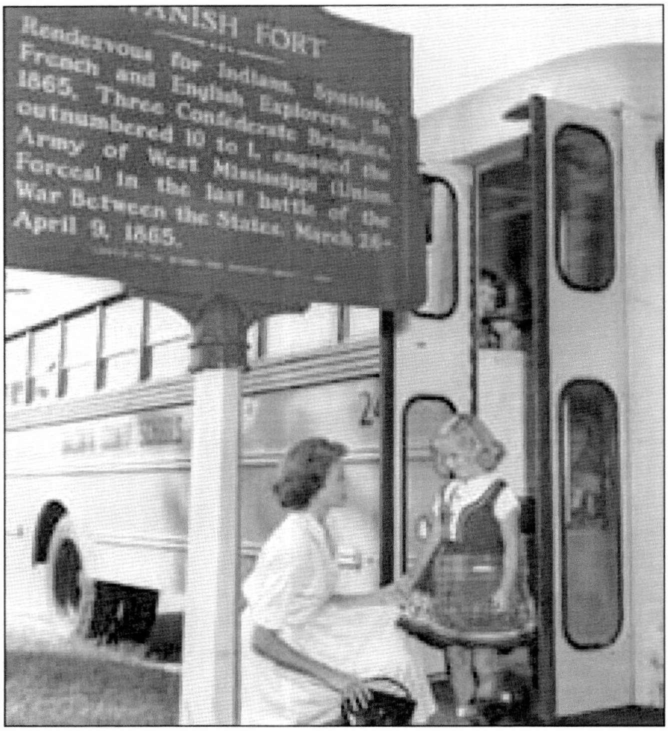

LIVING ON A HISTORIC SITE. Historic markers were placed throughout the developments to commemorate the value of the site as a battleground. In 1865, three Confederate brigades were under siege by Union troops until the fort fell and the battle moved north to Blakeley. This 1960 photograph shows a mother putting her child on a bus to the newly opened Spanish Fort School. (Charles "Chuck" Philipp.)

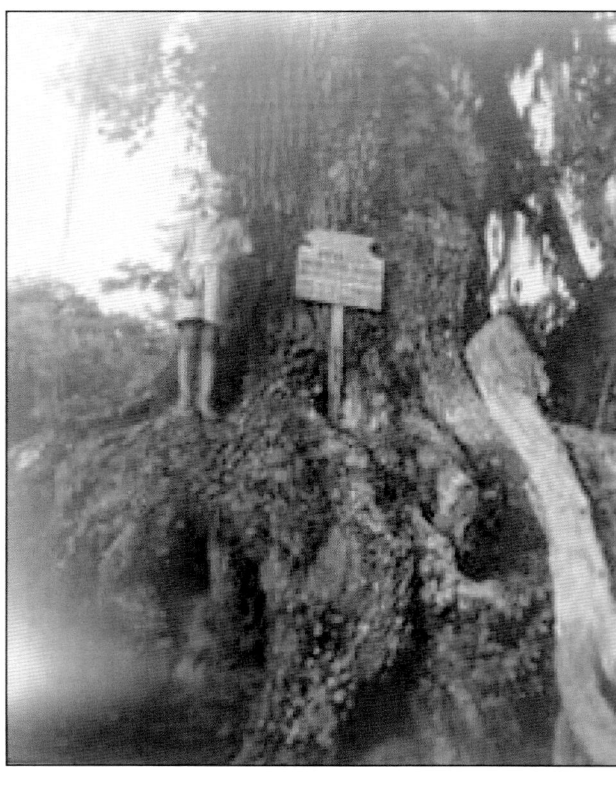

HISTORIC BLAKELEY. Five miles north of the community of Spanish Fort was Blakeley, the once-populous seat of Baldwin County. The vibrant city on the banks of the Tensaw succumbed to the ravages of yellow fever and flooding and was abandoned. Blakeley was the site of the last battle of the Civil War, during which time it remained the county seat. Marshall Carney is pictured here with an early sign at the Jury Oak, where Judge George Toulmin held court while the courthouse was under construction. (OMCMD, Carney Collection.)

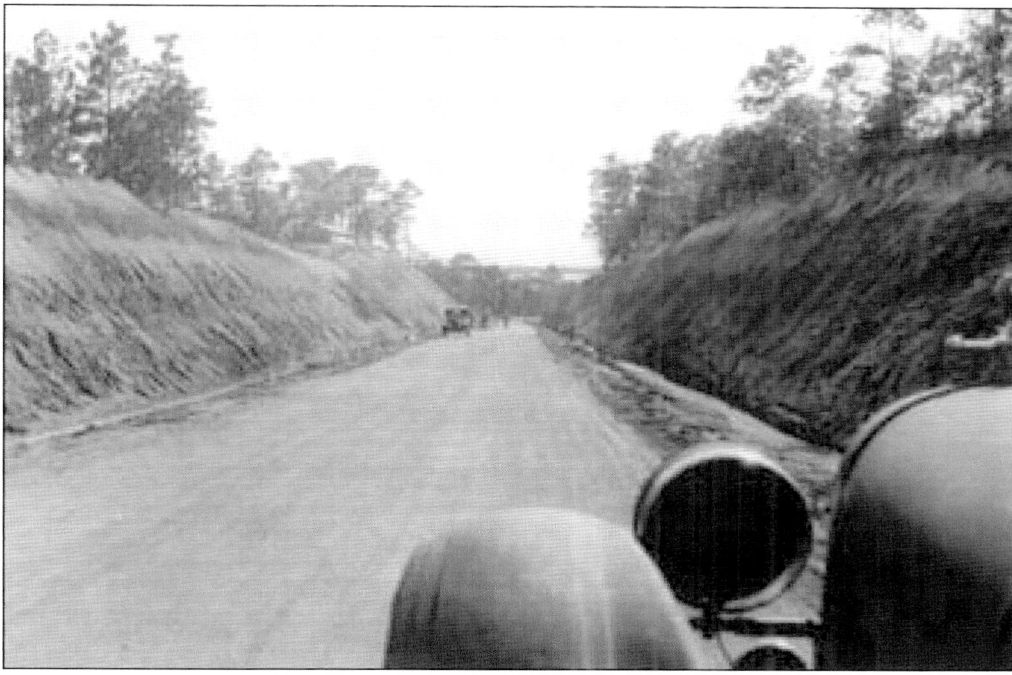

BUILDING A CAUSEWAY TO MOBILE. The 1920s saw an invasion of a different kind as Baldwin County was connected to Mobile via a causeway. Fill dirt joined islands in the delta area and bridges were constructed over the five rivers that flow into the bay. As roads were cut, there were always treasure hunters on hand to claim relics from the Revolutionary and Civil War battles held in the area. (Doy Leale McCall Rare Book and Manuscript Library, University of South Alabama.)

CAUSEWAY TO MOBILE. The road across Mobile Bay delta was completed in 1927, and the entire roadway was named Cochran Bridge. The Cochran Bridge at Magazine Point, Mobile, was the final phase of the connector to be completed. People were allowed to walk across the bridge on the opening day. In this 1930s image, a couple looks over the causeway from the bluff behind the Spanish Fort Tourist Court. (Doy Leale McCall Rare Book and Manuscript Library, University of South Alabama.)

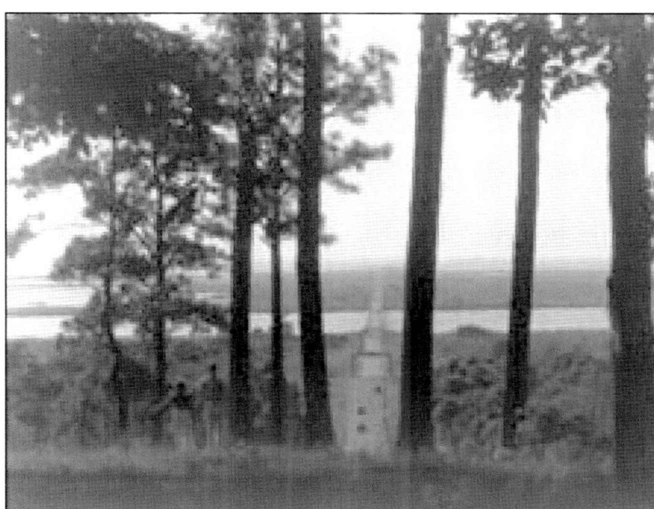

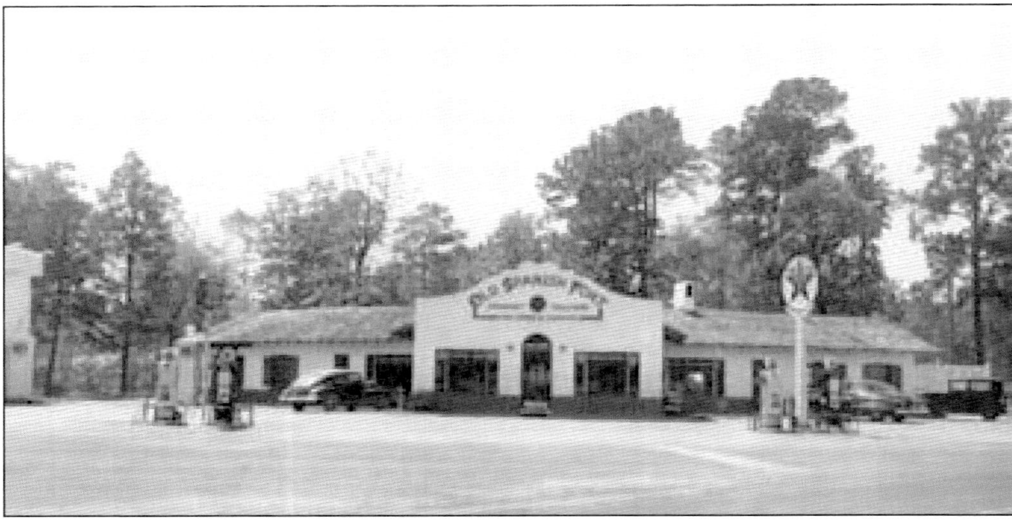

Old Spanish Fort Tourist Court. In the 1920s, George Fuller Sr. left his job as an assistant editor at the *Chicago Tribune* to develop a golf course at "Bridgehead," as Spanish Fort was known at the time. After the Depression-era decline of the venture, Fuller opened the Magnet Theater in Fairhope. As motor traffic increased, the Fullers once again established a business in Spanish Fort, this time in the form of a tourist court. (Charles "Chuck" Philipp.)

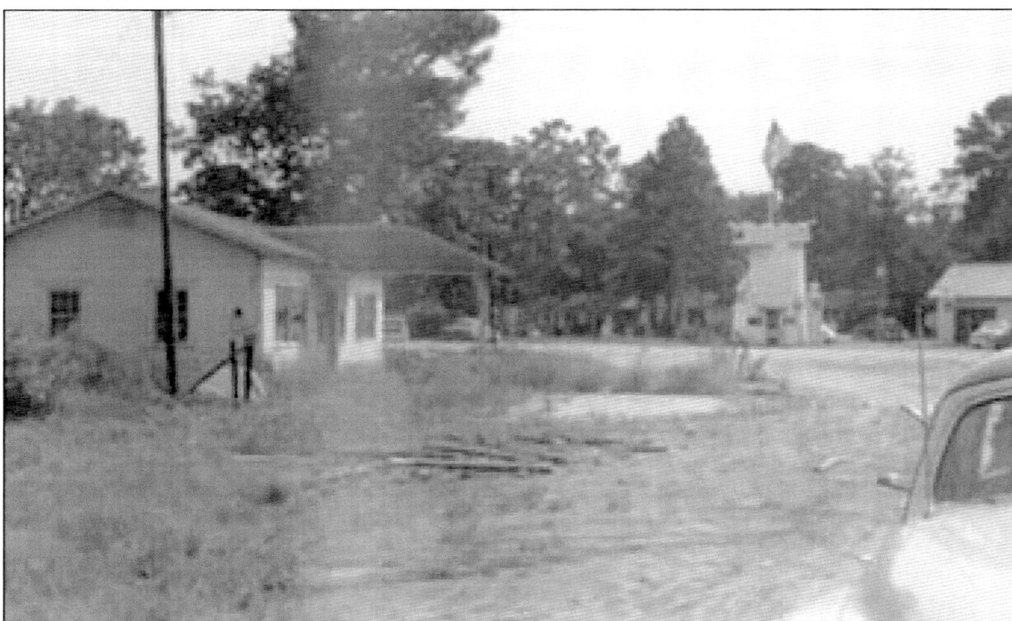

Cities Service Gas Station. One of the earliest grocery stores in Spanish Fort was the Cities Service gas and grocery market, which operated in the 1930s and 1940s. There was also a Gulf filling station and a fruit stand to entice travelers to stop at the historic spot. The Spanish Fort Methodist Church met in this building before the sanctuary was constructed. (Charles "Chuck" Philipp.)

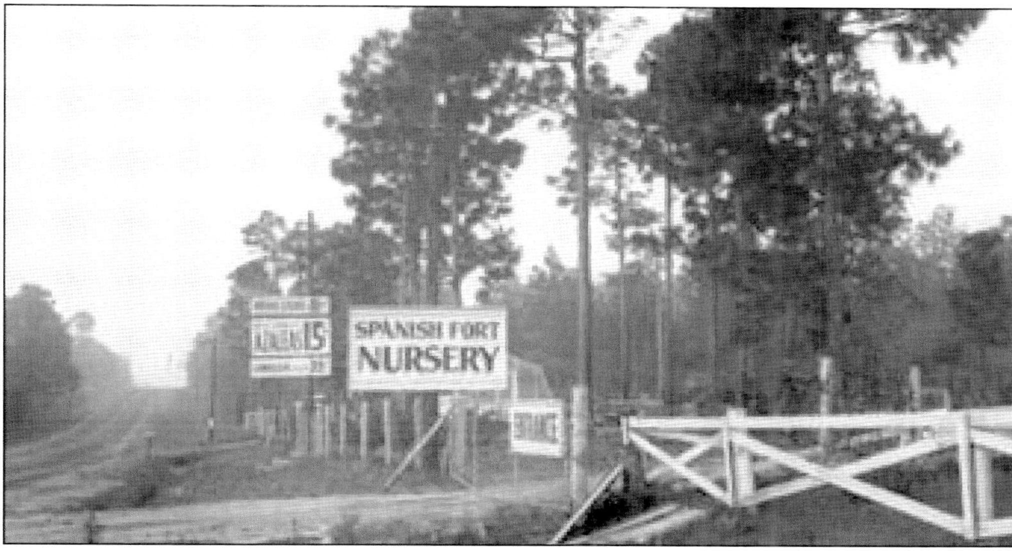

Landscaping for New Homes. The Spanish Fort Nursery, owned and operated by Johnny Moreland, was located at the entrance to Patrician Drive at the first housing development created by George and David Fuller in Spanish Fort. The nursery was successful during the 1950s as many people moved into new homes in the suburban community. (Charles "Chuck" Philipp.)

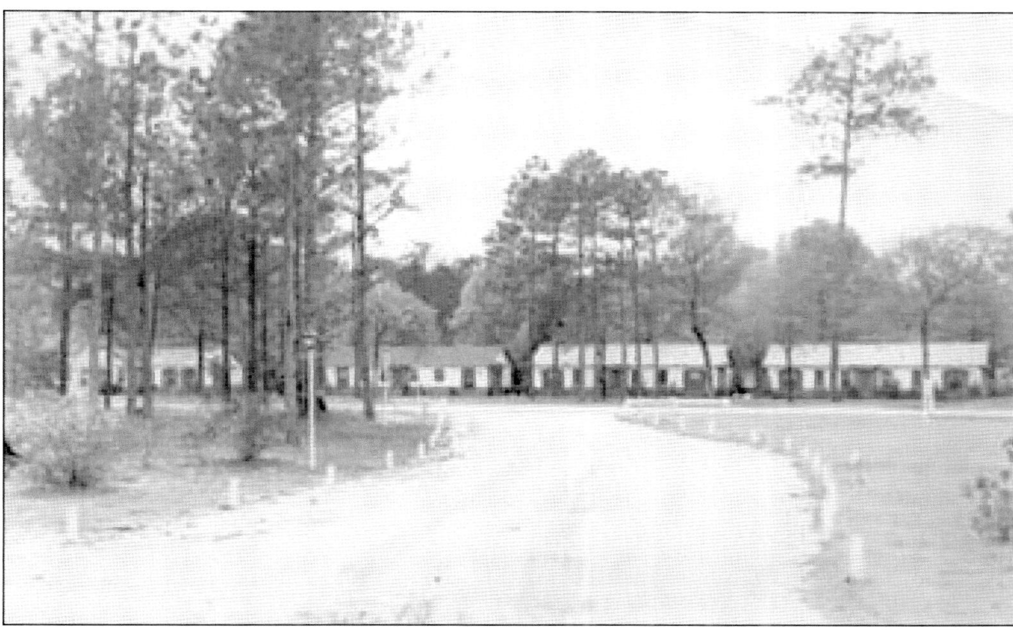

Motor Court. The cabins on the east side of the main highway, a part of the Spanish Fort Tourist Court, were replaced with a two-story motor court named Spanish Ranch Motel. The business was run by David Fuller and stayed busy until a bypass connected the causeway to Highway 90 south of Spanish Fort. (Charles "Chuck" Philipp.)

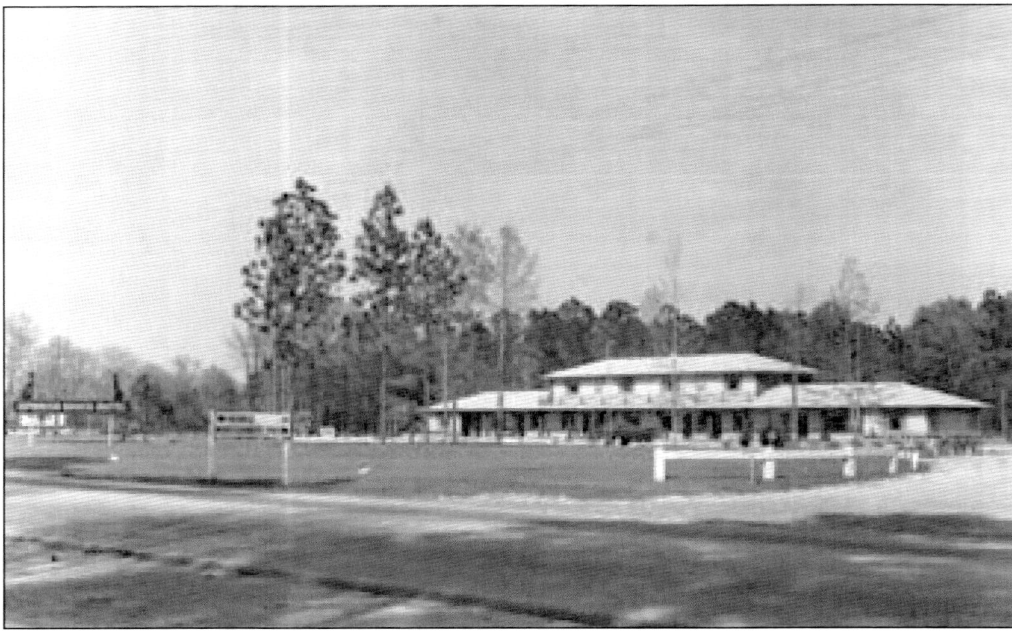

Spanish Ranch Motel. The Spanish Fort Motel operated until the late 1970s, when it was replaced by a new shopping center to meet the needs of the rapidly growing community. Locals mourned the loss of the neon sign, which showed a cannon firing a cannonball across the top of the sign. (Charles "Chuck" Philipp.)

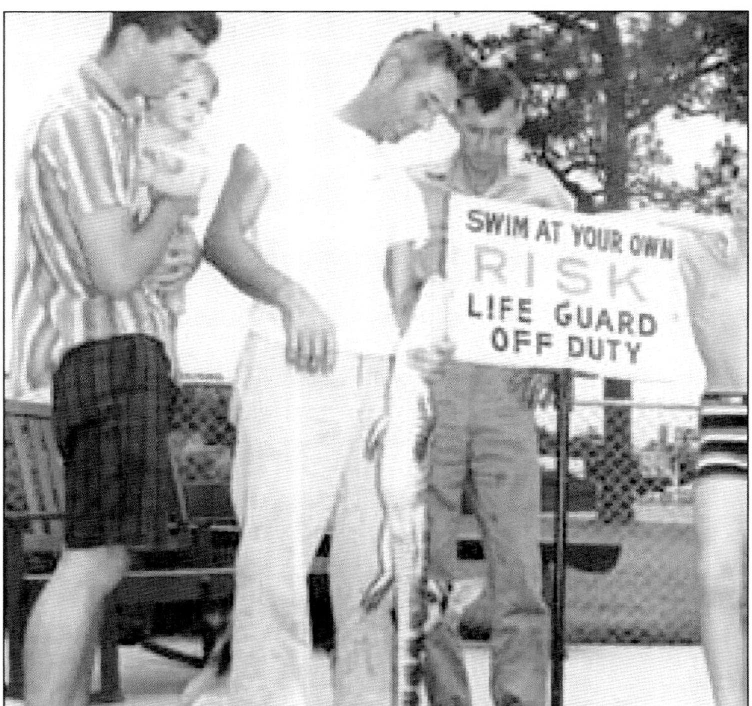

Swimming, Anyone? The Motor Court swimming pool became the gathering place for locals who bought summer memberships. Around 1977, the pool was filled in to make way for the new shopping center. Here, pool-goers crowd around a baby alligator that came for an overnight swim and surprised early swimmers. (Charles "Chuck" Philipp.)

Water Tower Sign. Behind the shopping center was the famous water tower, which was visible all the way across Mobile Bay. The neon "Spanish Fort" sign was designed by George Fuller Jr., who intended to dispel the idea that Spanish Fort was too far removed to be convenient for workers in Mobile and at the shipyards. Pictured for a 1920 news story are Martin Jones and Lois Creel in front of the water tower. (Charles "Chuck" Philipp.)

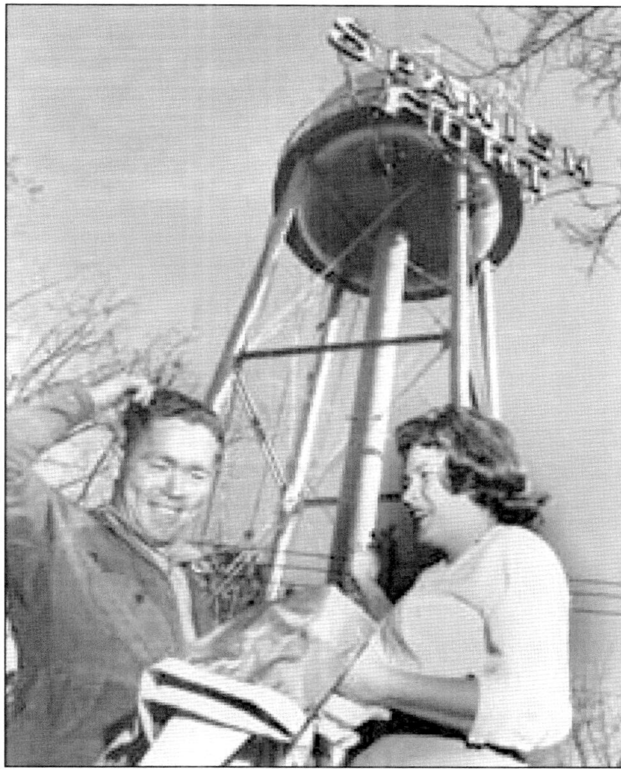

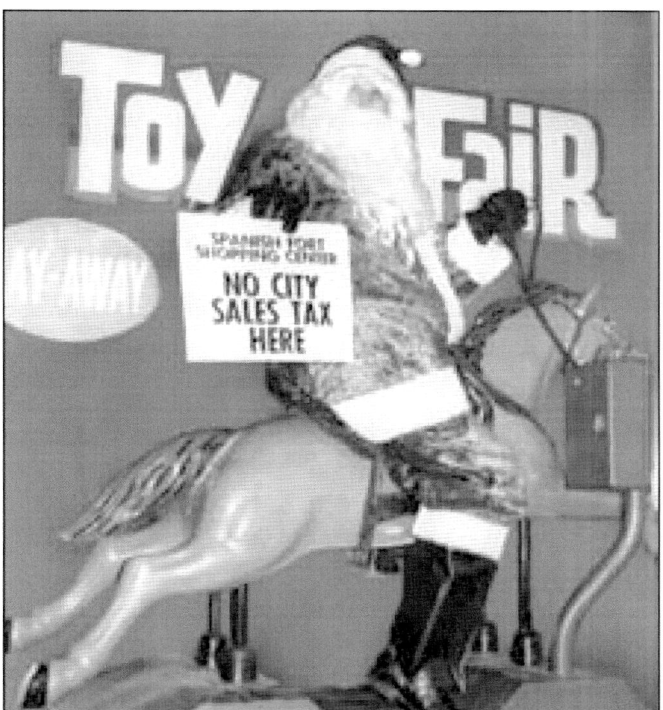

Shopping across the Bay. Santa Claus (marketing genius George Fuller Jr.) promotes a new shopping center in front of Toy Fair at the TG&Y Store. Every child in the community rode this arcade-style horse at one time or another. Fuller became Santa Claus every year at the shopping center, listening to the requests of little ones for at least two generations. (Charles "Chuck" Philipp.)

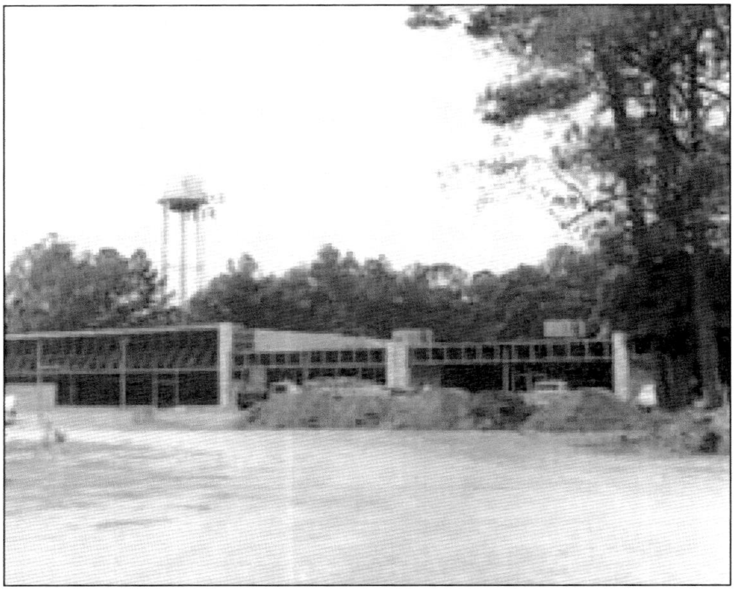

SHOPPING CENTER CONSTRUCTION. The Spanish Fort Tourist Court was demolished around 1961 to make way for the new shopping center. Most of the cabins were bulldozed, but a few were set on fire to provide practice for the volunteer fire department. Construction of the shopping center started in 1962. (Charles "Chuck" Philipp.)

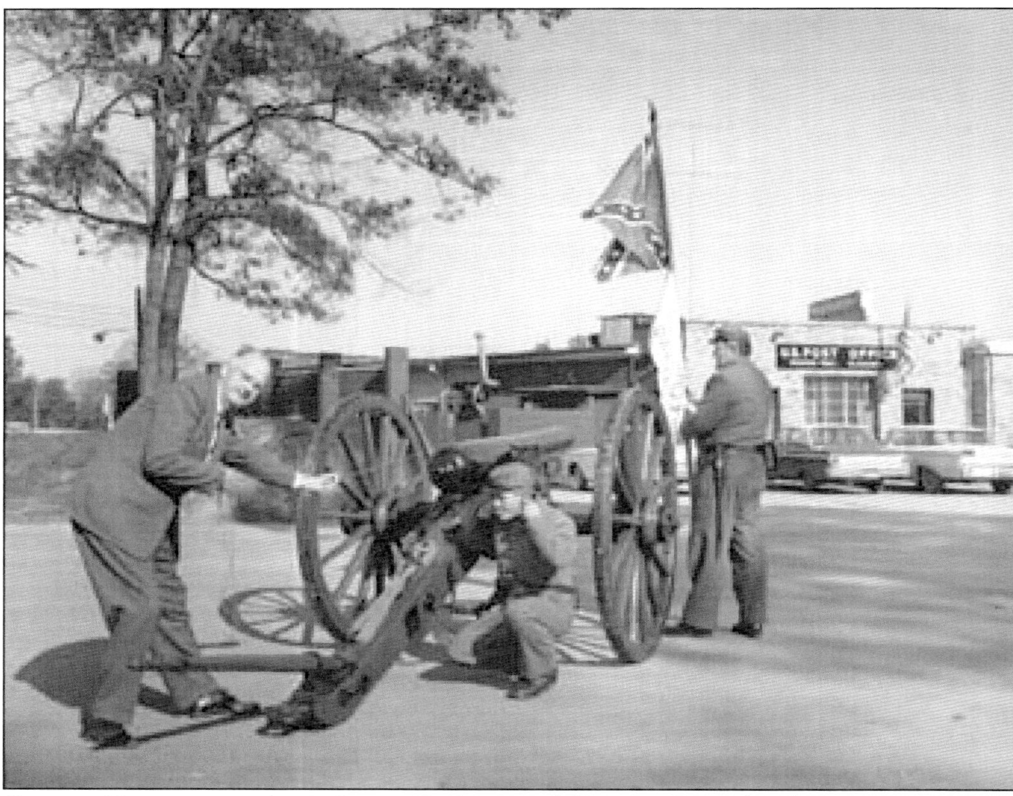

CANNON CELEBRATION. As a tribute to the history of the Spanish Fort battle site, postmaster Bud Hanson headed the artillery team firing the cannon for the 1961 opening of the new post office. The Spanish Fort post office—one of the first offices to open in the new shopping center—has moved four times, all within the same business complex. (Charles "Chuck" Philipp.)

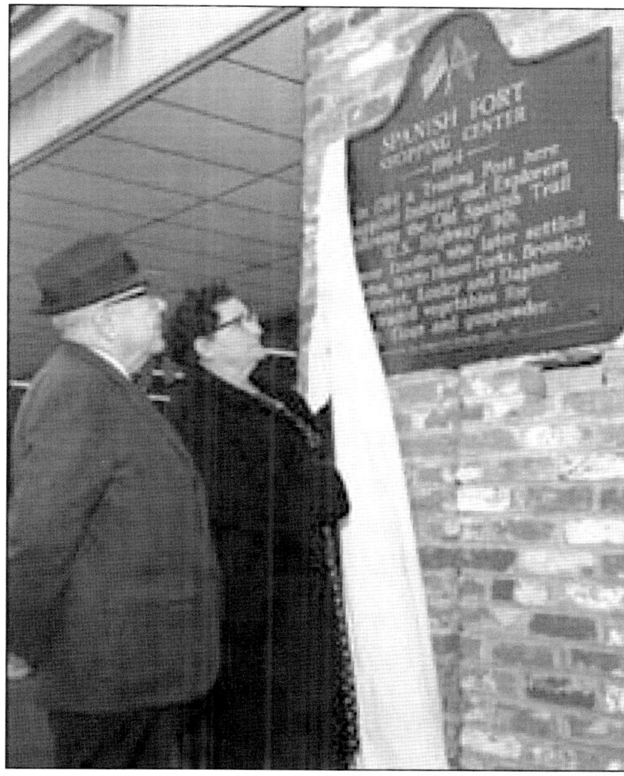

Unveiling the Marker. Murkey Bankster, granddaughter of early Stapleton homesteader Sam Rhodes, assists George Fuller in unveiling the marker at the Spanish Fort Shopping Center, which reads: "In 1764 a Trading Post here supplied Indians and Explorers following the Old Spanish Trail (US Highway 90). Pioneer families who later settled Stapleton, White House Forks, Bromley, Belforest, Loxley and Daphne traded vegetables for salt, flour and gunpowder." (Charles "Chuck" Philipp.)

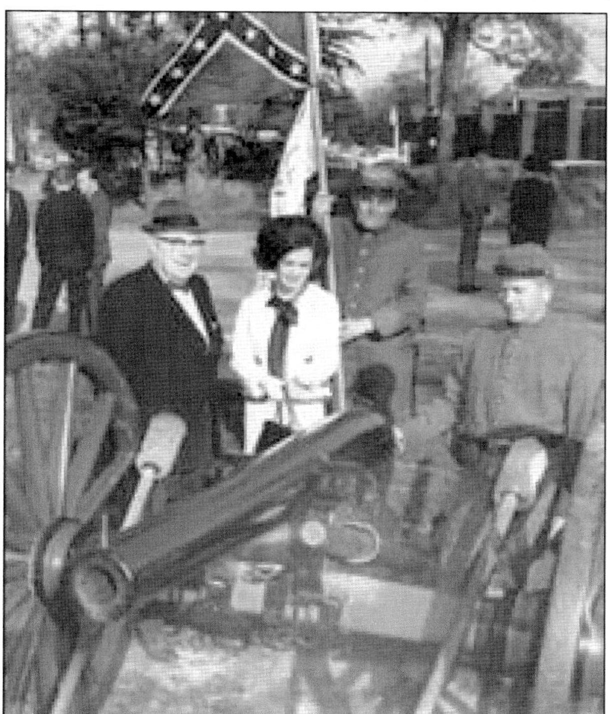

Grand Opening. The Spanish Fort Shopping Center was officially opened with the firing of the cannon by Mrs. Tommy Werneth, who is pictured with George Fuller Jr. (left) and unidentified Civil War reenactors. Many of the homesites in the area were once occupied by Confederate units and saw fighting for many days during the 1864 Battle of Spanish Fort. (Charles "Chuck" Philipp.)

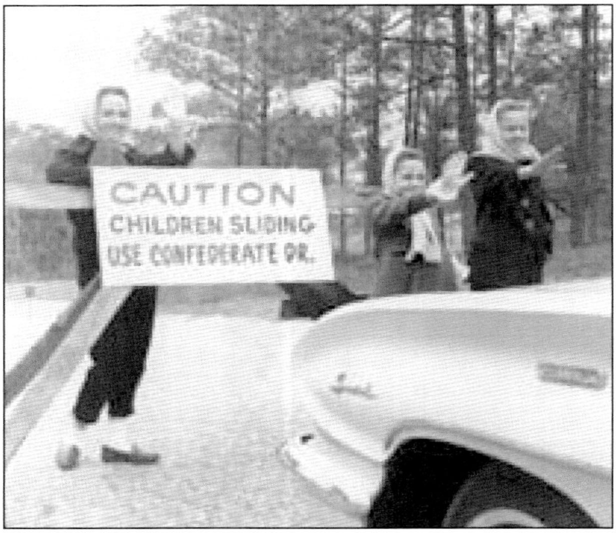

SPANISH FORT ESTATES. The first subdivision of Spanish Fort Estates overlooked the bay near the original Spanish Fort Tourist Court. A new phase was developed on the north side of the intersection, where the hilly terrain and earthen breastworks made for many steep roads. The main road in Spanish Fort Estates, Spanish Main, was soon dubbed "Butt Buster Hill" by the youngsters in the neighborhood, pictured here after a snowfall in 1965. (Charles "Chuck" Philipp.)

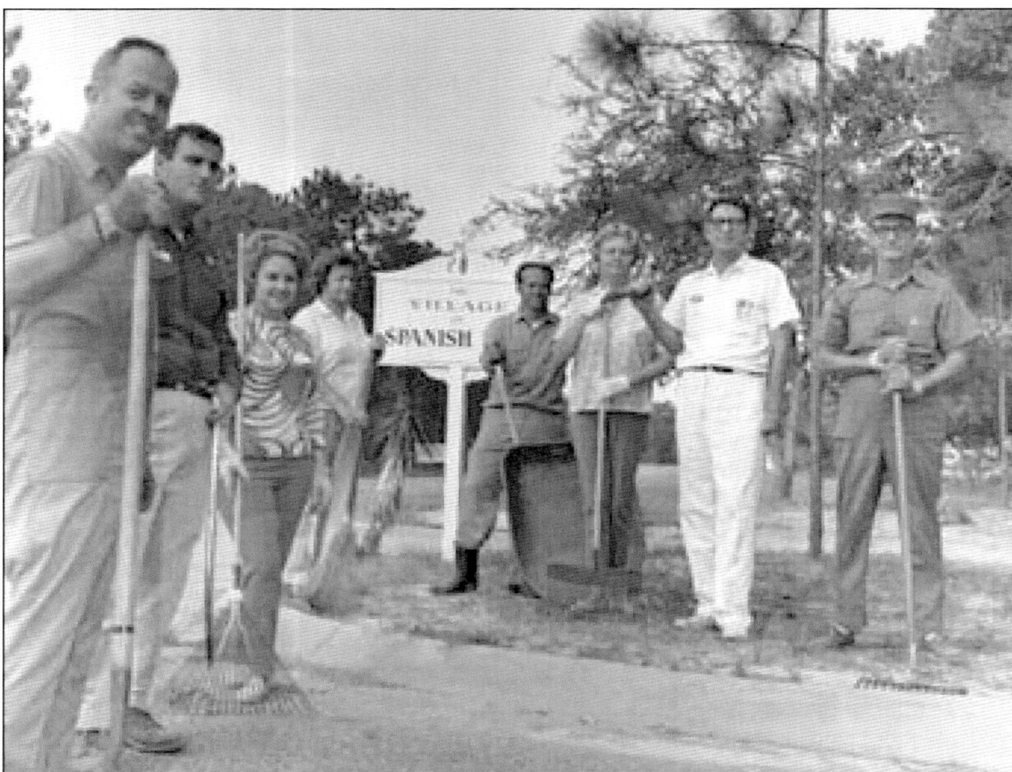

THE VILLAGE HOUSING DEVELOPMENT. Members of the Garden Club, an early version of a homeowners' association, work with their husbands to enhance the entrance to The Village, another housing development in Spanish Fort. Other subdivisions included Wilson Heights, Lee Circle, and the Buzbee Fishing Camp Road neighborhoods. Pictured from left to right are James Cameron, Barry Scheib, Judy Reid, Myrtis Taylor, James Ardis, Willie Thomas, Joe Thomas, and Jay Rawls. (Charles "Chuck" Philipp.)

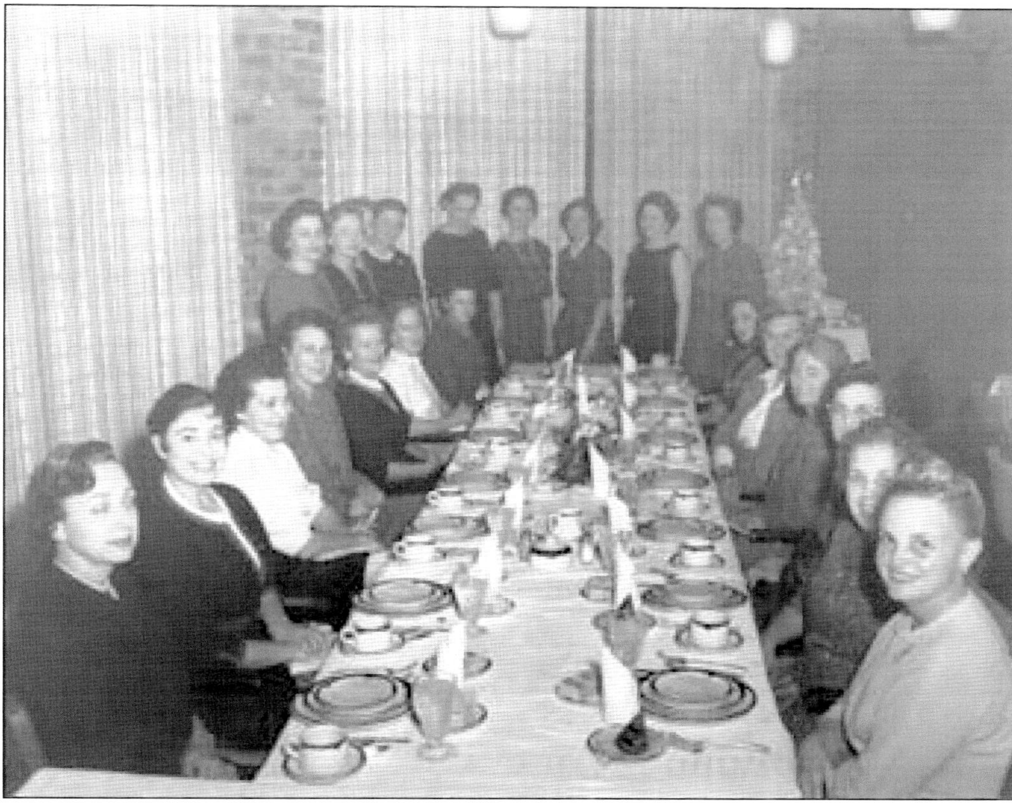

Garden Club Luncheon. The Spanish Fort Garden Club was established in 1956. A Christmas luncheon was held each year at the Spanish Fort Restaurant, an establishment that opened in the 1930s. The garden club has been active for more than 50 years. (Charles "Chuck" Philipp.)

Spanish Fort Restaurant. Until the 1980s, the Spanish Fort Restaurant was a gathering place for both locals and tourists. Even when a bypass routed causeway traffic around the intersection, the restaurant stayed busy. The round building was constructed around the reception office for the old tourist court. In the back of the building was the Spanish Clipper barbershop, where men swapped stories. (Charles "Chuck" Philipp.)

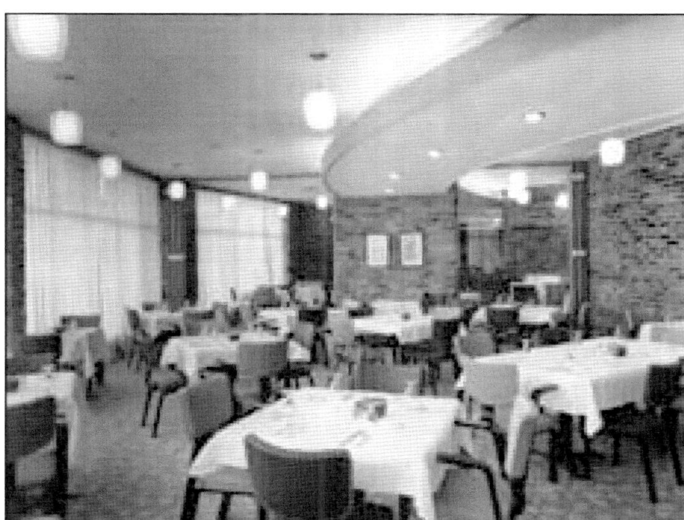

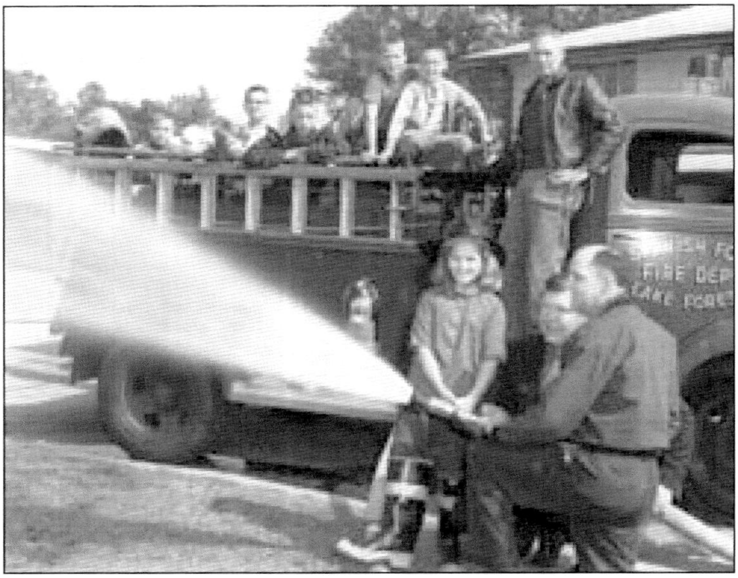

FIREMEN ANSWER THE CALL. From the earliest years of the community, a volunteer fire department has served Spanish Fort and Lake Forest residents. Here, schoolchildren learn about fire safety and the operation of the fire equipment. Note that the fire department served Lake Forest, south of Spanish Fort, as well. (Charles "Chuck" Philipp.)

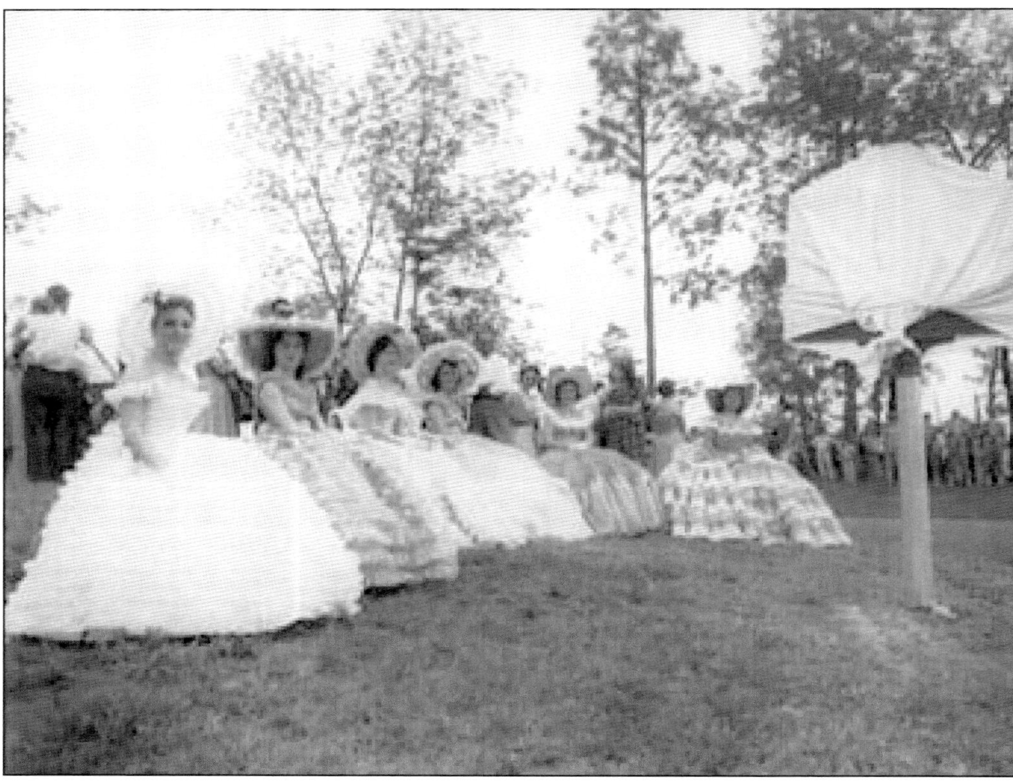

AZALEA TRAIL MAIDS. The Historical Society of Spanish Fort was diligent in erecting markers throughout the battlefield area to designate the sites of events of the Battle of Spanish Fort in 1864. Fuller Brothers Real Estate preserved the original Fort McDermott. Here, the Azalea Trial Maids from Mobile grace a marker dedication ceremony in 1957 at the entrance to the Spanish Fort Estates subdivision. (Charles "Chuck" Philipp.)

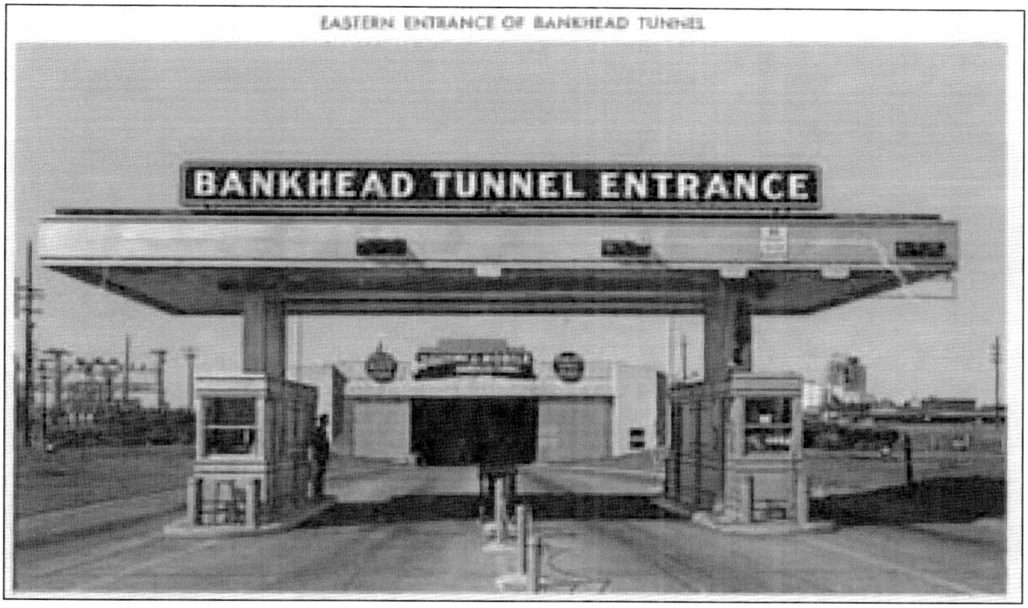

Bankhead Tunnel. In 1940, the tunnel under the Mobile River was completed, making the crossing of the causeway a much shorter journey. A toll of 25¢ could be paid at the tollbooths at the east entrance to the tunnel. With easier access to Mobile, growth was a given in Spanish Fort. This postcard photograph shows the tollbooths, which closed in 1974 when the toll fee was removed. (Harriet Outlaw.)

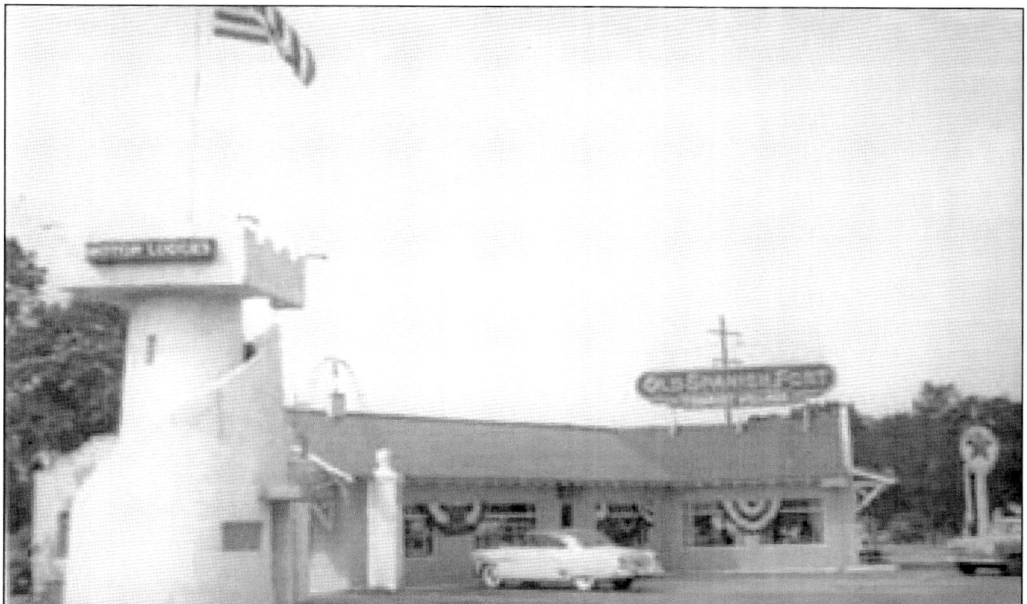

Spanish Fort Motor Lodge Updated. Until 1960, road trippers "stayed and ate on a battlefield," as touted in billboards across the south. The original tourist court was updated and served as a rest stop for many travelers. The cement tower was a landmark for many people who used the causeway across the Mobile Bay delta. (Dick Scott, Carney Collection.)

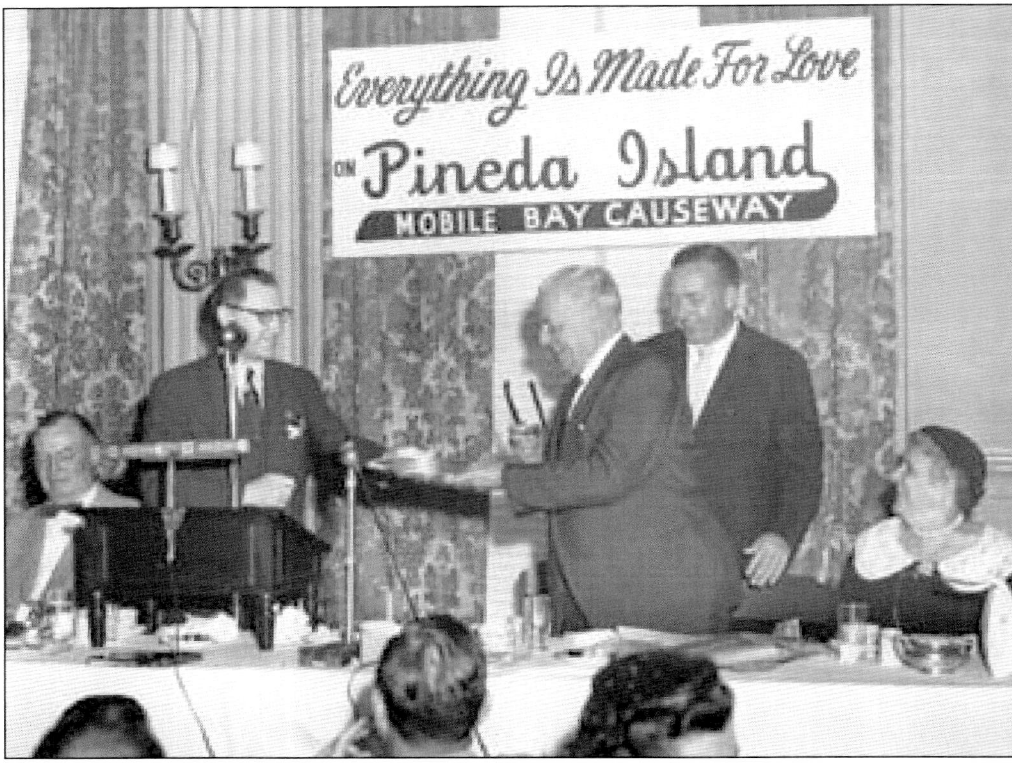

PINEDA ISLAND. The causeway affords beautiful views of Mobile Bay and the delta area. A venture to develop a high-end resort at the east end of the causeway, on Pineda Island, was begun by two corporations. The Olympic-size swimming and diving pool, a few homes and clubhouses were built, but the development never reached the success envisioned by the developers. (Charles "Chuck" Philipp.)

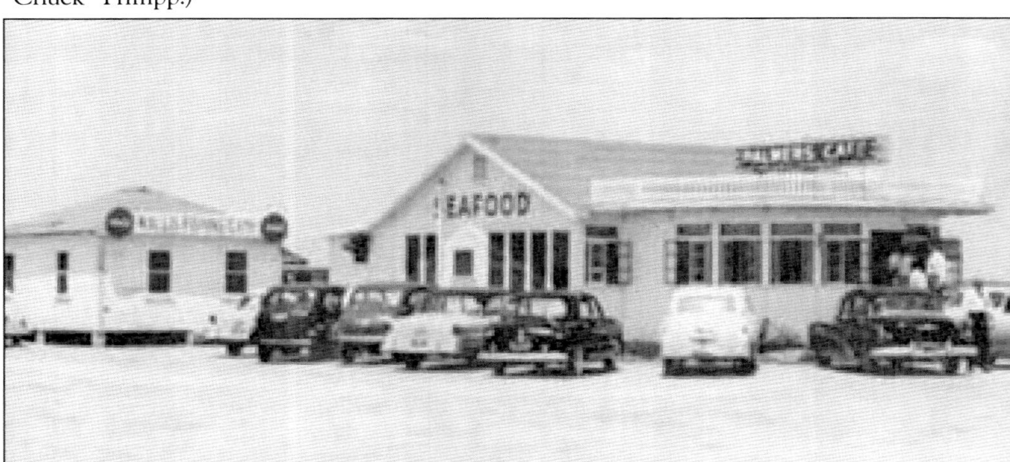

MOBILE BAY CAUSEWAY. Businesses along the waterway included fish markets, boat launches, and restaurants. One of the most famous was Palmer's Café, opened by Nancy McBride in 1950, who also opened the fish camp behind the restaurant. Her earliest menu offered a seafood platter for $1.25. Hurricane Camille destroyed this building in 1969. (Louise Goddin.)

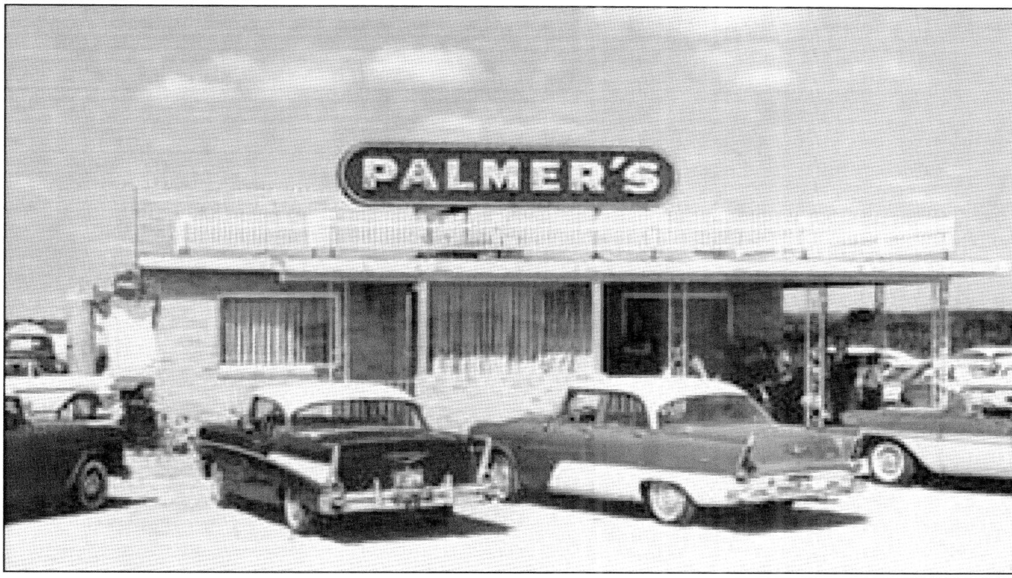

Palmer's Second Building. The owner of Palmer's rebuilt the restaurant after Hurricane Camille only to lose it to a fire in 1978. Hostess Louise Goddin, who began working there in 1953, remembers the faithful customers who came weekly to feast on the delicious T-bone steaks for $4.25 or a seafood platter for $1.95. (Louise Goddin.)

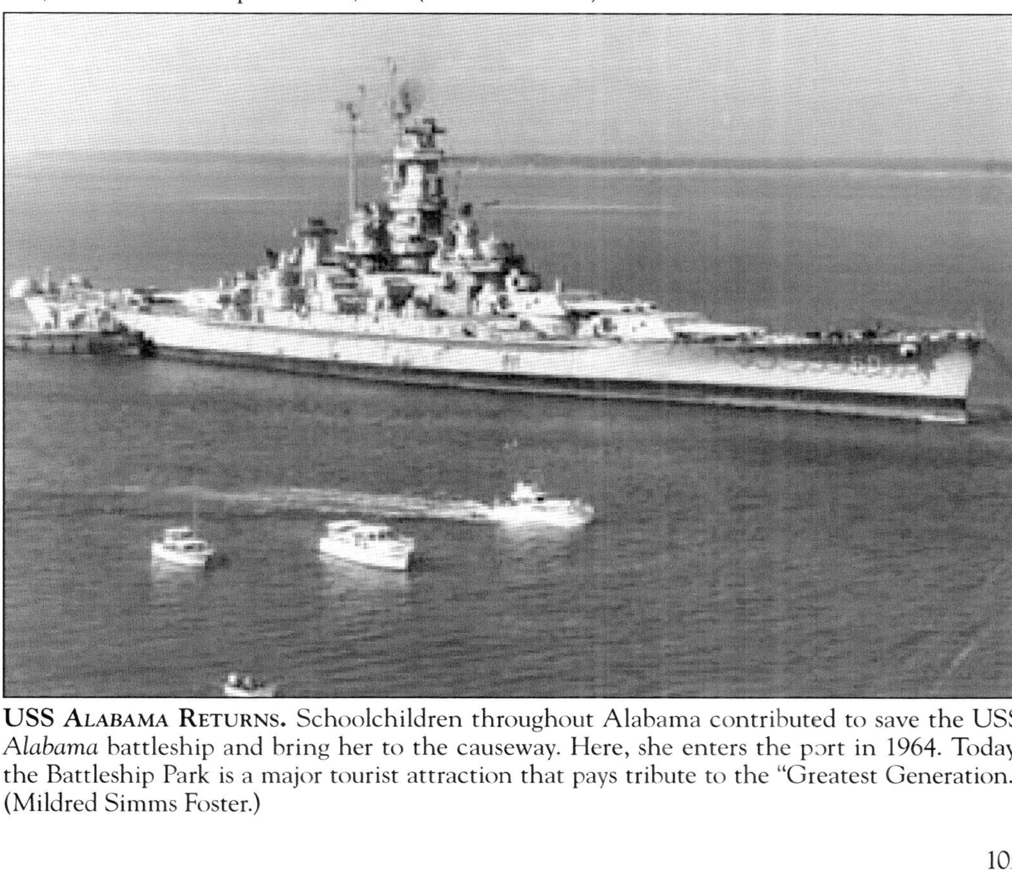

USS Alabama Returns. Schoolchildren throughout Alabama contributed to save the USS *Alabama* battleship and bring her to the causeway. Here, she enters the port in 1964. Today, the Battleship Park is a major tourist attraction that pays tribute to the "Greatest Generation." (Mildred Simms Foster.)

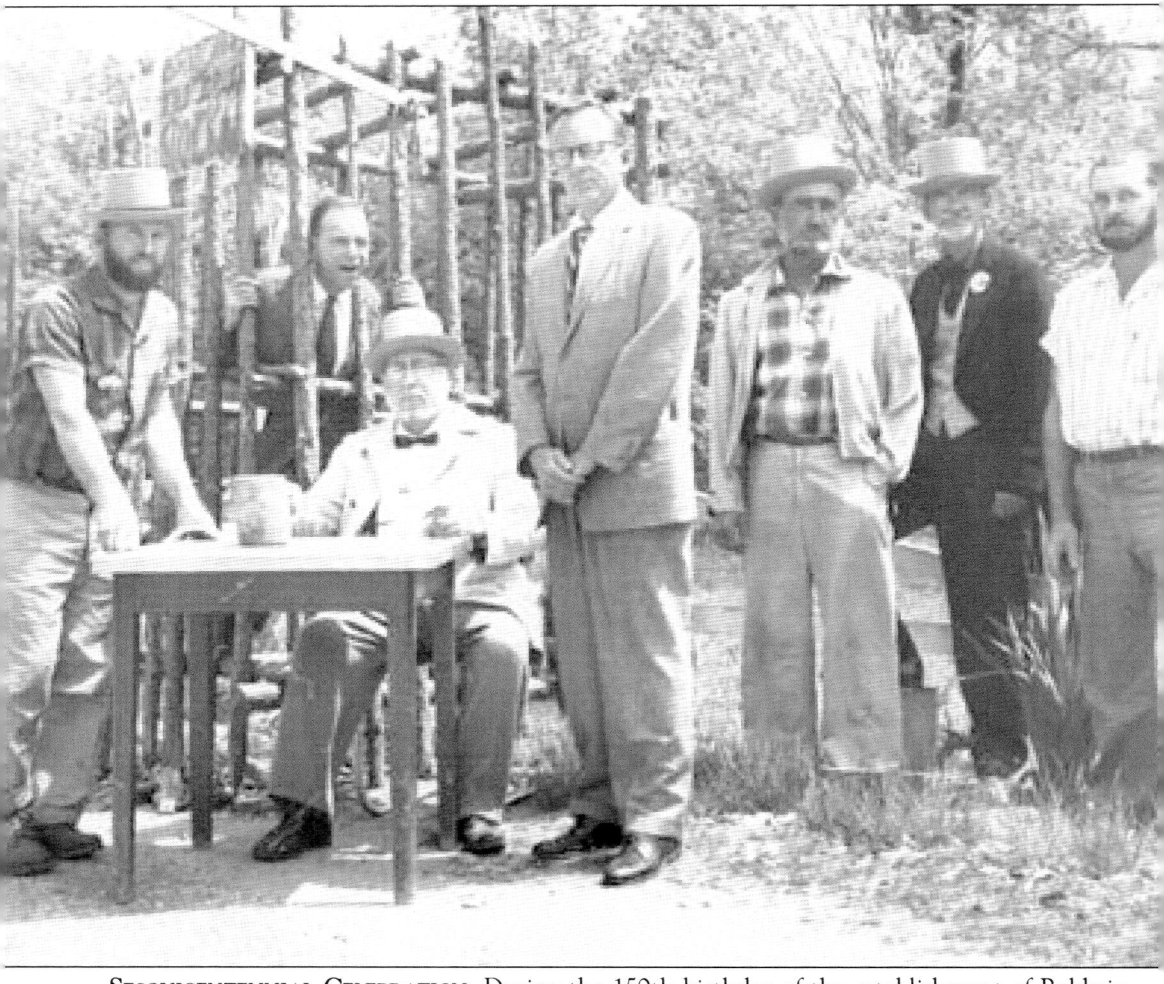

SESQUICENTENNIAL CELEBRATION. During the 150th birthday of the establishment of Baldwin County, men dressed up, with some sporting beards grown for the event. A community celebration held at the school featured a massive pageant performed by the students. Pictured here, from left to right, are Alex (Thumpsie) Trione, George Fuller (in the stockade), "Judge" Holly Rains, David Fuller, Angelo Trione, Felix Bigby, and Luther Wilkinson. Jailed men had to be bailed out by friends, whose contributions went to charity. This 1959 photograph appeared in the local newspaper, the *Spanish Fort Bulletin*, started by George Fuller Jr., who learned his communication skills in the European theater in World War II. He edited the paper until it was sold, then continued to write weekly columns. He was known for helping to build a sense of community and culture in Spanish Fort. (Charles "Chuck" Philipp.)

Eight

To the East
Belforest and Malbis

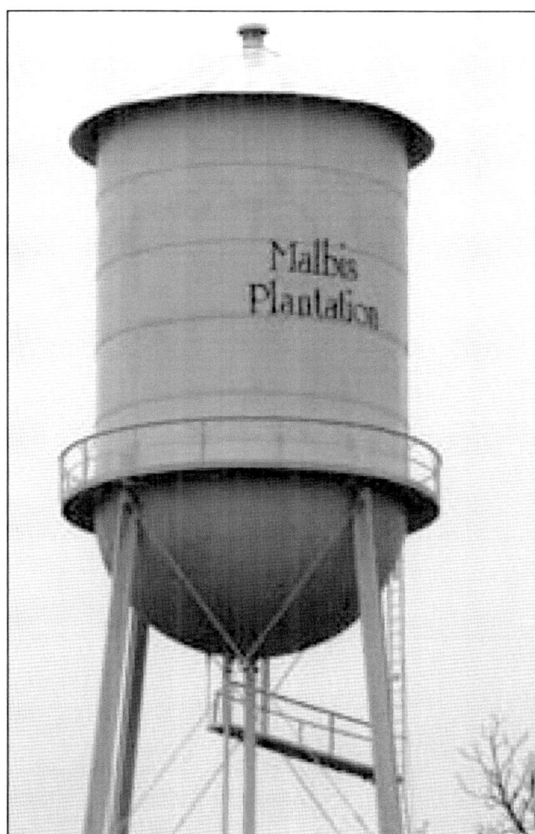

Historic Malbis. In 1906, Jason Malbis and William Papageorge invested in acreage just east of Daphne, creating a town that was eventually named Malbis. The historic water tank towered over the community, which was once a self-sufficient colony. (Photograph by Penny Taylor.)

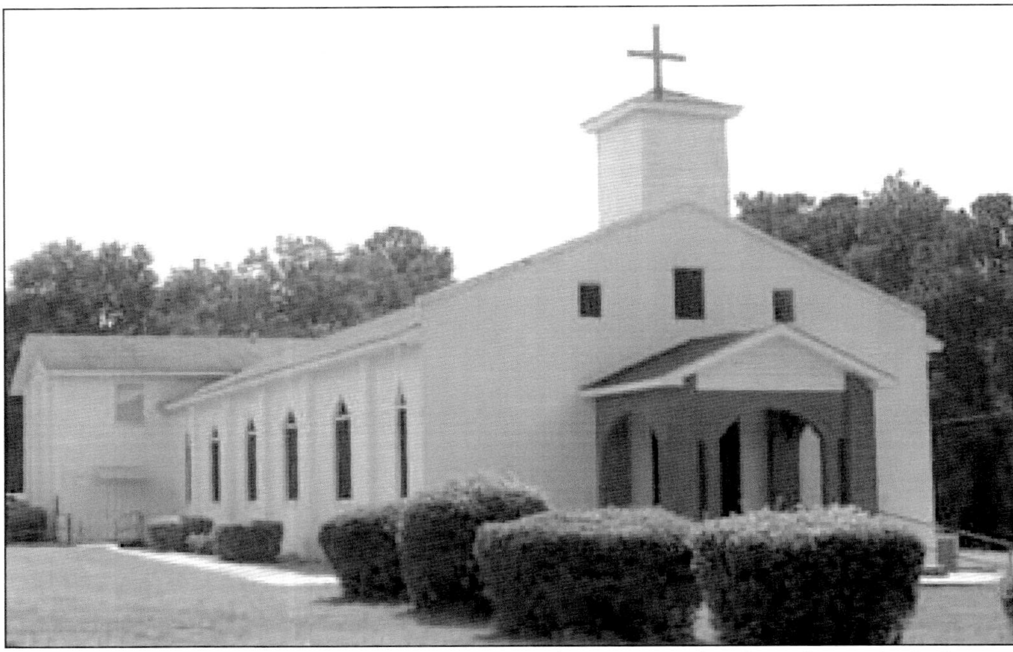

MOUNT AID MISSIONARY BAPTIST CHURCH. Near the scenic Turkey Branch stands the historic Mount Aid Missionary Baptist Church. Founded by the Reverend A.A. Williams in a little log cabin about two miles east of the present location, the church has consistently grown both in size and ministry. A larger church, purchased in 1923, was built on the current site. The present building was constructed in 1963, and major improvements were completed in 1977. (Photograph by Penny Taylor.)

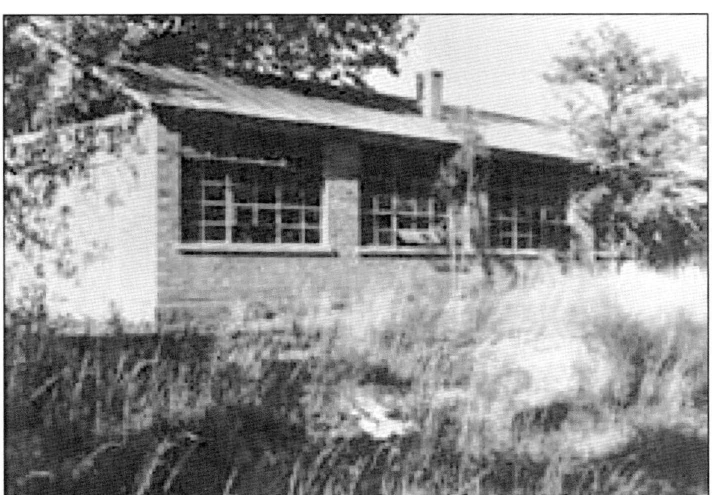

TURKEY BRANCH SCHOOL. The Turkey Branch School was one of the schools built in Baldwin County under the Julius Rosenwald program. The philanthropist set up a fund to provide schools for children of former slaves throughout the south. The school became part of the Mount Aid Missionary Baptist Church, where it was used as a fellowship hall and library. (Baldwin County Public Schools.)

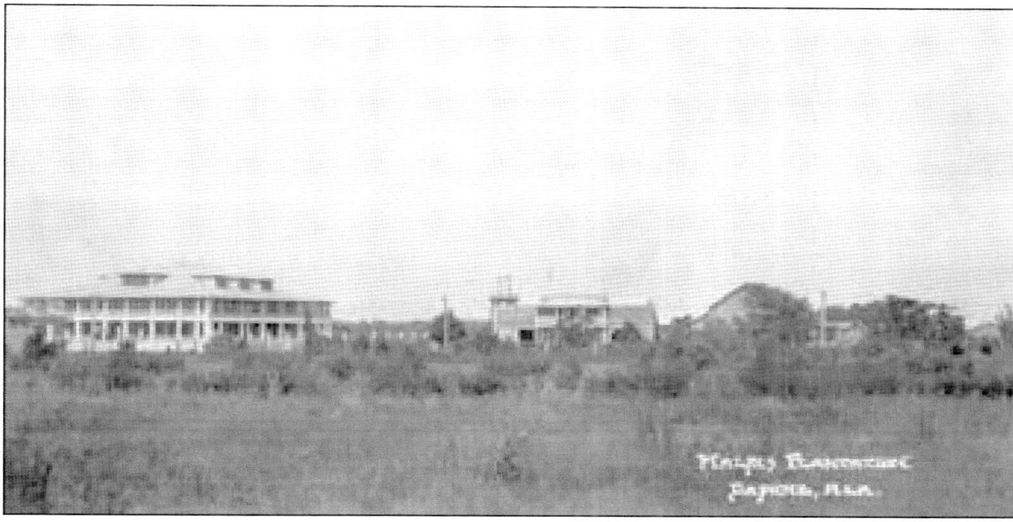

Malbis Plantation. This wide-angle view of the Malbis Plantation gives an indication of the extent of the operation. There were dormitories for workers, as well as residences for members of the religious order. Young men from Greece were offered work here and trained in skills enabling a successful life in America. (John Lewis, Willison Duck Collection.)

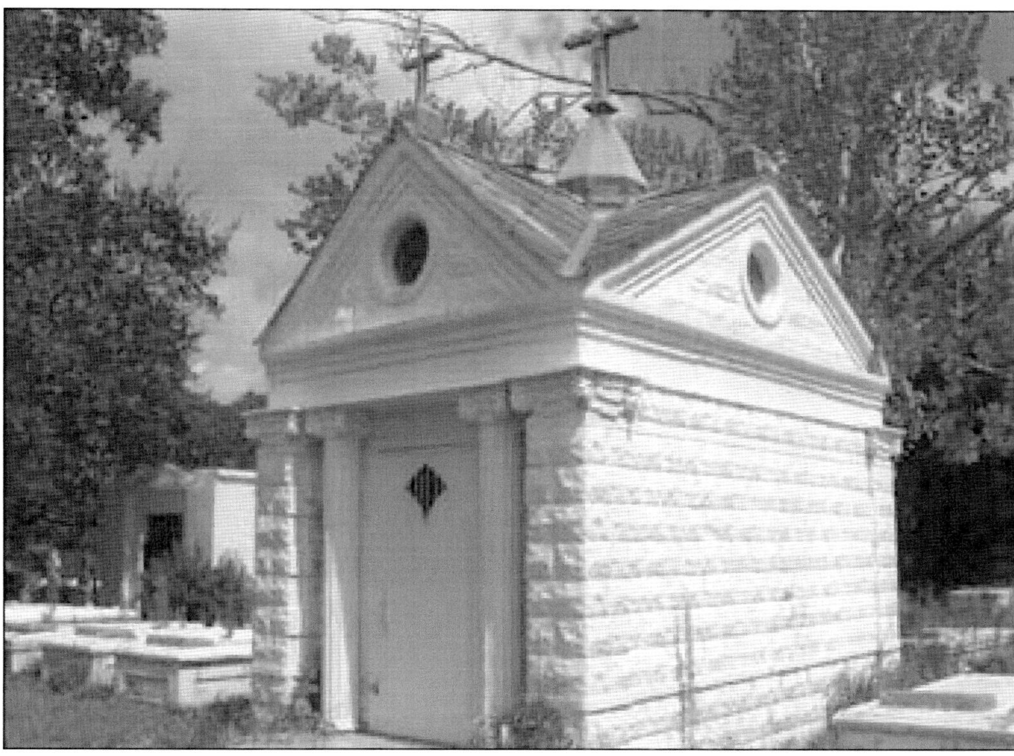

Greek Orthodox Cemetery. Following the customs of their heritage, members of the Greek community cherished the cemetery as a resting place for their loved ones. One of the oldest mausoleums was built in the early 20th century. This is the tomb of Fotene Chris Papageorge (1881–1918). (Photograph by Penny Taylor.)

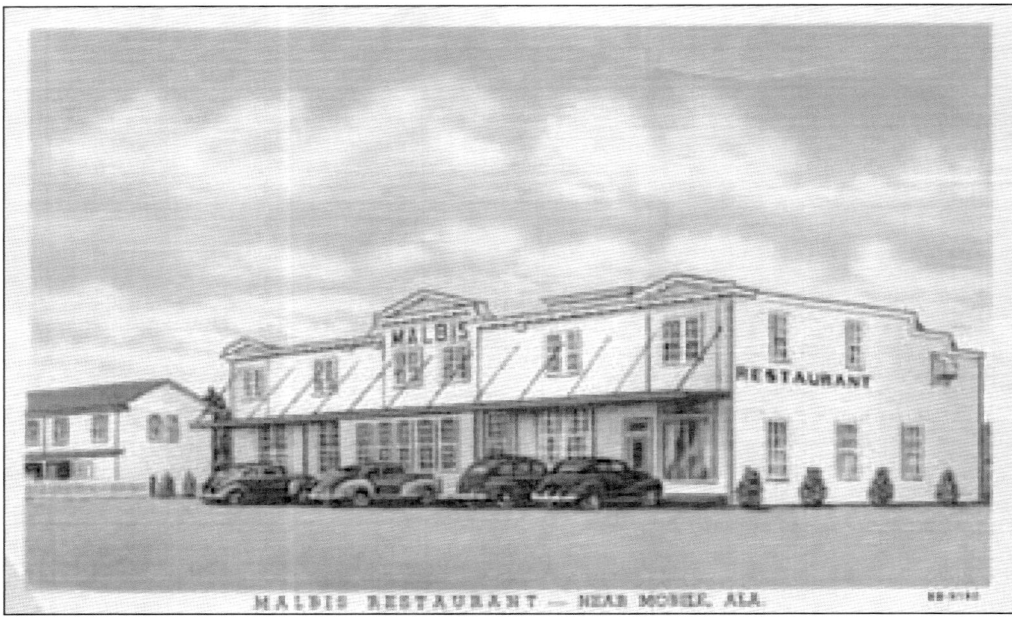

Malbis Motel and Restaurant. One of the Malbis family ventures was a hotel and restaurant on the Old Spanish Trail, aka Highway 90. The stopover for travelers burned down in 1947 and was rebuilt as a motel with a swimming pool shaped like the state of Alabama. The motel was demolished in the 1990s as the area developed into a major shopping and residential area. (Harriet Outlaw.)

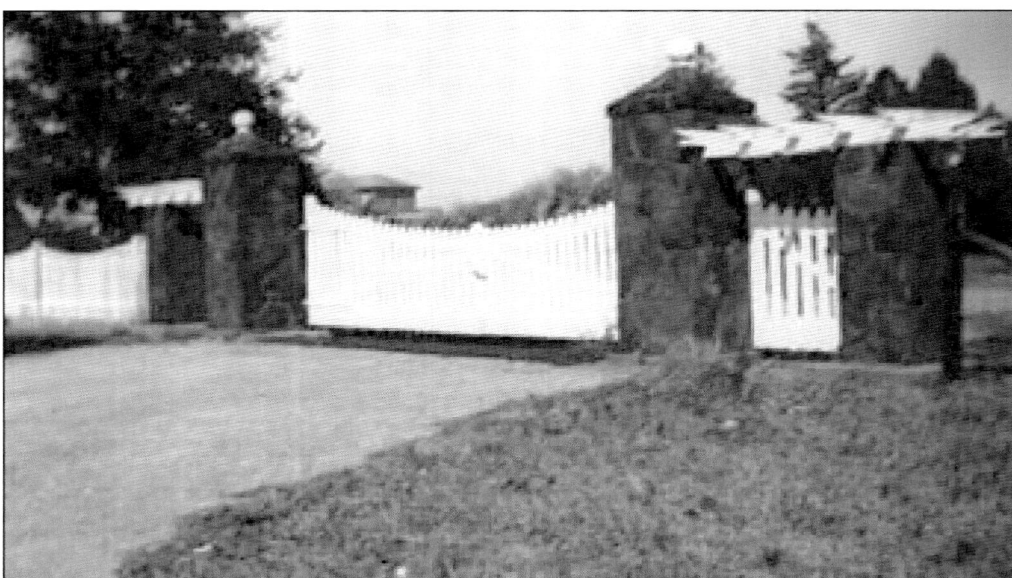

Malbis Enterprises. Malbis Plantation, Inc., included extensive farming and shipping operations, a cannery, a bank, a bakery, a dairy, and an icehouse. This is the entrance to the nursery business, on the north side of Highway 90, where greenhouses were set in beautifully manicured gardens. This photograph was featured in the 1950 publication *Gateways to History*, by Mary Carney. (Dick Scott, Carney Collection.)

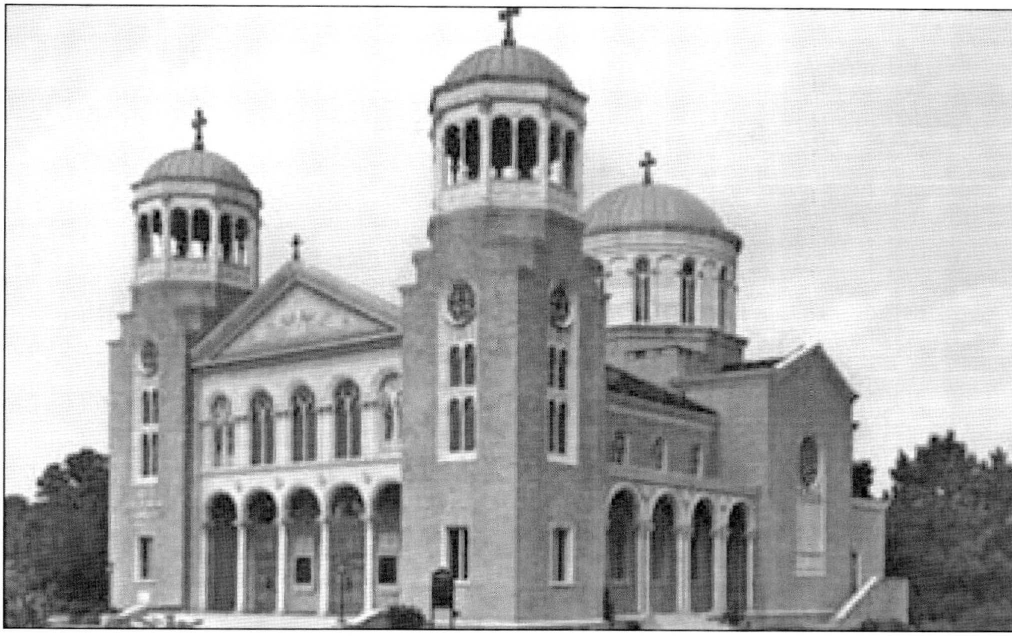

MALBIS MEMORIAL CHURCH. Town founder Jason Malbis was respected for his religious leadership. He had returned to Greece shortly before World War II, and died there in 1943. Before his death, he revealed his plan for a cathedral dreamed of by the colonists. Construction began almost 20 years later, with artisans brought from the old country. In 1965, the Greek Orthodox archbishop of North and South America dedicated the cathedral as a memorial to Jason Malbis. Its Byzantine architecture is a copy of a stately church in Athens, and marble was imported from the same quarries that provided stone for the Parthenon. Artists from Greece adorned the walls and domes with impressive icons and paintings. (Above, Harriet Outlaw; below, Elberta Heritage Museum.)

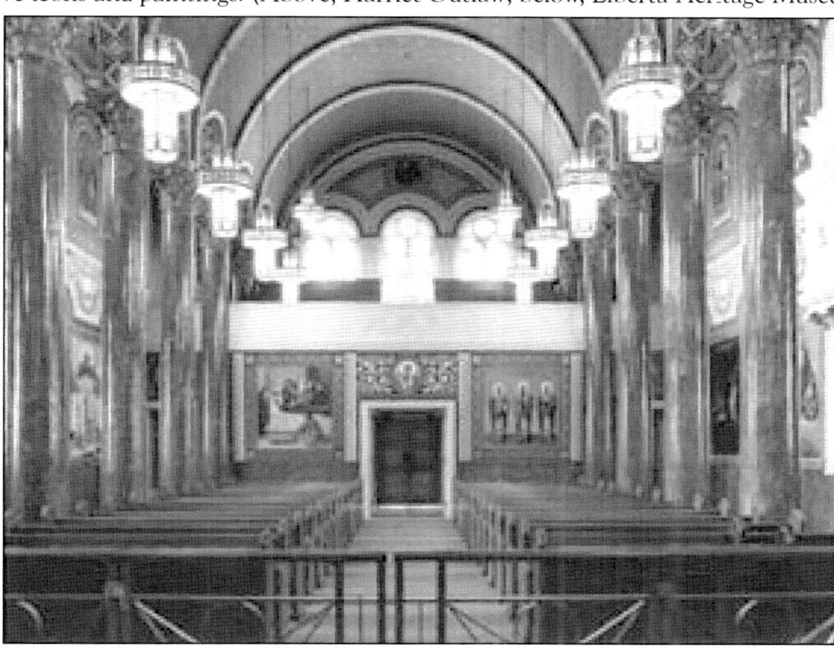

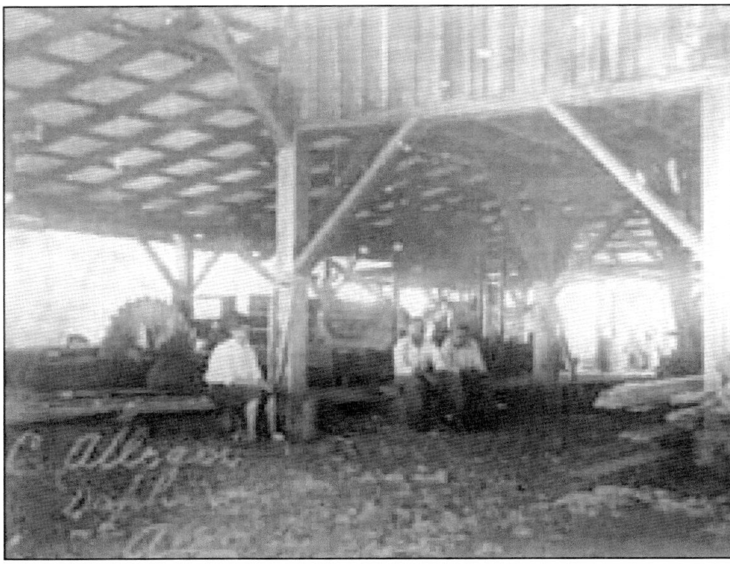

Allegri Saw Mill. Italian farming families settled the area immediately south of Malbis. The community became known as Belforest, and one of the largest families there was the Allegri family, who built a sawmill near their home. This view of the sawmill interior was taken about 1930. Vincent Allegri is the boy at left, with the bandaged toe. (Allegri-Volevecky families.)

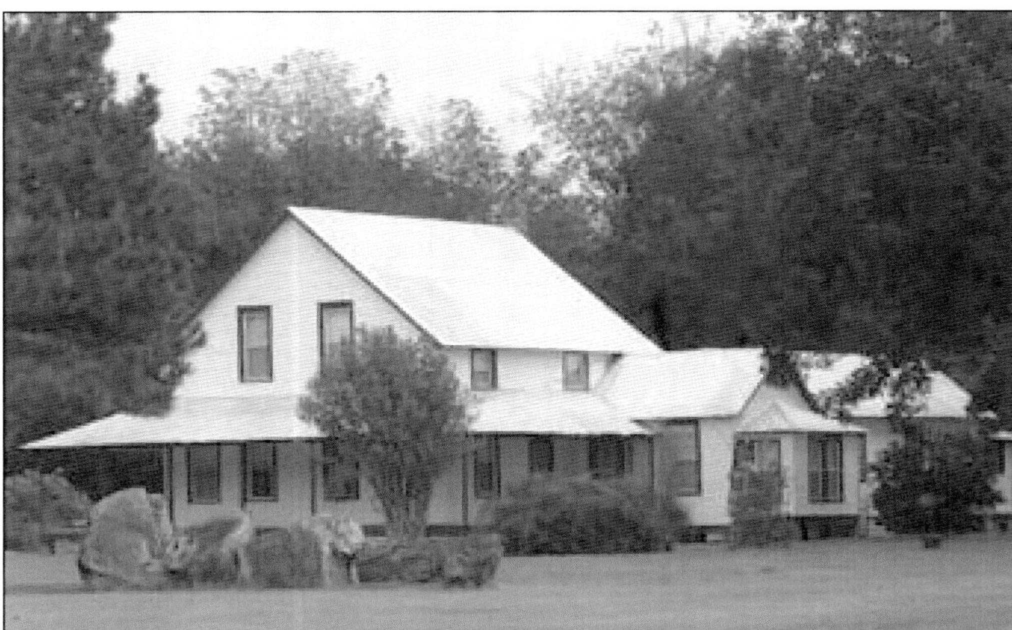

Allegri Home. Agostino Guarisco built the family home in 1906, high off the ground. The 1916 hurricane lifted the house off its foundation and set it down in one piece just a few feet from its original site. When it was raised again, it was still true and suffered very little damage. (Photograph by Penny Taylor.)

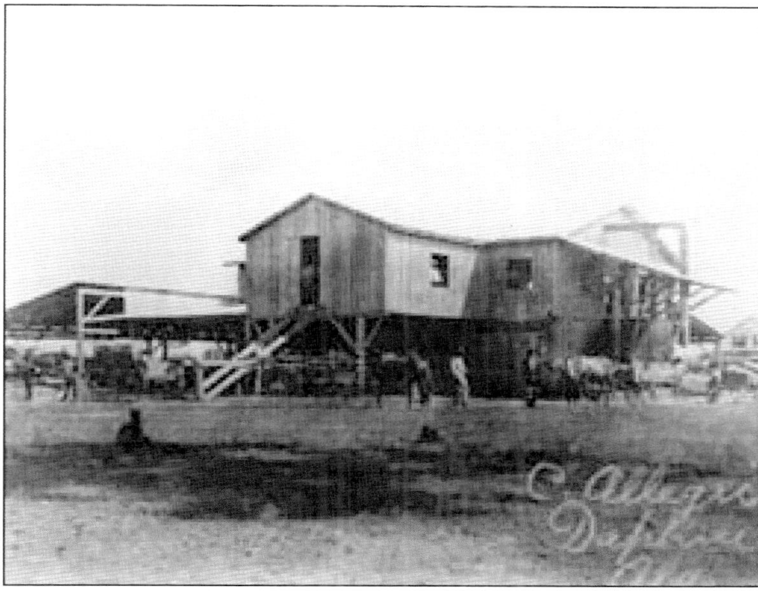

Cotton Gin. The large mill housed a gristmill (for grinding corn and wheat), the cotton gin, and the sawmill. The cotton gin removed the seeds from the cotton, which was then baled and carted by wagon to the bayfront for loading onto a packet. Usually, it was then sold to a cotton dealer in Mobile. (Allegri-Volevecky families.)

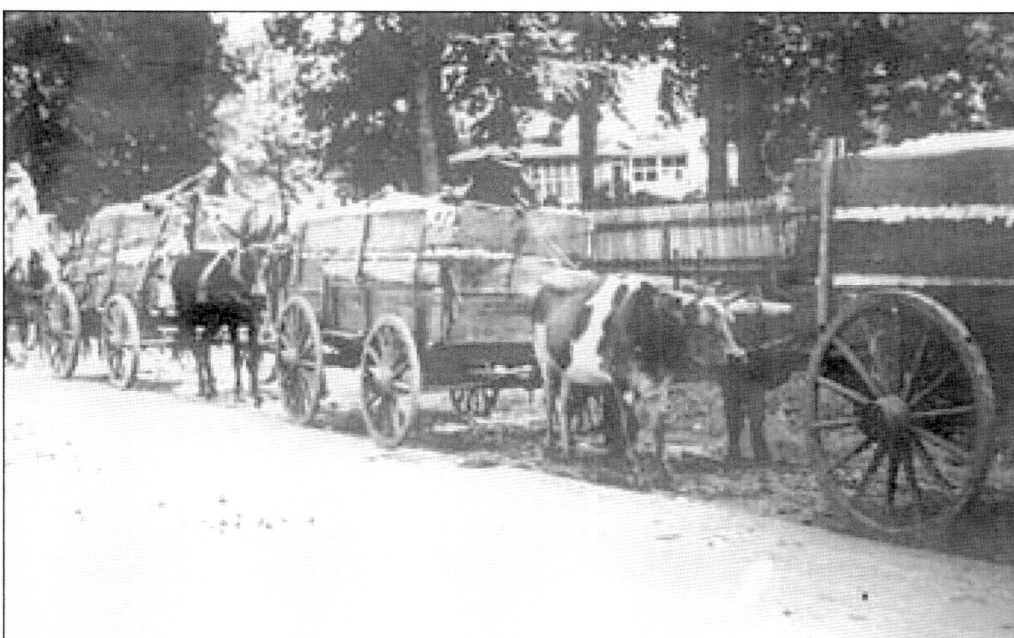

Hauling Cotton to the Gin. Men from surrounding farms carted their cotton to the Allegri gin via horse or mule and wagon. Loaded mostly by hand labor, the wagons were extremely heavy and dangerous. Roy Simms remembered delivering cotton to the mill when one of the workers grabbed his hat and threw it into the bin, where it was vacuumed with the cotton into the upper loft. Of course, the boys had to climb up into the loft to retrieve the cap. (OMCMD.)

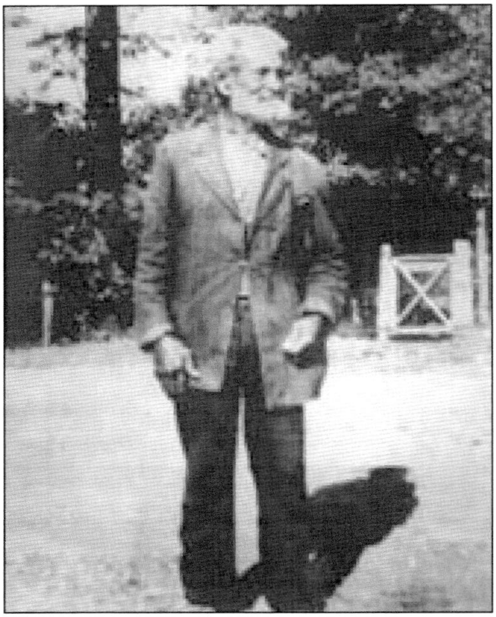

WALLIE VALRIE. After the Civil War, most of the former slaves in Daphne settled just east of the bayfront homes of their former masters. Their neighborhoods circled Main Street, and many of them worked in local businesses. However, there were also former slaves in the outlying farming plantations, like Wallie Valrie, who was born at the Greenwood Plantation near present-day Loxley. (Glenita Valrie Andrews.)

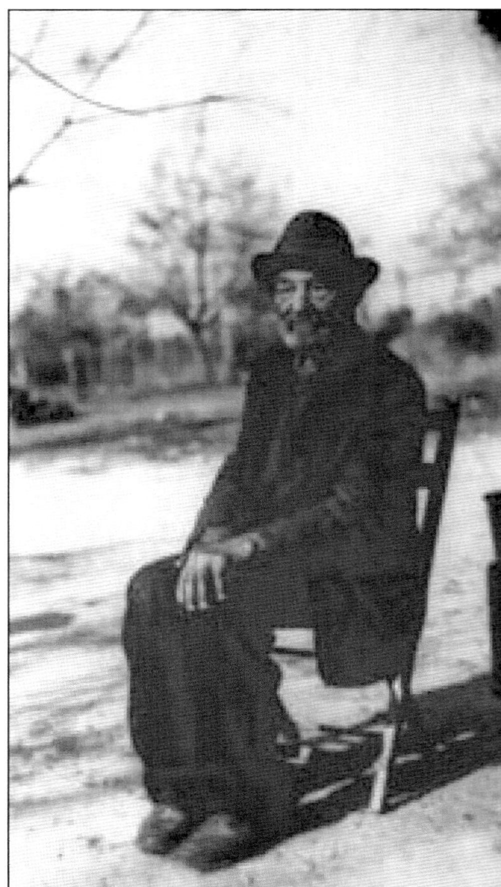

CENTENARIAN. Born in 1831 and living to the age of 117, Wallie Valrie well recalled the days he played marbles with his aging former owner, John Greenwood. Valrie later worked for the Greenwoods and married Melinda Webster, a Cherokee Indian. Wallie and Melinda Valrie lived most of their lives on their 30-acre farm near Montrose. (Glenita Valrie Andrews.)

BELFOREST SCHOOLHOUSE. The first community school in Belforest was a one-room wooden structure built in 1894. The teacher was Carrie Gregory. When it burned down, it was replaced with a more elaborate building with three classrooms. This structure stood until it burned down in 1937. (Mildred Simms Foster.)

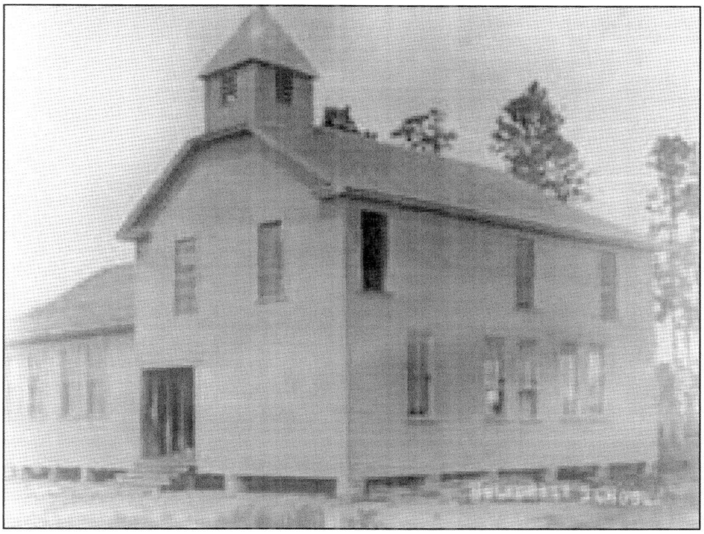

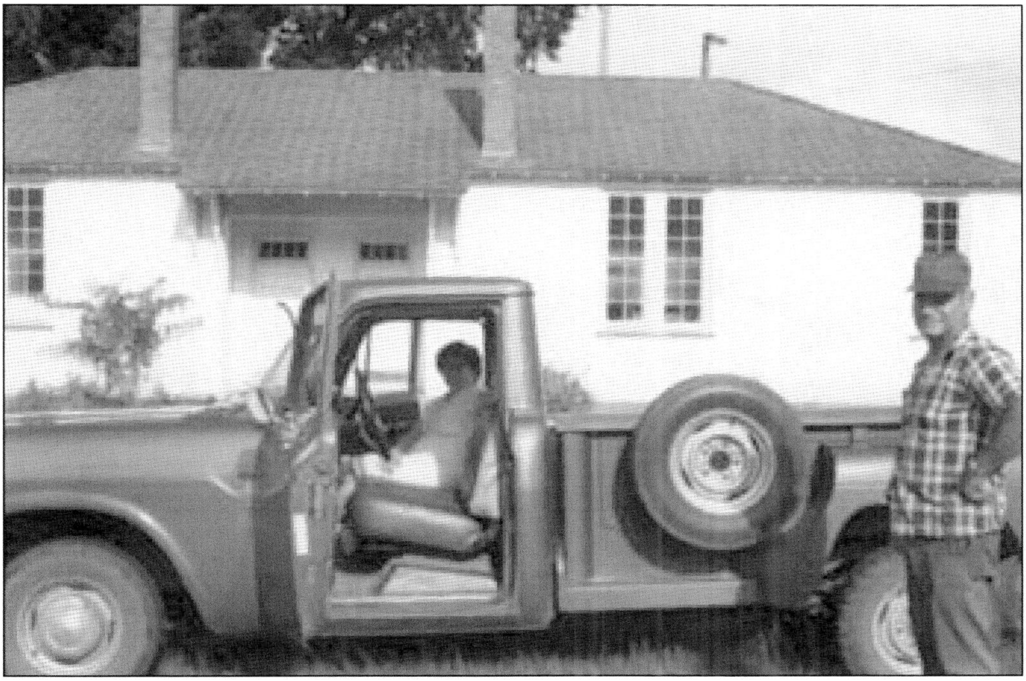

STUCCO SCHOOLHOUSE. The Baldwin County Board of Education built this stucco school in 1938. The two rooms were connected with sliding doors, and Edna Sirmon was remembered as a wonderful teacher. Pictured here is Jerry Volovecky, who brought his mother-in-law, Agnes Allegri, to visit the schoolhouse after it closed. (Allegri-Volevecky families.)

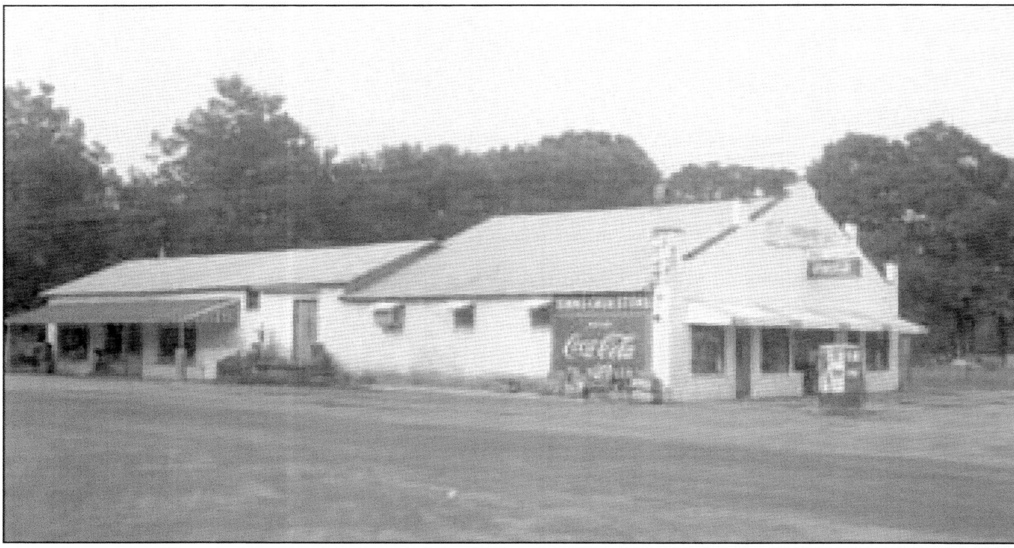

SIMMS CASH STORE. On the corner of County Road 64 and State Highway 181, the stucco building that was once Simms Store remains a symbol of Belforest. The store was built by Ben Edward Simms, who began the business around 1924 in a small shed where he sold drinks and snacks. Immediately behind the store is the Simms family home, built in 1920. Roy Simms completed an addition to the back of the store about 1941 and operated a hardware store there for 70 years until his death in 2011. The Simms family also ran a gas station and garage across the road. (Mildred Simms Foster.)

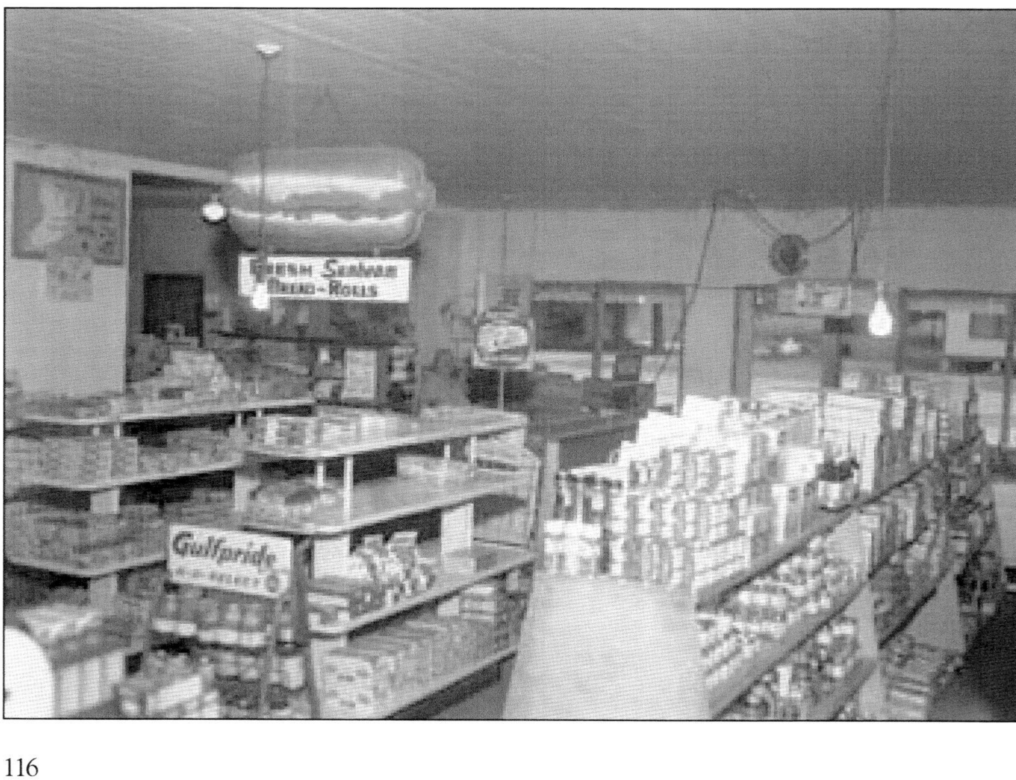

Nine

TO THE SOUTH

MONTROSE

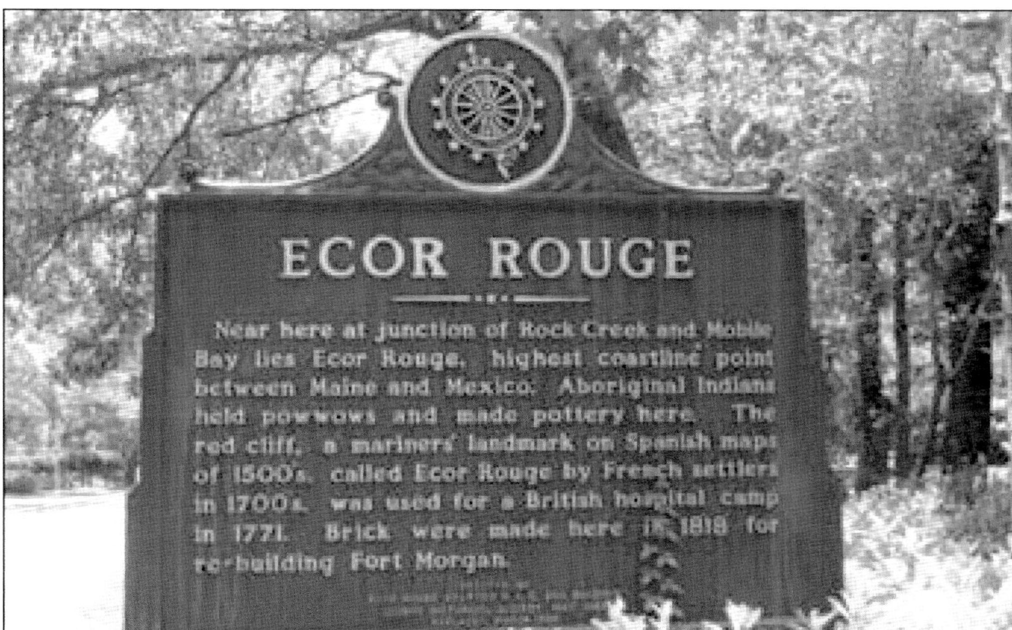

ECOR ROUGE HISTORIC MARKER. This historical marker, installed in 1966, reads: "Near here at junction of Rock Creek and Mobile Bay lies Ecor Rouge, highest coastline point between Maine and Mexico. Aboriginal Indians held powwows and made pottery here. The red cliff, a mariners' landmark on Spanish maps of 1500's, called Ecor Rouge by French settlers in 1700's, was used for a British hospital camp in 1771. Brick were made here in 1818 for re-building Fort Morgan." (Photograph by Harriet Outlaw.)

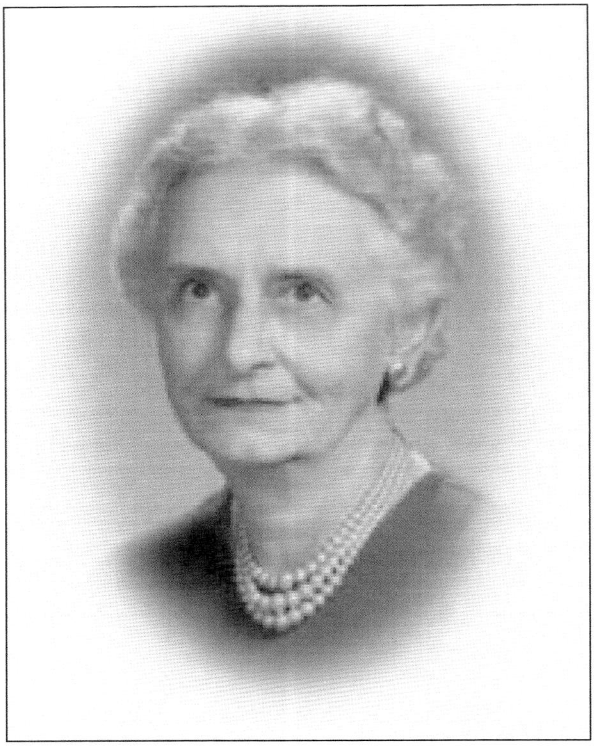

FLORENCE SCOTT. Richard Scott and his wife, Florence, were considered the utmost authority on Montrose history. Her diligent research and writings give a comprehensive account of local history in the three major works they published. Florence grew up in the family home in Montrose and attended the normal school in Daphne. She married Richard in Mobile, and they moved back to her family home in Montrose in 1927. (Dick Scott.)

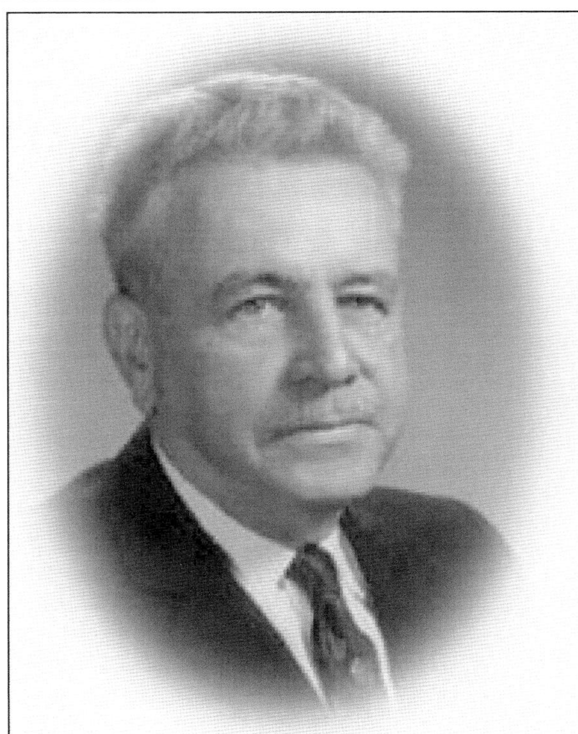

RICHARD SCOTT. Richard Scott met Florence while he was working in Mobile, building the Alabama State Docks. His exceptional artistic talent was helpful as the couple spent hours documenting the old structures of the Eastern Shore. His sketches were used in their published books and are included in this volume courtesy of their son, Dick. (Dick Scott.)

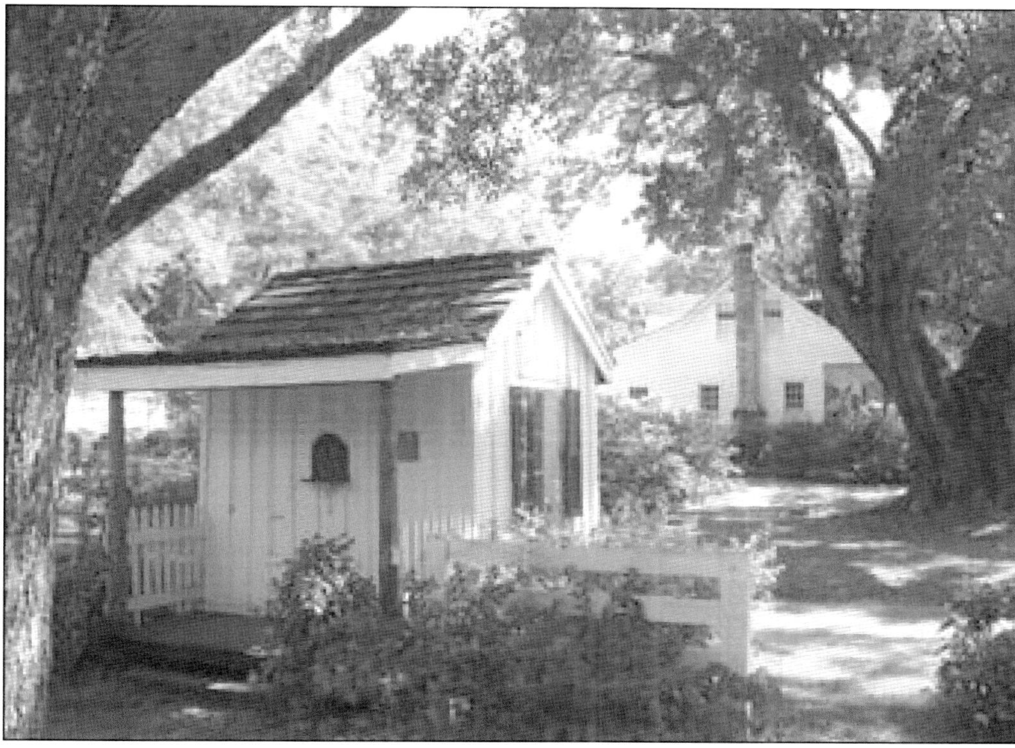

Montrose Post Office. This historical marker reads: "When retired riverboat Captain Thomas W. Marshall and his wife and family moved to Montrose and made their home here in 1883, he was appointed Postmaster and served until his death in 1890. His widow was appointed to take his place and had this building constructed on the home property. Built in 1890 by Postmaster Ida Babb Marshall, this building served residents of Montrose for many years. In those days, mail arrived from Mobile by boat. Mrs. Marshall would take any unclaimed mail to the house every evening and residents sometimes would knock on the door at night to get their mail." This building was last used as a post office in 1913. The home in the background later became the residence of Richard and Florence Scott. (Above, Penny Taylor; below, photograph by Harriet Outlaw.)

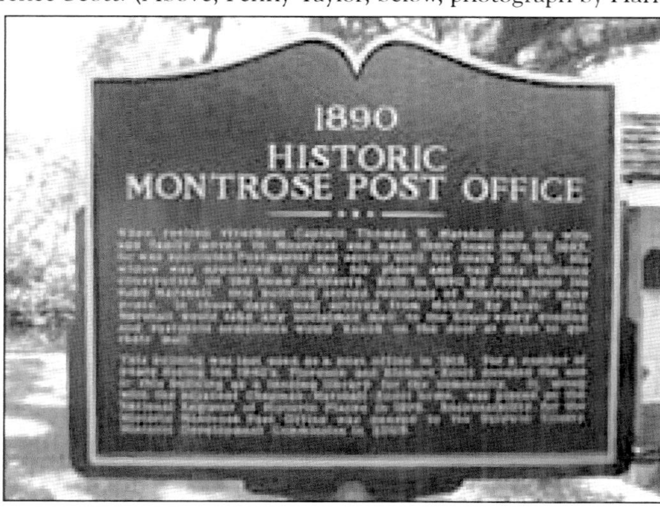

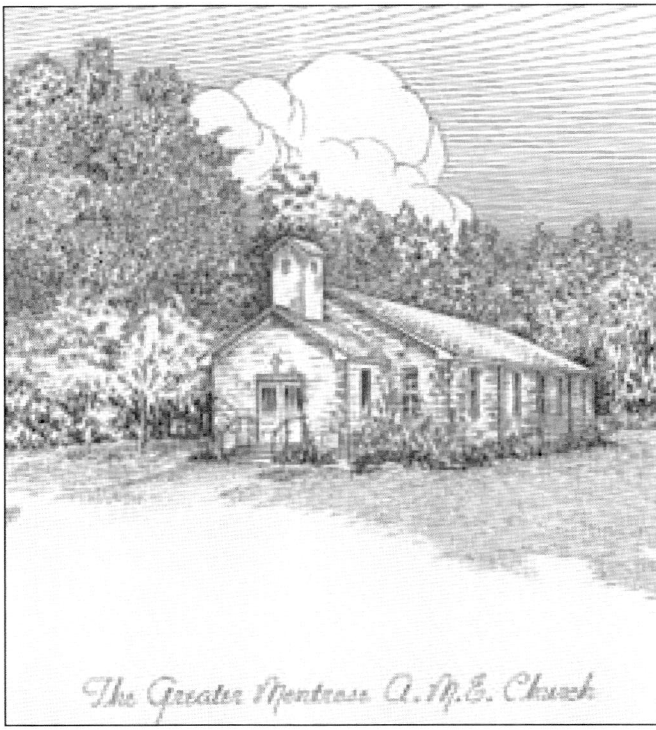

Greater Montrose AME Church. Ruth Smith Rhone records that the first group of citizens met in 1867 to form a church meeting in a store at Red Gulley. Later, they met in a brush arbor on land deeded to the church in 1870, where the Greater Montrose AME Church, built in 1957, still stands today. (Dick Scott, sketch by Richard Scott.)

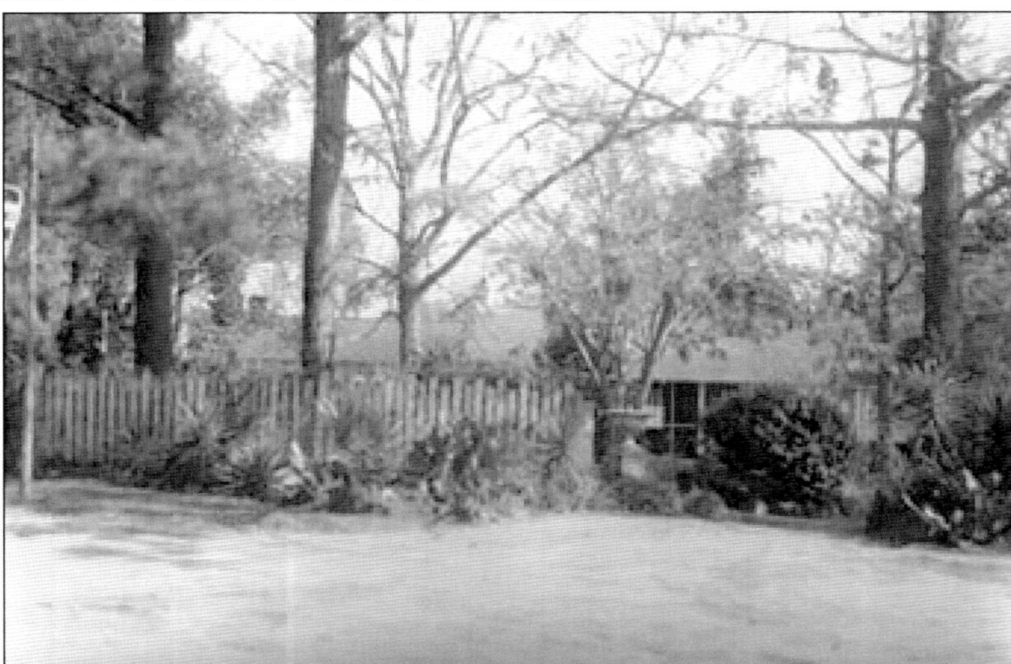

Sibley Home. Known as "the Cottage," this home had been in Mrs. Jack Oliver's family since her grandfather Cyrus Sibley bought the whole of Montrose for $850 before 1839. Sibley laid out the town of Montrose in lots and marketed the homesites wisely. (Dick Scott, Carney Collection.)

Seven Gables. A group of ladies stands on the steps of one of the most legendary homes in Montrose—Seven Gables. Built in 1855, it was first known as the Brainard Place. During the Civil War, as Adm. David Farragut's Union fleet advanced up Mobile Bay, residents of the house came out on the gallery to watch, only to be fired upon. Fortunately, no one was injured, and Mary Jane Convington offered rooms to Union officers to ensure the safety of the house. (Dick Scott, Carney Collection.)

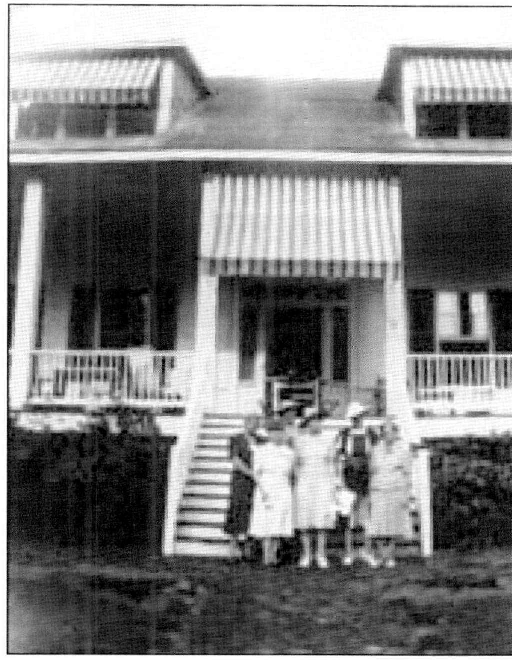

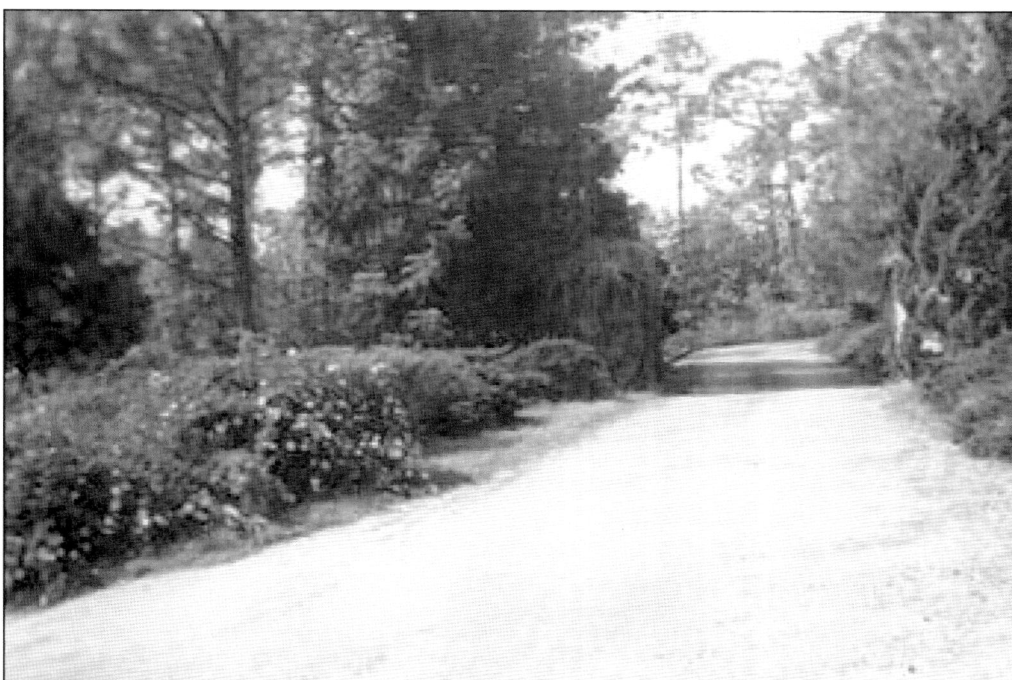

Highlands-Croftown. One of the highest bluffs in Montrose is near Rock Creek. Ira Jones, of Chicago, owned the home, dubbed "Happy Landings." The site, recorded as Croftown in 1770, was the summer encampment of the English army on the bluffs north of Rock Creek. There were barracks, a guardhouse on the cliff, and a provision storehouse on the beach below. Pictured is the drive to Happy Landing as it appeared in 1950. (Dick Scott, Carney Collection.)

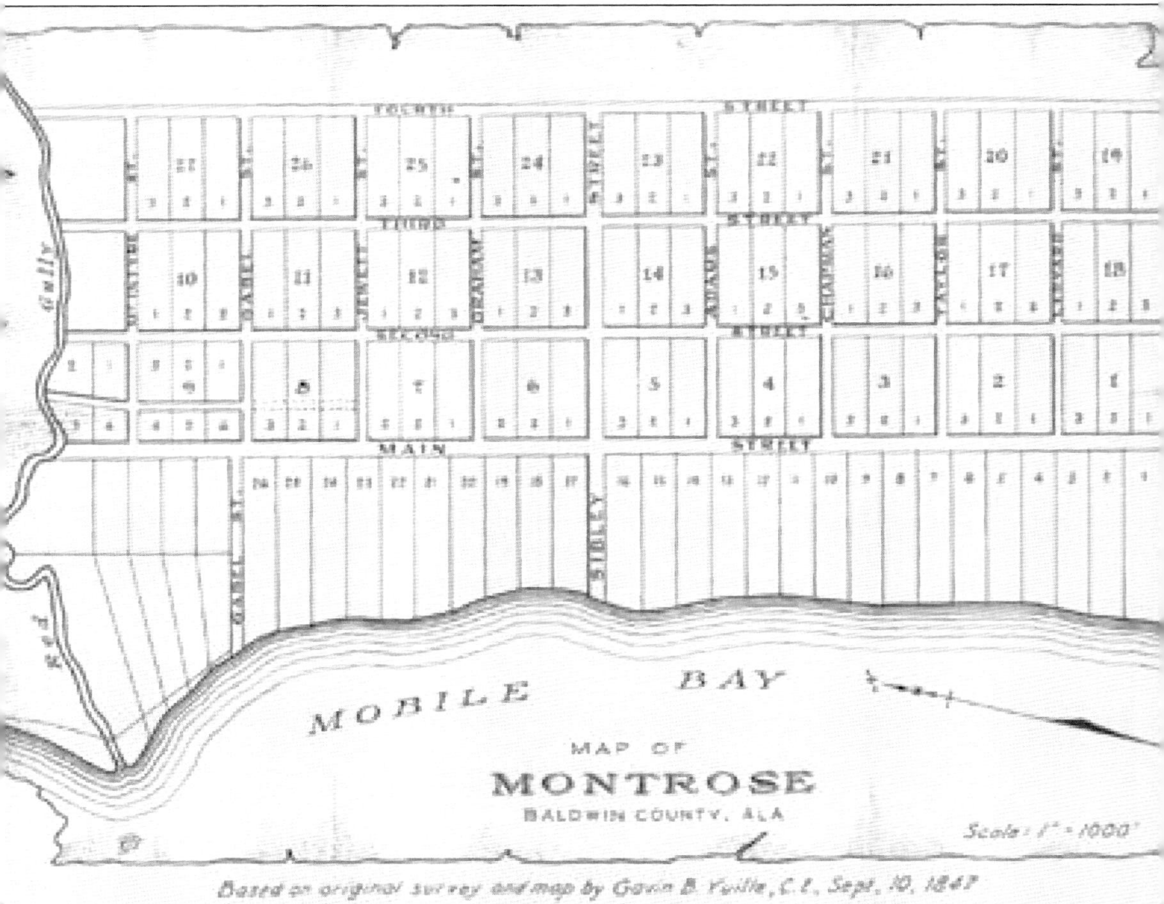

Plat of Old Montrose. Land along the bluff known as Ecor Rouge was owned by Isabelle Narbonne Campbell, who had established a brickyard there by 1811. Cyrus Sibley purchased the land and developed a town he first called Sibley City. He hired Gavin Yuille to draw the plat shown above. The streets were named for residents of the area and lots were sold. Theodore Graham, who purchased lots 19 and 20, suggested changing the name to Montrose after the Duke of Montrose in Scotland. The landing dock at Montrose was named Steadman's Landing on many older maps. (Dick Scott.)

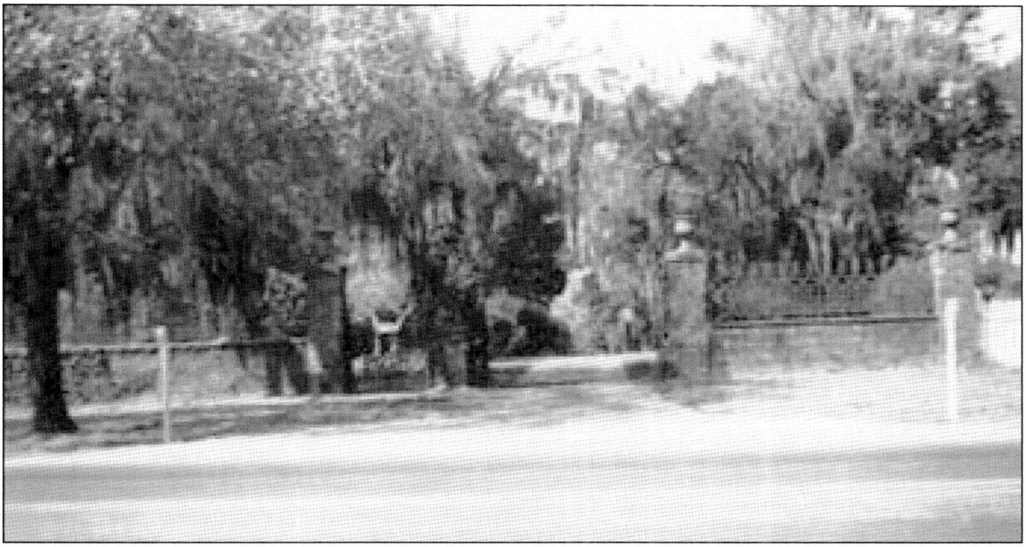

ANDERSON-MOSES. Pictured here is a formal gateway to a cedar grove, great oaks, and azaleas that almost hide the gravesite of the Judge Decatur Anderson family, which purchased a home from the Ledyards around 1866. The white frame house was built by E.D. Ledyard in 1853 and was used as an inn for Confederate officers. Grandson Ashleigh Moses owned the Montrose Pottery until Prohibition eliminated the demand for jugs. (Dick Scott, Carney Collection.)

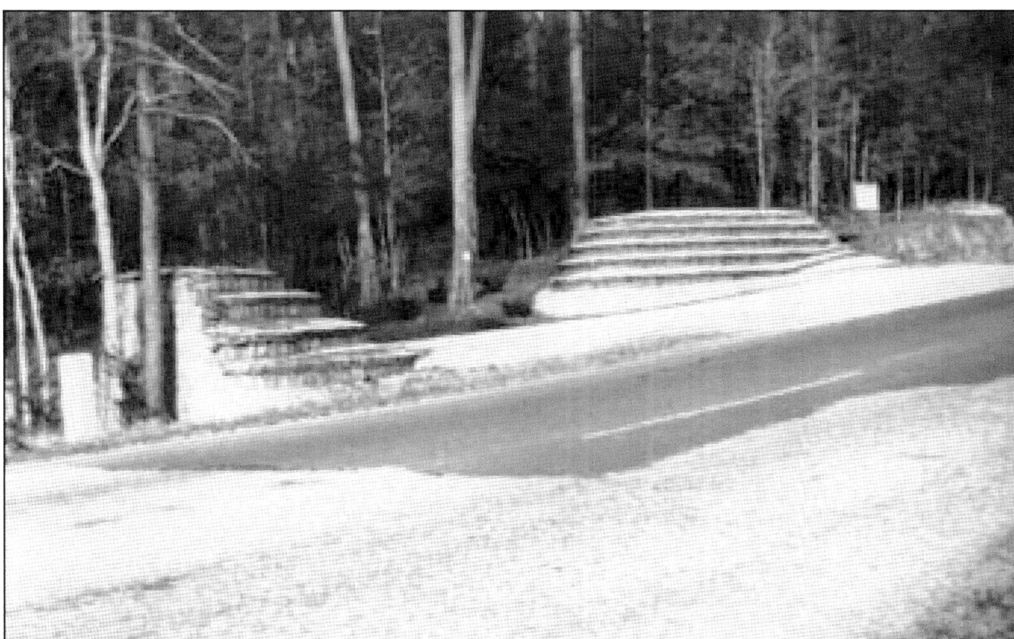

ENTRANCE TO ECOR ROUGE NEIGHBORHOOD. Seacliff, south of Rock Creek, was a Mobile colony for many years. The house nearest the beach was home of Dr. Gardiner Tucker, rector of St. John's Episcopal Church in Mobile for more than 50 years. Just north of Seacliff is the entrance (pictured) to a neighborhood. These sturdy gateways built of bricks salvaged from a Spanish kiln on the beach have withstood the flooding of Rock Creek for almost 100 years. (Dick Scott, Carney Collection.)

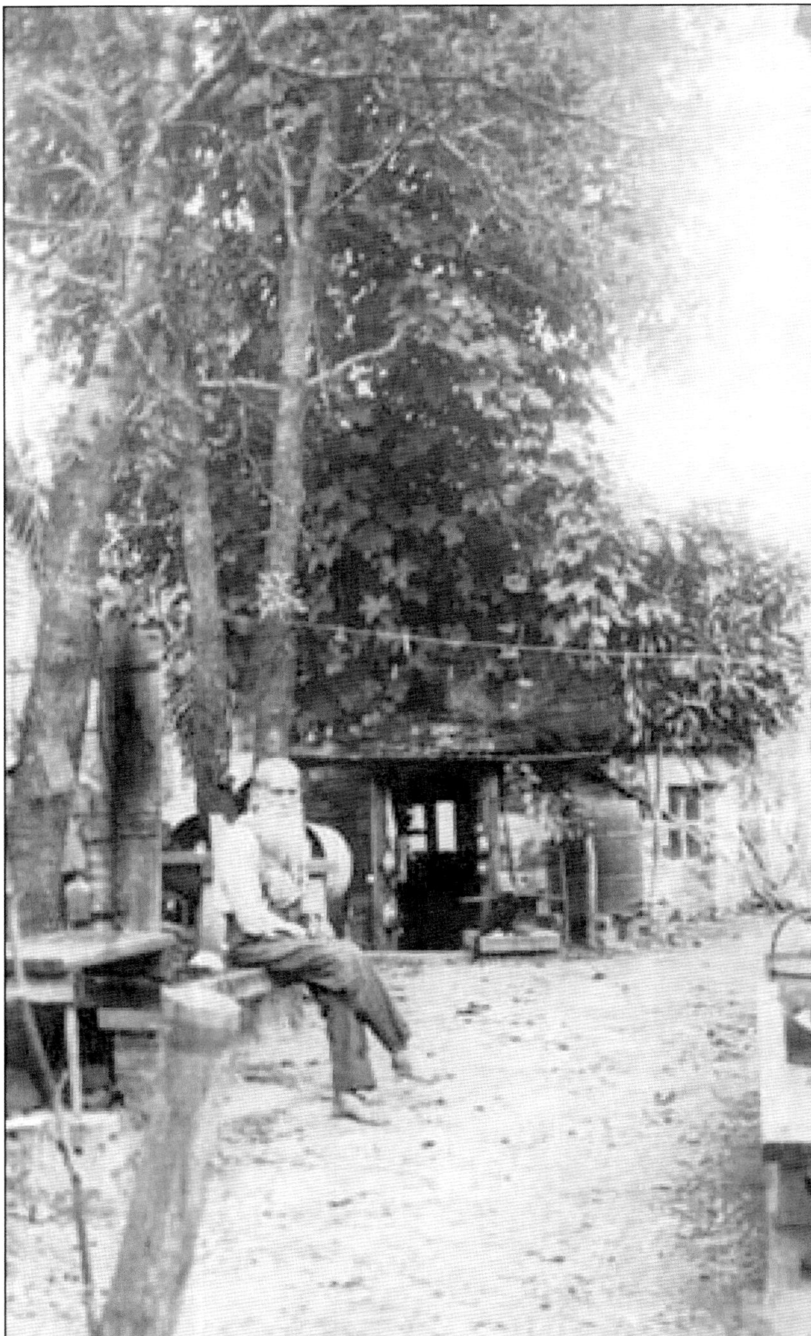

HERMIT OF TOLSTOY PARK. Idahoan Henry Stuart purchased 10 acres in the south part of Montrose, near Fairhope, in 1925. Stuart had been told he had one year to live and so moved to a warmer climate to "perfect the soul awarded him." He lived for many years in the round house he built, naming it Tolstoy Park. His life inspired the novel *Poet of Tolstoy Park*, by Sonny Brewer. (Dick Scott, Carney Collection.)

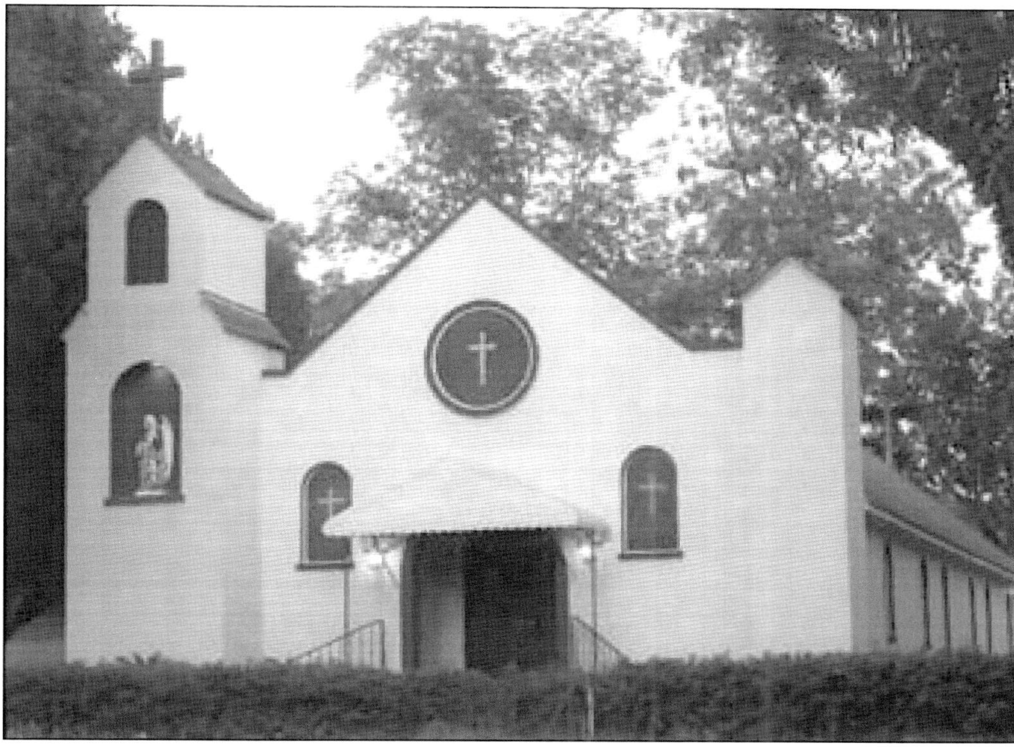

Shrine of the Holy Cross. Near Daphne, at 612 Main Street, a mission to serve the needs of African Americans was established by Rev. Vincent W. Warren, a Josephite priest. Under his leadership, catechism was taught to children of all races, together. The stucco and orange-tile building was constructed around a World War II surplus Quonset hut. (Photograph by Penny Taylor.)

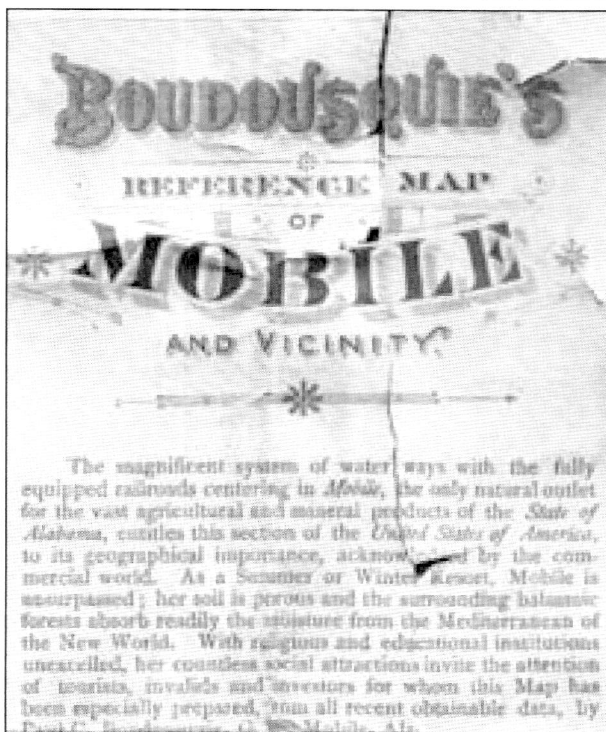

An Ideal Place to Live. The caption on this map made by Boudousquie in 1889 boasts of the magnificent system of waterways, commercial center, perfect climate, agricultural and mineral products, abundant forests, religious and educational institutions, and countless social attractions. Just add the word "jubilee," and it becomes clear that Daphne is the stuff of which a perfect home is made. (OMCMD.)

BIBLIOGRAPHY

Carney, Mary Owen. *The Yanks Take Over the Eastern Shore*, 1949.

———. *Gateways to History*. Self-published, 1949.

Comings, L.J. Newcomb, and Martha M. Albers. *A Brief History of Baldwin County*. Fairhope, AL: Baldwin County Historical Society, 1969.

Crowder, Joan. *Tell It to an Old Hollow Log.* Bay Minette, AL: Lavender Publishing, 2000.

Danley, Nancy. *The History of Baldwin County Training School.* Bay Minette, AL: Baldwin County Public Schools, 2009.

Gardner, David Manci. *A Tour of Historic Olde Towne Daphne*. Self-published, 2002.

Gums, Bonnie L. *Made of Alabama Clay*. Mobile, AL: University of South Alabama Center for Archaeological Studies, 2001.

Lewis, John C., and Harriet Brill Outlaw. Images of America: *Baldwin County*. Charleston, SC: Arcadia Publishing, 2005.

Nuzam, Kay. *A History of Baldwin County*. Bay Minette, AL: *The Baldwin Times*, 1971.

Scott, Florence, and Richard Scott. *Daphne*. Bay Minette, AL: Lavender Press, 2003.

———. Montrose. Montrose, AL: Montrose Garden Club, 1959.

About the Museum

Stepping into the shadow of the museum and being as still as a church mouse, one may hear the clash of boards slamming together and the resounding whack of a hammer on a wooden peg as the wall goes up, 25 feet straight up to the Lord, giving the slave in the upper-deck gallery enough room to keep on his hat before service begins. One may even hear the newly installed bell pealing its arrival every day—morning, noon, and night—for a month; its voice, a beacon of sound, calling the community to worship in the new church. A walk through the cemetery may bring to life those who have stories to tell of the earliest years of the town of Daphne.

The 1858 Methodist Church tells the story of those who built it on land donated by William "Billy" Howard. It tells the story of those who worshipped within the church's walls, of the Union soldiers who camped there in 1865, and of those put to rest in its graveyard.

The church tells the story because it is still alive and well. Even after the congregation built a new church on Main Street, the old building was used as a gathering place for community events. Hurricane damage and old age threatened its life. When a preservation committee prevailed upon Daphne to lease the property for a museum, the church's walls were restored and preserved to house the treasures of the past. The Old Methodist Church Museum of Daphne opened to the public in 2001. Its mission statement presses and forms its boundaries: "The Old Methodist Church Museum of Daphne will preserve the heritage of the citizens of Daphne through the collection and exhibition of records, artifacts, photographs, and other memorabilia, which portray the history and evolution of the City. The museum will further provide educational programs that will enhance the cultural experiences of residents and visitors."

The museum is located at 405 Dryer Avenue and is open to the public each Friday, Saturday, and Sunday from 1:00 p.m. to 4:00 p.m. Additional information can be found at www.daphnemuseumalabama.com. Admission is free; donations are welcome.

Consistent with our mission to preserve history on a local level, this book was printed in South Carolina on American-made paper and manufactured entirely in the United States. Products carrying the accredited Forest Stewardship Council (FSC) label are printed on 100 percent FSC-certified paper.

MADE IN THE USA